THE MAYFAIR MAFIA

DICK KIRBY
has also written

Praise for Dick Kirby's Books

His style of writing pulls no punches and he tells it like it is. Highly recommended.

Police History Society Journal

Its no-nonsense portrayal of life in the police will give readers a memorable literary experience.

Suffolk Journal

All of the stories are told with Dick Kirby's acerbic, black humour in a compelling style, by a detective who was there.

American Police Beat

. . . a series of gripping, individual stories.

Daily Express

A superb description of crime-busting at the front end.

Bertram's Books

Dick Kirby . . . knows how to bring his coppers to life on each page.

Joseph Wambaugh, Author of The Choirboys

. . . impeccable research, interviews and documentation, written in Kirby's delightful, conversational style.

Police Memorabilia Collectors' Club

Kirby writes with authority and clarity . . . highly recommended.

Real Crime Magazine

A well-researched book . . . written by an experienced, natural raconteur.

History By The Yard

He is uniquely placed to draw on those sources which really matter.

London Police Pensioner

To Ann
When love speaks,
The voice of all the gods
Makes heaven drowsy with the harmony.

Shakespeare's *Love's Labour's Lost*

An extract of a song from the Australian outback; it might have been composed with 'The Queens of Maddox Street' in mind.

For the day's growing short, the night's coming on;
Well, darling – just gimme yer arm and we'll joggle along,
We'll joggle and joggle and joggle along.

The Mayfair Mafia

The Lives and Crimes of the Messina Brothers

DICK KIRBY

PEN & SWORD
TRUE CRIME

First published in Great Britain in 2019 by
Pen & Sword True Crime
An imprint of
Pen & Sword Books Ltd
Yorkshire – Philadelphia

Copyright © Dick Kirby 2019

ISBN 978 1 52674 261 2

Printed and bound in the UK by TJ International Ltd,
Padstow, Cornwall

Pen & Sword Books Limited incorporates the imprints of Atlas,
Archaeology, Aviation, Discovery, Family History, Fiction, History,
Maritime, Military, Military Classics, Politics, Select, Transport, True
Crime, Air World, Frontline Publishing, Leo Cooper, Remember
When, Seaforth Publishing, The Praetorian Press, Wharncliffe
Local History, Wharncliffe Transport, Wharncliffe True Crime
and White Owl.

For a complete list of Pen & Sword titles please contact

PEN & SWORD BOOKS LIMITED
47 Church Street, Barnsley, South Yorkshire, S70 2AS, England
E-mail: enquiries@pen-and-sword.co.uk
Website: www.pen-and-sword.co.uk

Or
PEN AND SWORD BOOKS
1950 Lawrence Rd, Havertown, PA 19083, USA
E-mail: Uspen-and-sword@casematepublishers.com
Website: www.penandswordbooks.com

Contents

About the Author

Dick Kirby was born in 1943 in the East End of London and joined the Metropolitan Police in 1967. Half of his twenty-six years' service as a detective was spent with the Yard's Serious Crime Squad and the Flying Squad.

Married, with four children and five grandchildren, Kirby lives in a Suffolk village with his wife. He reviews books, films and music, is a consultant for a television series and writes memoirs, biographies and true crime books – this is his seventeenth.

Kirby can be visited on his website: www.dickkirby.com.

Acknowledgements

A brief historical and biographical note, before I delve into the 'acknowledgements' section. Over fifty years ago, as a brand new police constable in East London, I quickly discovered that many of my contemporaries were among the most idle, column-dodging, piss-taking – and, on occasion, cowardly – police officers whom God ever blew breath into. Salvation came from the west, when a constable from King's Cross was transferred to my station. Well-educated, tough – he had been a member of the 'N' Division boxing team – yet surprisingly compassionate to the criminals he encountered, Ed Williams and I hit it off immediately. We carried out the very last arrest of 'a suspected person, loitering with intent to commit a felony'; the next day, felonies were struck off the statute books, to be replaced with 'arrestable offences'.

That friendship has endured unabated for over half a century, and I am most grateful to Ed for his extremely kind and thoughtful foreword to this book.

My thanks also go to Brigadier Henry Wilson and Matt Jones of Pen & Sword Books for their help, assistance and encouragement, plus George Chamier for his careful overview to check and eradicate my mistakes.

A number of people came forward to assist with researching this book, but top of the tree was Michael Nesbitt, editor of *Britain's Gangland* magazine, who provided me with enormous assistance and to whom I'm most grateful. In addition, I should like to thank the following: John Lewis; Dave Allen of the Bow Street Police Station Website; Mick Carter of the ReCIDivists' Luncheon Club; Siobhan Clark, archivist for the Metropolitan Women Police Association; Bob Fenton, QGM of the Ex-CID Officers' Association; Alan Moss of the *History by the Yard* website: Susi Rogol, Editor of the *London Police Pensioners' Magazine*; Dr Clare Smith of the Metropolitan Police Heritage Centre; Barry Walsh of the Friends of the Met Police Historical Collection; Neil Fraser of Fraser & Fraser, Probate Researchers; Ellie Longman of Bury St Edmunds library; P. Feakins and D. Hjiej-Andaloussi of the Freedom of Information Team; HM Passport Office; and the staff at Gunnersbury Cemetery.

I'm most grateful to those who stretched their memories and contributed to the book. In alphabetical order they are: Ken Davies, John Falconer, Ron Feldman, Derek Lawbuary, Thomas Proudfoot and Gordon Walker.

Whilst some of the photographs come from the author's private collection, every effort has been made to trace the copyright holders of the others, and the publishers and I apologise for any inadvertent omissions.

By now I should have been able to hold my own in the complex world of cyberspace, but old age, decrepitude and general ignorance has denied me that privilege; thankfully, my daughter Suzanne Cowper and her husband Steve have come to my rescue more times than I care to remember, and I am hugely indebted to them.

Similarly, I am most grateful for the love and support I have received from my sons, Mark and Robert, my daughter Barbara Jerreat, her husband Rich and their children, Sam and Annie Grace, plus my other grandchildren, Emma Cowper B Mus, Jessica Cowper B Mus and Harry Cowper.

Last, and by no means least, my wife Ann, who for over fifty-five years has been the mainstay of my life.

Dick Kirby
Suffolk, 2019

Foreword

by ex-Detective Superintendent, Metropolitan Police
Edwin Williams BA (Joint Hons), PGCE,
MBPsS, Dip. NEBSS

What are we faced with in the 19th century? An age where women were sacred; and where you could buy a 13-year-old girl for a few pounds, a few shillings if you only wanted her for an hour or two.
John Fowles, *The French Lieutenant's Woman*

I count myself fortunate indeed to have served in the Metropolitan Police with Dick Kirby. Not because he was an outstanding 'thief taker' in the days when, together, we worked the streets of London's East End, and not because of his enviable Flying Squad and Serious Crime Squad expertise. The real joy in working with Dick Kirby came from watching him tease away at the battlements of the seemingly unassailable castle walls of the criminal fraternity. Those enemies of society who, backed by an army of well paid lawyers, were able to flip an Agincourt salute at the police, the courts and those victims left crushed on crime's battlefield. Dick Kirby's sophisticated intelligence found the cracks in those castle walls, and, pen and warrant card in hand, he stormed the inner sanctum. Criminals lost their liberty.

Now, minus his warrant card, but not his pen, he is still fighting those battles. Dick Kirby was an exceptional detective because he paid attention to the details that mattered. Blessed with a truly formidable memory, he was more than a match for the criminals and legal scoundrels who lived off the proceeds of crime. Those superb attributes he now applies to the intricacies of *The Mayfair Mafia,* a complex history of the notorious Messina Brothers. Kirby's fastidious research brings alive once more the Messinas' world of wickedness and debauchery, the days when they were reputed to have as many as two hundred prostitutes working in and around London's Mayfair immediately before, during and after the Second World War.

Frankly, a book about prostitutes, pimps and ponces is not what we expect from Dick Kirby, so why has this highly regarded detective and author devoted his talents to such a theme? After all, those who live on immoral earnings barely rank above paedophiles in the criminal hierarchy. Small fry for Kirby. The answer is revealed when Kirby links the baiting methods of the Messina Brothers to those who, in today's modern world, exploit the newly pubescent girls of England's broken industrial heartland. Gullible girls and young women, starved of love and affection and lacking self-esteem, hooked remorselessly into a life of prostitution with promises of love and material reward. Neither came their way; instead of the promised rewards there were venereal disease and drugs. *Plus ça change.*

Step to the front of the stage Dick Kirby, crusader against the most wicked crime of all, the theft of innocence. A dedicated family man (I love you too, Ann!), Dick Kirby laments the apathy with which we treat the victims of human trafficking and sexual exploitation. He understands that, if we want to find solutions, one way of doing so is to look not just at contemporary trends, but also at how prostitutes and prostitution were viewed in generations past.

After policing Kings Cross, Mayfair, Knightsbridge and Hyde Park, I can justify my claim to know a little about the women who, in the depths of winter, presented a sad sight dressed in miniskirts, touting, frozen-faced, for clients on London's streets. Their lives were, in the words of the philosopher Thomas Hobbes, 'Nasty, brutish and short'.

The public, anxious for shorthand explanations of the inexplicable, tend to see prostitutes as either 'fallen women' or 'happy harlots'. Back in the 1970s and 1980s, the press gorged on the antics of Cynthia Payne, otherwise known as 'Madam Sin', who police say ran a brothel in Streatham. Compliant men paid for sadistic sexual services with 'luncheon vouchers'; Cynthia would then joyfully spank their bottoms, a woman delighting in her work. She, despite a short prison sentence, became a minor celebrity. When she died in 2015, I almost expected a State funeral, with sore-bottomed public school types lining the route.

Contrast Cynthia's story with that of a prostitute witness from the Serious Crime Squad days of Dick Kirby and myself, whose ponce forced her to lie face down on the ground and 'punished' her for talking to the police by firing a 9mm parabellum bullet into her lower spine; crippled and wheelchair-bound, she still courageously gave evidence against him. No surprise then that Mr Kirby has not lost the determination to keep the spotlight on those who control prostitutes.

I mention Cynthia to demonstrate the immense power of the press. Journalists can reshape social opinion, a fact that Dick Kirby recognized by honouring the role of Duncan Webb, a Fleet Street journalist employed by the *People* newspaper. Duncan literally put his life on the line to expose the Messina Brothers and the full extent of their sex trade empire.

Yet some sections of the press of the 1950s chose to extol the life of luxury allegedly enjoyed by some 'Messina Girls', adorned with jewellery and silver fox fur coats and driven to their pavement positions in the Messinas' yellow Rolls-Royce. But for every gift there was a blow, a cutting, a murder. The Messina Bothers ruled by fear and they shared Parent-Duchâtelet's 1836 notion that prostitutes were nothing but human sewers. One of the Messina prostitutes is reputed to have had sex with forty-nine clients in one day, so what else could she be but a human sewer? Your child? My daughter? Prostitutes are human beings, and so very few are 'happy harlots'.

Assistant Chief Constable Dan Vajzovic, the National Police Chiefs' Council lead for prostitution and sex working, is quoted in *The Times* on 18 April 2018 as saying, 'Enforcement alone has proven to be an inadequate response to prostitution.' He is right, and today's police must take note of extensive current and past research, if only to build a framework for understanding the role of prostitution in today's society. French philosopher and historian, Michel Foucault (1926–1984), a critical thinker and engine for social debate, suggested that we must look at prostitution in conjunction with the power and influence of the state, with social, medical, cultural and judicial opinion taken into account. Please let that happen.

I sincerely hope that Dick Kirby's *Mayfair Mafia* will come to be recognized not just as a brilliant read for cops and fans of policing, but also as a literary work of significant social importance. The 2015 Rochdale Child Abuse Ring, infamous for the sexual exploitation and human trafficking of underage girls by up to a score of men, proves that prostitution does not fade away. It is here, it is now, it is brutal. We owe Dick Kirby a debt of gratitude for this book and his important contribution to this debate. Never stop storming the battlements, Mr Kirby, and may your pen never run dry.

Suffolk, 2018

Prologue

Sicily – that island situated on the toe of Italy, surrounded by the Tyrrhenian, Ionian and Mediterranean Seas – is where our story begins. It's an island which, over the years, has had its fair share of problems. In 1169 an earthquake killed 15,000 of the island's inhabitants, and among a series of invasions was that by the French in 1266. The islanders fought back, and their insurrection of 1282 was captured in Verdi's opera, *The Sicilian Vespers*; in the final act, when the lovers Elena and Arrigo are about to be wed, the church bells sound. Elena sings, 'It's the bells announcing . . .' and Arrigo, interrupting and finishing her sentence for her, cries, 'Joy!'

Unfortunately, it's also the signal for rebellion, and Procida (a patriot and a thoroughly nasty bit of work) adds his own interpretation to the chimes – 'Vengeance!'

'This is the happiest day of my life!' sings an exuberant Arrigo – 'And your last!' adds Procida, and to prove his point, as the bells toll, Sicilians of both sexes, brandishing torches, swords and daggers, rush in from all directions and muller the French.

I mention this because there are some who believe that what became known as the Mafia started there and then. Difficult to say, because another theory is that organization commenced its activities in the early nineteenth century. But whatever way you look at it, Sicily was undeniably the Mafia's birthplace. It offered protection to those unable to protect themselves; a bit, I suppose, like Freemasonry, although with their special hand signals to communicate with each other and their contempt for the law, as time went by the Mafia expanded and took on a more sinister aspect, offering assassinations, smuggling and prostitution as part of their agenda. The origins of the word are diverse: some say it comes from the Sicilian *mafiusu*, meaning swagger or boldness, others from the Arabic *mahyah*, meaning bragging, but in any event, the first official use of the term 'Mafia' was in a communication from the Prefect of Palermo (Sicily's capital) to Rome in 1865. And the Italian government was determined to stamp out the Mafia – in February 1898 soldiers arrested 64 suspects in Palermo.

The pretty village of Linguaglossa, situated in the east of the island at the foot of Mount Etna, was not thought to be an area

of Mafia activity at that time, although surrounding villages –
Castiglione to the north-west and Piedimonte and Fiumefreddo to
the south-east – were.

One of the inhabitants of Linguaglossa was Giuseppe Messina.
He was the son of peasants, born on 6 October 1878. However, he
would later state that he had been born in 1879. Giuseppe was not
renowned for his accuracy or truthfulness; he simply lied for the
sake of lying. He would pass this trait on to his sons, and it's as well
that the reader should be aware of this, right from the start. It will,
I assure you, make for a much easier read; instead of looking at an
alarming, perhaps implausible passage in the book and thinking,
'But how on earth could they possibly . . . ?', it will make matters
so much simpler if you accept that the Messinas were unable to lie
straight in bed.

The Messinas lied about everything: their names, their dates
and places of birth, their addresses and their occupations. Others
were drawn into their net; their legal representatives lied for them,
and the prostitutes they ran not only lied for them, they went into
courts of law and perjured themselves as well. So did the Messinas;
as will be shown, they committed perjury on a grand scale when
they appeared in court, so much so that in the words of Hilaire
Belloc's poem about Matilda (who told lies and was burnt to
death), 'It made one gasp, and stretch one's eyes.'

No aspect of untruthfulness was considered so small as to be
disregarded by the brothers, and only one Government department
was untarnished by their mendacity. That was the Inland Revenue,
and the reason was simple; none of them ever submitted an income
tax return.

★

During the late nineteenth century, Giuseppe Messina was dealing
in prostitution and white slavery and had earned the antagonism
of some of the local inhabitants and the enmity of the local Mafia.

Before the Italian round-up of the Mafiosi commenced,
Giuseppe could see the way the wind was blowing; so before they
could demonstrate their knifing skills on him, he beat a hasty retreat
from the island. In 1896 he sailed 58 miles south, to the island of
Malta, and although he would later say that by trade he was a
carpenter and a furniture repairer, at the time Giuseppe reached
his destination, renovating cabinets and sawing and shaping wood
was furthest from his mind.

Nowadays, in Malta, if you were to mention the names Arthur
Evans, Alfred Martin, Edward Marshall, Raymond Maynard

and Charles Maitland to any of the more mature citizens of that island, you would probably be rewarded with polite puzzlement or perhaps a careless shrug of the shoulders.

But mention their baptismal names – Salvatore, Alfredo, Eugenio, Attilio and Carmelo Messina – to the same people, and I'm reliably informed that those staunchly Catholic citizens would experience a sharp intake of breath, lower their eyes and piously cross themselves.

In time, the Mafia would spread its tentacles far and wide, across Europe and to the United States of America; also, to London. Over sixty years have passed since the worst of the brothers' depredations, and all of them are now dead. However, Giuseppe had spawned sons so depraved, with absolute contempt for law and order, coupled with ruthlessness, that following their arrival in London they could rightly be described as 'The Mayfair Mafia'.

CHAPTER 1

The Start of the Family Business

Malta is a small island in the Mediterranean, just 122 square miles in size, and like Sicily it has had its fair share of invaders, among them the British. At the time that Giuseppe set sail from his homeland, the Grand Harbour in the island's capital, Valletta, accommodated the Royal and Merchant Navies' biggest vessels, and the six Government dry docks could contain the largest men-of-war. These ships also transported British servicemen to and from the Suez Canal, and whilst the island carried out some shipbuilding and its trade included grain, wine, fruits and cotton, it also needed to cater for the appetites of the sex-hungry troops who disembarked there.

Strait Street (or *Stada Stretta*) in Valletta is a narrow road. Known to the troops as 'The Gut', at the time of Giuseppe's arrival it was a thoroughfare crammed with bars and brothels.

But it was not Valletta where Giuseppe settled; the native Maltese competition in poncing was far too strong there. Instead, he went to Ħamrun, which is situated two miles south-west of the capital, and there was a good reason for his going there. Many of the inhabitants of that town were descendants of Sicilians who had settled there in the sixteenth century. In fact, the townspeople were known as *Tas-Sikkina* ('of the knife' or 'those who carry a knife') or as *Ta'Werwer* ('those who scare' or 'the scary ones'), so Giuseppe was in pretty solid company. It was a fairly insular society (much as exists in many British communities of immigrants nowadays) and, in addition, there was more than a sufficiency of brothels in the area.

It was in one of these brothels that Giuseppe secured a job as an assistant; he also married a Maltese girl from the town of Żejtun named Virginia de Bono, who had been born on 10 January 1878 (although the year of her birth was later 'estimated' to be 1877). In 1898 the first of their sons, Salvatore, was born, and in 1901 Alfredo arrived; both were born in Ħamrun.

The Treaty of Paris in 1814 had made Malta part of the British Empire. Therefore Virginia could claim British citizenship, which was handy for her offspring, because at that time Malta observed the *jus soli*, meaning 'right of the soil' – in other words, citizenship was conferred on children born in the country providing one of the parents was a citizen of that country; so because of their mother's status both Salvatore and Alfredo became British citizens.

Moreover, it appeared – at that time, at least – that when a foreigner married a Maltese citizen, British citizenship was conferred on the spouse. Parish registers commenced in 1863 for the registration of marriages, but certificates were often missing or damaged and the records are incomplete. Some records were not entered in the registers at all, and in others the handwriting of the *Kappillans* (parish priests) was so poor it could not be deciphered either on the marriage certificate or in the register. This begs the question: were Giuseppe and Virginia actually married? Who knows?

In the meantime, Giuseppe prospered. In fact, he worked so hard that he amassed a considerable sum of money, so much that in 1904 he decided to take himself and his family on the 946-mile journey to Egypt, where in Alexandria there were even richer pickings to be had.

★

In 1837 Muhammad Ali Pasha had outlawed prostitution in Egypt. Article 240 of the Mixed Penal Code (1867) decreed: 'A pimp who incites young men or women below the age of twenty-one to evil practices leading to rape, is to be punished by a period of imprisonment, not less than one month and not more than one year.' Article 241, by the way, increased the penalty if the offence was committed by the father, mother or guardian of the minor.

The British had occupied Egypt since 1882 and were concerned – quite rightly, too – that their troops should be protected from the ravages of venereal disease which was endemic amongst the local prostitutes, many of whom had been slaves prior to the abolition of slavery in 1877.

In July 1885 Egypt's Minister of the Interior introduced regulations for health inspections of prostitutes, and in 1896 further rules were issued to control brothels.

There was also the problem of 'White Slavery' – the import and export of women for the purposes of prostitution – and in 1904 the Alexandria Committee for the Suppression of the Traffic in Women was set up.

The same year that the Messina family arrived, the British Colonial authorities set out a series of regulations: prostitution had to be conducted from registered premises in certain locations;

the prostitutes must not be minors; and they had to obtain police permits which displayed their photograph. Furthermore, they had to undergo weekly examinations in order to detect venereal disease; if they were infected, they were obliged to stop working, their permit was withdrawn and they were obliged to get treatment at their own expense. Only when the treatment was satisfactorily concluded would their licence be restored.

Enforcement of these procedures proved difficult, and someone as adept as Giuseppe was cunning enough to be able to drive a horse and cart right through the rules and regulations.

The Egyptian authorities were aware of Giuseppe's activities by 1908 although they did little or nothing to curb them. It was a pity, because in 1910 alone there were 71 reported cases of illegal prostitution involving girls mainly aged between fourteen and sixteen, but also as young as six, eight and ten and, in one case, only four.

So with waterside pimps regaling the British troops with irresistible offers – 'You like my sister? She all pink inside like Queen Victoria – only sick twice!' Giuseppe's coffers swelled and so did his family. Eugenio was born in 1908, Attilio in 1910 and Carmelo in 1915. But under Egyptian law, persons born in Egypt could only gain citizenship if the father had been born there; and since Giuseppe had been born in Sicily (part of a united Italy since 1861) all three births were registered with the Italian Consul in Alexandria. In addition, a daughter, Margherita, was born; she would take no part in the family business.

Egypt was a pretty rough place to be a prostitute. Giuseppe was what was known as a *sahăbat*, a person who brought young women into the profession; nor were the *sahăbats* particularly choosy about how they acquired them. Girls would often be abducted and raped in order to force them into prostitution. Excessive violence would sometimes be used: beatings, mutilation, the use of acid and even putting chilli in their sensitive bodily areas. On the face of it, these methods appear to be rather counter-productive for a ponce demanding an income from women who, in Victorian and Edwardian times, were dubbed 'Unfortunates'; these extreme measures were probably only used on the most recalcitrant of girls, as a warning to the others.

With the advent of the First World War, the Secretary of State for War, Lord Kitchener KG, KP, GCB, OM, GCSI, GCMG, GCIE, PC, famous for his recruiting poster: 'BRITONS [followed by a photograph depicting a stern looking Secretary of State] wants you. Join your country's Army! God save the King', offered the following advice to recruits:

> Your duty cannot be done unless your health is sound. So keep constantly on your guard against any excesses. In this new experience you may find temptations both in wine and women. You must entirely resist both temptations and while treating all women with perfect courtesy, you should avoid any intimacy. Do your duty bravely. Fear God, honour the King.

Unsurprisingly, the young Tommies who had come to the conclusion that they were likely to be slaughtered in very short order, thanks to the incompetence of their senior officers, largely disregarded the crusty old bachelor's advice. Kitchener was blamed for the shortage of shells in the 1915 Spring Offensive. He should have been criticized for neglecting to issue condoms to the troops.

With the First World War underway, Giuseppe expanded his businesses even further afield. Now he set up a chain of brothels right across Egypt, in Cairo, Suez and Port Said, and further to Morocco, where he sold girls to the dregs of that country, Bedouins, gangsters and bandits. He had a bit of competition, namely Ibrahim al-Gharbi, whose father was, like Giuseppe, a slave trader. Al-Gharbi had moved to Cairo and in 1912 was running fifteen brothels in the Azbakiya district, each containing ten women. When al-Gharbi was arrested in 1923, due to the fact that he dressed as a woman and wore a veil, the authorities accurately deduced that he was a homosexual. The Egyptians had (and still have) a fairly ambivalent attitude to homosexuality, it not being an actual offence to be homosexual. However, there were certain morality laws under which, if it is proved that a person has acted in a way thought to be immoral, scandalous or offensive, he can be sentenced to up to seventeen years' imprisonment, with or without hard labour, and fined into the bargain. Perhaps al-Gharbi thought that he'd got a result when he was given just five years' imprisonment, but in any event, he died within the first year of his sentence.

Also in 1923, the International Criminal Police Organization (Interpol) set up an office in the Rue Paul Valéry, Paris to provide international assistance to worldwide police forces battling sophisticated criminality. In January 1930, at the sixth session of the General Assembly, a committee was set up to address the problem of white slavery. Its resolutions were:

1. Strict control of employment agencies where work in a foreign country is offered.

2. Establishment of offices to ensure that women artistes abroad, whose contracts are withdrawn, are returned to their country of origin.
3. Careful scrutiny of all applications to work abroad and checking of contracts offered.
4. Women police officers to be available in all countries to work in liaison with the social services to help women in difficulties.

Interpol was so pleased with their resolutions that they were repeated at the General Assemblies of 1932, 1934 and 1936. Unfortunately, they did not even scratch the surface of the problem.

Just to eliminate a misconception, there was an ITV television series named *Interpol Calling!* which ran for 39 episodes, mercifully for one season only, between 1959 and 1960. In each of the black and white episodes, flinty-eyed, granite-jawed Interpol detectives were depicted dashing about, making sensational arrests and, what was more, solving their cases, all in the space of 25 minutes. I have endeavoured, without success, to discover who the police consultant was for the series and have come to the conclusion that there probably wasn't one. The series was, of course, tripe, since Interpol is, in the main, staffed by detectives who are sick, lame or dying. Their days are spent shuffling paper, they do not go out and make arrests and in most cases they are not fired with enthusiasm.

Should any active officers slip through the net, or be posted there because they had offended against the discipline code which made Interpol 'a punishment posting', they were mostly prepared to take any risk in order to be transferred elsewhere. These included simulating lunacy, attempted bribery and endeavouring to shag the senior officer's wife, anything to get out of that cheerless 2-year posting. Those ruses were usually accurately identified for what they were, and were seldom successful.

★

Since the Messina brothers had grown up in surroundings where their playmates were mainly prostitutes, it was hardly surprising that they should have joined the family firm; by 1928 Alfredo had a bank account with the Crédit Lyonnais in Egypt and also the Bank Italo Egyptano where, stating that he was in the furniture business with his father, he deposited a total of £1,659. During the same year, Eugenio was in trouble with the Egyptian authorities on charges of gun-running and drug-smuggling; but for whatever reason, no prosecutions followed.

However, by 1932 a cabinet decree in Egypt had abolished prostitutes' licences and established 'The Public Morals Police'. The following year, this gave the authorities (who by now were sick and tired of Giuseppe and his family) the excuse to kick them straight out of the country. The decision was given extra impetus when Salvatore was sentenced to six months' imprisonment for living on immoral earnings.

However, to do so required the family to be in possession of passports, which had been used by European countries since the First World War. They had not been necessary when the Messinas had arrived in Egypt almost thirty years' previously; now, they were. The familiar 32-page British passport (known as 'the old blue style') came into use in 1920. It was valid for two years, until 1924 when it became valid for five. It contained the bearer's name, profession, place and date of birth, country of residence, height, eye and hair colour, signature and photograph.

Salvatore was first in the queue. At the British Consulate at Cairo on 29 May 1924 he gave his date of birth as 8 (instead of 20) August 1898 and was issued with British passport No. 3541. This was replaced at the British Consulate at Tangier on 15 March 1934 with passport No. 557, and then his passport was renewed, some time between 1936 and 1945, at a place unknown.

Following his brother's example, on 25 July 1924, Alfredo, giving his date of birth as 2 May (as opposed to 6 February) 1901, applied for a British passport at the British Consulate at Alexandria and was duly issued with one, No. 1821. He acquired a fresh passport, No. 558, in Tangier at the same time as brother Salvatore obtained his, and it would be extended on 16 April 1939 at a place unknown.

Although Egypt gained its independence in 1922, British influence still dominated that country's political life and fostered fiscal, administrative and governmental reforms. Britain retained control of the Canal Zone, Sudan and Egypt's external protection; this included the police, army, communications, railways – and the protection of foreigners.

So on the morning of Monday, 3 July 1933 Virginia Messina went to the British Consul in Alexandria and applied for and duly received a British passport, No. 5473. Her nationality was shown as 'British subject by birth. The wife of a British subject by birth'.

Formal records of British passports have been kept since 1794; however, a thorough search has since been carried out, at my request, which reveals that there is no record of a British passport being issued in the name of Giuseppe Messina, nor one using his alias of Giuseppe de Bono. This does not mean, of course, that a passport was not issued to him, but it would have been one for which he had provided a different identity.

Coincidentally, on the same day at the same place, British passport No. 5474 was issued to Attilio. He gave his date of birth as 20 March (as opposed to the correct one, 24 March) 1910, and the passport was extended on 29 June 1938 at a place unknown. A fresh one, No. 374440, was issued some time between 1946 and 1947, once more at a place unknown.

A third passport was issued to the Messina family on that day at that location: No. 5472 was issued to Carmelo Messina, who produced a baptismal certificate which showed that although he had been born in Alexandria he was a citizen of Malta. This, of course, was a lie, because like his brother Attilio he was registered as an Italian national. He gave his date of birth as 27 June 1915, although when he came to renew it at a place unknown in July 1938 he gave his correct birth date, 29 June 1915. In fact, it would be reissued by the Foreign Office on 31 October 1946, before being impounded in 1951, it having been discovered that Carmelo – by then, he was referred to as 'Signor Messina' – was not a British subject. However, we have something like twenty years of Messina-inspired depravity to trawl through, before that juncture is reached.

So – since the two brothers had been born in Alexandria to a father who was Sicilian and whose births had been registered at the Italian consulate – how was it they had been granted British passports? Had a little illicit money changed hands from the brothers who would become known for offering bribes to officialdom in order to get their own way? Surely not. There must have been some rational explanation for their acquisition of those very important Government documents. However, if there was, it was not one which the Consul General in Alexandria wished to share with me, despite three requests to do so.

★

From Egypt, Salvatore went to Madrid, Marrakesh and Casablanca, where, along the way, he married a Frenchwoman, Maria Burratti; following a further confrontation with the law, he moved to Pau, a French border town near the Pyrenees. It was also in Pau that brother Carmelo married Ida Poumirou. Thanks to the brothers being in possession of British passports, this permitted two more 'British wives' to be admitted to the shores of England.

Initially, most of the family returned to Malta but then, one by one, the Messinas made their way to London.

If either the Maltese or the Egyptian officials, all of them signed up to the Interpol agreement, had been aware of their destination, it would have been helpful if those chairbound warriors had informed their counterparts, the recumbent gladiators based at Scotland Yard, of the imminent arrival of this revolting family.

Unfortunately, it appears they did not.

CHAPTER 2

Marriages and Importations

The Messinas were either really well informed or downright lucky, because by the time of their arrival in Britain, brothel-keeping and the running of prostitutes in London were up for grabs. There were two main reasons for this.

The first were the laws governing prostitution, most of which were pretty archaic. These were the Disorderly Houses Act, 1751; the Disorderly Houses Act, 1818; the Vagrancy Act, 1824; the Town Police Clauses Act, 1847; the Criminal Law Amendment Act, 1885; the Vagrancy Act, 1898; and the Criminal Law Amendment Act, 1912.

It was the Vagrancy Act 1824 and the Town Police Clauses Act, 1847 which dealt with prostitutes, who once convicted became known as 'common prostitutes'; this expression continued in use for almost two hundred years, until political correctness abolished the title and changed it to 'person'. However, in London, Section 54, sub-section 11 of the Metropolitan Police Act, 1839 was used to effect the arrests of prostitutes who solicited to the annoyance of passers-by, and the maximum fine was £2, or forty shillings. That penalty – or less – was imposed by magistrates for well in excess of a hundred years. This sum might have inflicted financial hardship on the 'Tom' (prostitute) of 1839, but by the time the Messinas arrived, such a pecuniary penalty was laughable.

Next, permitting prostitutes to assemble in premises used for the sale of refreshments was punished by virtue of the two Disorderly Houses Act of 1751 and 1818 – penalty, £5.

The two Criminal Law Amendment Acts of 1885 and 1912 dealt with procuring women to become common prostitutes, for which the penalty was a maximum of two years' imprisonment. However, there was a get-out clause; it was not an offence to procure a woman who was already a common prostitute. This anomaly was finally eliminated in 1951.

The offence of keeping a brothel was a real can of worms. A brothel was defined as a place where people of the opposite sex met for sexual intercourse for payment; it required at least two women to inhabit the premises for it to constitute a brothel, although neither woman needed to have been a common prostitute. If a woman rented a room or flat and used it for the purposes of her own prostitution, it was not a brothel; she committed no offence. Even if she used the premises for habitual prostitution, she could not be prosecuted. But if she permitted just one other prostitute to use the premises, as well as herself, then it became a brothel within the meaning of Section 13 of the Criminal Law Amendment Act as amended by Section 4 of the 1912 Act.

In the case of the landlord of such premises, he could be guilty of allowing it to be used for 'habitual prostitution' – but not by any of the tenants, who could not be prosecuted. But if a landlord controlled a block of flats in which each one was inhabited by a single prostitute, then that could constitute a brothel.

See? Clear as mud.

The penalties for brothel-keeping were hardly dire: a fine not exceeding £100 or three months' imprisonment for an initial offence, and for a second or subsequent offence a fine not exceeding £250 or six months' imprisonment or, by virtue of Section 3 of the Criminal Law Amendment Act, 1922, both.

With all of the 'ifs, ands or buts' contained in that ancient legislation, plus the insignificance of the fines, the Messinas must have rubbed their hands with glee.

As well as the limits of the legislation, the English attitude to ponces was not quite the same as in France; there, they could be excluded from major urban areas, although in both countries ponces could be placed under surveillance.

The second reason for the Messinas' good fortune was the lack of opposition.

★

In 1926 a French pimp, Charles Baladda, had been shot dead by a fellow undesirable, one Emile Berthier aka 'Mad Emile', in London. Found guilty but insane, Berthier was later deported to France; he had been an associate of Juan Antonio Castanar, a Spaniard believed to have introduced the tango to Britain. Castanar was also credited with exporting prostitutes to the Middle East. Casimir Micheletti was a violent French pimp who due to his expertise with a knife was known as 'The Assassin', and he and Castanar were – no pun intended – at daggers drawn with each other.

Micheletti's club, 'Le Mirage', and Castanar's dancing school in Archer Street, London, W1 were both firebombed, there was a spate of stabbings and shootings, and in 1929 both men were deported. They came to sticky ends the following year; Micheletti was shot dead in Paris, and his murderer, Castanar, was sent to Devil's Island for life.

Then there was Eddie Manning (dubbed, with complete justification, 'Eddie the Villain' and 'The Worst Man in London'), who had forsaken his Jamaican roots to run prostitutes and distribute drugs in Soho on a commercial scale; he died in 1933 of syphilis in Parkhurst prison's infirmary whilst serving a 3-year term of penal servitude. So that was that rather objectionable bunch out of the way.

Who did it leave? Well, there was Max Kassel – otherwise known as Emile Allard, Red Max, Max the Red, Ginger Max and Max le Rouquin – who had been busily involved in white slave trafficking, but his activities came to an abrupt end when he was found murdered in January 1936. There was no involvement by the Messina brothers; Kassel's murderer was later sentenced in France.

After Kassel's demise there really wasn't anybody else of any note. There were a few French ponces in the areas of Soho and Tottenham Court Road, and Charles 'Darby' Sabini and his gang had a toehold in Soho. However, they were also occupied in continual running battles with the Hoxton Gang, the Bethnal Green Mob and the Birmingham Boys for control of the racetracks, so they were happy to step aside for the newcomers.[1]

★

To coincide with the Messina family's arrival in Britain, steps were already being taken to keep a lid on prostitution and white slavery, although those in authority often held opposing views on the subject. 'I think there is more rot written about white slavery, as it is called', wrote Detective Chief Inspector Fred 'Nutty' Sharpe, who investigated the Max Kassel murder, 'than any other subject in crime.' However, one person who would have disagreed with those sentiments was the rather formidable Superintendent Dorothy Olivia Georgiana Peto OBE, KPM (she frightened her male counterparts witless by dressing as a man, wearing a jacket, shirt, tie and trilby), who had taken command of A4 Branch at the Yard which catered for women police. She built up the A4 Index, which noted details of prostitutes and

---

1 For more details of these activities during the 1920s and 1930s, see *The Guv'nors: Ten of Scotland Yard's Greatest Detectives*, Wharncliffe True Crime, 2010 and *The Sweeney: The First Sixty Years of Scotland Yard's Crimebusting Flying Squad 1919-1978*, Wharncliffe True Crime, 2011.

missing girls and supervised young women leaving the country
on theatrical contracts; in addition, she set up a good working
relationship with educational authorities and juvenile courts and
she wanted women officers appointed court officers and gaolers
at Police Courts.

As with many concepts, Miss Peto's was good in theory but,
due to the lack of personnel, not so helpful in practice. In 1917 the
Commissioner of Police had formed a body of 100 women patrols
and twelve sergeants for welfare work amongst women and children.
The Sex Disqualification Removal Act, 1919 lifted the legal barrier
which had hitherto prevented their enrolment as regular constables.
However, the Geddes economy measures which followed the First
World War meant that by 1922 the women's numbers were reduced
to twenty. Two years later, the figure was increased to fifty, but
although their official establishment was raised to 200, their actual
numbers were woefully far below that figure. The full complement
would not be reached until the advent of the Second World War.

There had, however, been a number of murders of prostitutes
in London in which the finger of guilt was pointed in the direction
of perpetrators of foreign origin. The matter was raised in the
House on 18 May 1936 by George Mathers, Labour MP (later
1st Baron Mathers KT, PC, DL), who asked the Home Secretary
if he was aware that three women had been murdered in Soho in
the previous seven months, that no arrests had been made and that
women in Soho were going in fear of their lives; would he assure
the House that everything possible was being done to bring those
responsible to justice?

The Home Secretary, Sir John Simon, was regrettably absent,
so it fell to the Under Secretary of State for the Home Department,
Geoffrey Lloyd (later Baron Geoffrey-Lloyd PC) to murmur a
few placatory words to soothe the inflamed breast of the Right
Honourable Member for Linlithgow.

But Mr Mathers was having none of it; he demanded to know,
'Has the Home Secretary observed the ugly words, including
blackmail, that have been used in connection with these tragic
occurrences and has he not thought that a searching enquiry into
the whole of the circumstances is called for?'

This was precisely what the Under Secretary of State did not
wish to hear.

'The most searching investigation is now in progress', he
replied. 'While I appreciate the anxiety of the honourable member,
I should deprecate any suggestions which are liable to create an
exaggerated impression of the situation or to arouse unnecessary
alarm.'

But that was exactly what did happen. The 23 May 1936 edition of *John Bull* magazine, under the heading of 'London's Murder Land' contained the words, 'Decent hardworking, clean-living foreigners, as good citizens as any Briton, living cheek by jowl with the scum of continental gutters. And now the mixture is getting too strong for anybody's taste.'

The very next day, blame was apportioned by the *News of the World*, which pointed an accusing finger at 'Foreigners – men who prey upon the women of the streets'.

However, if 'foreigners' were responsible for one or more of the murders, nobody was ever charged; and meanwhile, the Messina family got to work.

To start with, in 1934 Eugenio had already been busy. On 28 July at Bow Street Police Court, Charles Haddon Redvers Gray, a 33-year-old solicitor of Crown Court, Chancery Lane, pleaded guilty to making a false declaration by saying that Hilda Ward, a 20-year-old barmaid, was a fit and proper person to receive a passport. In mitigation, Mr J. Thompson Halsall told the magistrate, Sir Rollo Frederick Graham-Campbell, that his client had been introduced to the girl by an estate agent with whom he had had many dealings and had no reason to disbelieve, and added that Gray was 'more foolish than knavish'. Fining Gray £50 and ordering him to pay ten guineas costs, Sir Rollo sternly informed the prisoner that the offence was a serious one, punishable with a maximum sentence of two years' imprisonment and a fine of £100.

It was a serious matter for two other reasons: first, the Director of Public Prosecutions thought the matter sufficiently grave to instruct a barrister, Mr R. L. Jackson (later Assistant Commissioner [Crime] Sir Richard Jackson CBE) to represent the prosecution, even though the defendant had pleaded guilty. Second, the arresting officer, Divisional Detective Inspector Leonard Burt of 'D' Division (later Commander Burt CVO, CBE), informed Sir Rollo that he believed this to be a case of attempted procuration but that the solicitor had been unaware of it.

What was not mentioned in court but was privately passed between 'tec and barrister, was that the person behind the whole business was one Eugenio Messina.

So Miss Ward tottered off, hopefully still a virtuous, albeit a sadder and wiser, girl, and whilst Eugenio's plans were frustrated, he was temporarily down but not out.

Two years previously, in France, Eugenio had married a prostitute, Andrée Astier – she was also known as Colette – who of course was able to claim British citizenship thanks to Eugenio's blue British passport. And that raises an anomaly.

Eugenio must have possessed a British passport, but it was not in his own name, nor was one issued using his alias of Eugenio de Bono. Where and when it was issued – and in which name – is a mystery. The first record that the Passport Office possesses is when passport No. 412201 was issued to 'Eugene Messina' on 2 February 1938. His date and place of birth was not shown, neither was the place of issue. The same applied when it was renewed on 2 May 1946, as it did when a fresh one, No. 23959, was provided for him on 5 August 1949.

But whatever name Colette was using, she arrived in England in 1934 and it took just one month for her to collect her first conviction for soliciting; by 1956 she had collected 127 more. It was with her assistance that by 1945 Eugenio's earnings amounted to £1,000 per week.

Between 1934 and 1937 Eugenio made frequent trips to the continent and, whilst he paid the passages for a number of attractive young women to return with him, oddly, as they passed through customs, he gave no indication to officials that he was acquainted with them, or they with him. And when matters became too tiring for Eugenio, his brothers helped out with the human import business. So did his parents.

Alfredo was the next brother to marry, in 1935: this was to Mary (he was unable to recall her maiden name) in Madrid. She was also known as 'Marcelle', and accompanying her 'husband' to London she was promptly put to work; between September 1935 and June 1936 she had acquired fifteen convictions for soliciting. By 1951 they would total 122. During the same year as his marriage, whilst making a trip to Belgium, Alfredo also met (and imported) a prostitute named Georgette Borg. She would later figure prominently in his affairs.

★

At this time, many foreign prostitutes used addresses in and around the area of Tottenham Court Road – Whitfield Street, Grafton Street, Goodge Street and Fitzroy Street – and their ponces were also foreigners, some Italian, others French. Therefore, the Messinas gave the area a wide berth, for two main reasons. First, there were the problems which would have arisen because of the number of prostitutes the Messinas were importing – the beats would have become overcrowded – plus the strong probability of confrontations between the girls, and also with their ponces, thereby drawing attention to the Messinas themselves. It was probably a lesson passed on to the brothers from their father;

after all, with his arrival in Malta, hadn't Giuseppe stayed clear of the streets of Valletta with its home-grown ponces and gone instead to Ḥamrun with its friendlier inhabitants?

The second reason was this: the streets around the Tottenham Court Road area were pretty sleazy, and the Messinas thought themselves a cut above those surroundings. So whilst the brothers would not find the same ex-pats as their father had found in Ḥamrun, they could – and did – pass themselves off as diplomats and dealers in precious gems to gain acceptance amongst the inhabitants of Mayfair.

They couldn't have chosen better. Much of the land belonged to the wealthy Grosvenor family, who had developed it into the most affluent area of London. From Park Lane in the west to Oxford Street in the north, from Regent Street in the east to Piccadilly in the south, it was policed by the Metropolitan Police's 'C' Division from West End Central police station. Since 'CD' (which was the code by which West End Central was known) also covered Soho, it became unwieldy and in the 1960s was split into two areas, 'CD1' and 'CD2'.

The name of the region came from 'May Fair', an annual celebration held at Great Brookfield between 1686 and 1764. That area later became part of Curzon Street and Shepherd Market, which attracted an unpleasant crowd; the fair was abolished but the seediness of Shepherd Market remained.

But that was a small blip in such a prosperous area; there were upmarket residential properties, embassies, shops and restaurants. In addition, there were the hotels, which included the Ritz, the Grosvenor House, Claridges and the Berkeley. It was to this last hotel that, at about the same time as the entrance of the Messina family, a travel-worn young adventurer from Tasmania arrived. He was not exactly penniless; he had two shillings in his pocket, and since the taxi from Waterloo station had cost 1s 9d, he gave all of his fortune to the cab driver. He was booked into the Berkeley's Royal Suite, and when financial assistance from his anthropologist father failed to arrive, 24-year-old Errol Flynn turned in one of his earliest acting performances with a convincing (but contrived) case of appendicitis, whereupon he was shipped out to a private nursing home. It was from there that Mr Flynn's career took off; so did that of the Messinas.

As the Messinas rented and bought properties in and around the Mayfair district, the girls continued to arrive; at one stage, they had thirty-two under their control, and their earnings flowed into the Messinas' coffers.

On 11 November 1935 John Horwell, the Chief Constable of the CID, sent a report to the Assistant Commissioner (Crime), Sir Norman Kendall:

It would be difficult to find a street prostitute in the West End without bruises, even around the neck. They daily come up against vicious men, and always demand more money than they bargained for.

However, not all of the 'vicious men' they encountered were customers.

The girls were incredibly strictly supervised; the charm used to entice them into the Messinas' net soon wore off and they were subjected to bullying, beatings and threats of disfigurement and death if they failed to toe the Messina line.

On 23 April 1936 the Assistant Commissioner (Crime), Sir Norman Kendall CBE, authorized John Horwell, the Chief Constable of the CID, to compile a list of 102 foreign prostitutes in London who accounted for 28.8 per cent of the total number of arrests. This would be known as 'The Secret Foreign Prostitutes' and Associates' Album'. However, the prostitutes and ponces were not receiving the practical attention from the police and the courts that they really merited. During the 1920s there had been a series of high-profile scandals involving the arrests of prostitutes, and the police – perhaps a little unfairly – had received a great deal of criticism from the judiciary and Parliament. By way of example, 2,291 arrests for soliciting were carried out in London in 1922; the following year, the number had dropped to 650, and due to the barrackings that the police often received in court, along with allegations of heavy-handedness and exhibitions of disbelief, their rationale was, 'Why should I bother?'

The Commissioner, Brigadier General Sir William Thomas Francis Horwood GBE, KCB, DSO, could not be said to be 'a father to his men'; he was detested by them and was described by a clerk in his office as 'an unattractive man who mistook arrogance for leadership'. Nevertheless, he appeared to sympathize with them when he wrote in his annual report for 1923:

No cases of a controversial nature have arisen in connection with sexual offences during the year, presumably on account of the extreme reluctance of police officers to take action which they feel may bring them into collision with the magistrates, the press and the public. It is not at all a satisfactory condition of affairs, but in all circumstances it is not to be wondered at.

The Commissioner was perhaps being a little premature in speaking of 'cases of a controversial nature'; by 1928 the rate of prostitutes' arrests had crept up to a fairly respectable 2,315, but during that year there were three enormous scandals of a sexual nature in the Metropolitan Police Area, and although the Lee Commission was set up under Lord Lee of Fareham to examine the first two cases, the third, involving club and brothel owners bribing a police officer on a massive scale, all but brought the Met to its knees. Horwood resigned, and the following year, prostitutes' arrests fell to 723 and to 695 by 1930.[2]

One female magistrate refused to believe that it was possible to have sexual intercourse standing up; any such cases – they were colloquially known as 'knee-tremblers' – which came before her were summarily dismissed. One such case (it was not heard in her court) was brought before the bench; the charge was one of 'outraging public decency'. The arrest had been made after the arresting officer had seen a prostitute and her client engaged in the aforementioned 'knee-trembler' against a brick wall, the unyielding surface of which was necessary to give them some sort of stability during their exertions. To this charge, both pleaded not guilty.

In giving his evidence, the officer told the court, 'The defendants had just completed an act of sexual intercourse when I arrested them.'

'Just a moment!' interrupted the defence solicitor. 'How did you know they'd just completed an act of sexual intercourse?'

This statement had attracted the attention of the magistrate, as well. 'Yes', he exclaimed. 'How *did* you know?'

Completely unfazed by this left and right attack on his probity, the officer coolly replied, 'There was a smell of fornication in the air!'

Views on the prosecution of prostitutes changed in 1937 with the forthcoming coronation of King George VI; Mayfair residents were sick and tired of the girls plying their trade in that area. In no time at all, the Government acted; after all, nobody in authority wanted Mayfair residents to be disgruntled. Their votes were valued and in addition, there was the 1938 Honours List to be considered. The necessary orders were passed downwards to the police, and 'C' Division – which covered the Mayfair area – struck, making 1,571 arrests. The following year, that number increased to 2,298.

---

2 For further details of these scandals, see *Whitechapel's Sherlock Holmes: The Casebook of Fred Wensley OBE, KPM, Victorian Crime Buster*, Pen & Sword True Crime, 2014.

Now, it was noted that of the 102 prostitutes listed in Horwell's index, 87 per cent solicited in the Piccadilly and Mayfair areas of London, more of them were attracting a 'limited clientele' in the upper classes of Mayfair and some were actually living there. As the decade came to a close, property owners and agents became so concerned that they formed a committee to tackle the problem; in doing so, they hoped that the police would become more involved.

However, in an attempt to downplay matters (and in an effort to preserve credibility for his position), Superintendent Cole of 'C' Division sent a report to the Deputy Assistant Commissioner of No. 1 District, dated 28 August 1939, informing his senior officer that 'It was unlikely that more than a few offenders were "professionals" for whom crime was the principal source of income.'

Superintendent Cole was either naïve, badly misinformed or downright mendacious – or perhaps he was relying on past glories, since in 1936, twenty-three of the sixty ponces who had been documented had been deported. Whatever his reasoning, within a week he would be proved to be hugely wrong because the Second World War would break out, and whilst the Messinas' income was already substantial, their profits would now go sky-high.

CHAPTER 3

Marthe Watts and the War Years

With the advent of a second world war, the Metropolitan Police Commissioner, Sir Philip Woolcott Game GCB, GCVO, GBE, KCMG, DSO, rose to the occasion. He was now almost sixty-five and his health was poor but nevertheless, he patriotically decided to remain as head of the police for the duration. With war inevitable, on 31 August 1939, 1,764 police pensioners and special constables were recruited to form a war reserve; then 18,868 war reservists, 5,380 special constables and 2,737 pensioners were called up, and they would soon number 26,985. They would be much needed; at the commencement of hostilities, the establishment of the Metropolitan Police was 19,465, although the actual strength was 18,805, but by the end of the year, recruiting for the regular Force had ceased. Furthermore, within two years 4,000 of them had left to join the armed services.[1]

Within days of war being declared, the Emergency Powers Bill was passed and, believing that air attacks from Germany were imminent, the evacuation of schoolchildren and those described as belonging to 'priority classes' commenced, and identity cards were introduced. At that time, the average weekly wage was £4 9s 0d; one month after the commencement of war, income tax was raised to 7s 6d in the pound, and shortly afterwards to 10s 0d in the pound. Those who were considered high earners had to pay 19s 6d in the pound – but that did not include the Messinas, who decided that they were exempt and not only from paying income tax, either.

On 2 December 1939 conscription for the armed forces was expanded to include men aged between nineteen and forty-one – bad news for all five brothers. Their British citizenship had rebounded badly on them since they had adopted English-sounding names: Salvatore was Arthur Evans, Attilio became Raymond Maynard and Carmelo was transformed into Charles Maitland. After failing to report for military service, warrants were issued for their arrests, but although Alfredo (in his guise as

---

1 For further information of those times, the austerity measures and black-marketeering, see *Scotland Yard's Ghost Squad: The Secret Weapon Against Post-War Crime*, Wharncliffe Local History, 2011.

Alfred Martin) was ordered to report to attend a medical board on 17 August 1943, he simply refused to go. Eugenio was rather more subtle. He utilized his redundant skills as a carpenter to fashion a set of bookshelves which fitted exactly in front of a wall cupboard in his Lowndes Street flat. The bottom shelf was hinged so that if an unexpected caller rang the doorbell, up came the flap, Eugenio's tubby little body squeezed through the aperture, the flap was closed and anybody who demanded his services for King and Country was doomed to disappointment. The other brothers used a series of front-men to ensure that no unwelcome visitors invaded their personal space.

They could have used the services of some decidedly dodgy doctors; Dr William St John Sutton was one who dished out untruthful certificates, and when he appeared at the Old Bailey he asked for fifty other offences to be taken into consideration and was jailed for nine months; incidentally, the prosecution barrister was Christmas Humphreys, who would later play a prominent part in Alfredo's downfall.

So it would have made sense for the Messinas to have utilized someone of Dr Sutton's skills, or at least for them to have gone to ground, but they did not; they had a business to run, they continued to rent properties, employ girls and marry them off to vagrants and drunks; and with troops flooding into London demanding the services of the Messina women, the brothers had sufficient money to thoroughly enjoy themselves.

*

In February 1940 a visitor arrived on these shores (for the second time) who was to play a decisive role in Eugenio Messina's life. She had been born Marie Julie Marthe Hucbourg in 1913 at Neuville-au-Pont, Marne, France, and at an early age she became a prostitute in France, Italy and Spain, before deciding to settle in London to ply her trade. However, she was fully aware that if she were caught she could be deported; the Aliens Act, 1905 had provided for the expulsion of 'improper and scandalous foreigners' (especially of those convicted of offences linked to prostitution).

However, deportation could be circumvented by marrying an Englishman; this ruse was known as 'an arranged marriage' or 'a marriage of convenience'. Only 35.9 per cent of these arranged marriages were carried out in England, because it made sense to evade the eye of the British police by carrying them out abroad, often (although not always) in British consulates; not that they were considered illegal in the sense that it was not an offence for a man to marry a known foreign prostitute. This deception had already been carried out by the Messina brothers on the continent; in the same way that they had apparently claimed residency on their mother's citizenship, it meant that their 'wives' – and for that read 'sources of income' – now being the holders of British passports, could not be deported.

Reports varied as to the cost of such an agreement – anything from £10 to £300. Therefore (and at a cost – she said – of 30,000 francs or £240) a marriage was arranged between 24-year-old Mlle Hucbourg (always known as Marthe) and a 63-year-old Englishman named Arthur David Watts. A widower, previously married to the late Annie Eliza Rogers, Watts was also an impecunious drunk. This travesty was carried out at the *mairie* in Barbizon, near the Forest of Fontainebleau on 12 November 1937, and with marriage certificate No. KB63362 tucked into Mrs Watts' handbag, the couple made their way to the British Consulate in Paris. There their ruse became so blatantly obvious – neither bride nor groom could speak the other's language – that her application for a British passport was refused. Nevertheless, they took a one-way ticket to Victoria station using her French passport, although it was possible that having unsuccessfully applied for a British passport, the consulate would have passed her details on to the Passport Office in London. After her arrival, it took Marthe no time at all to collect her first conviction for soliciting. It was more difficult when she was charged with keeping a brothel; in the absence of a British passport, she was in danger of being deported. After several remands at Bow Street Police Court, she was fortunate in locating her bibulous husband at his salubrious London residence, 34 Harcombe Road, Stoke Newington; through a mist of whisky fumes he was able to authenticate her claim that they were married. The result was a £50 fine with £35 costs on the brothel-keeping charge, a bursary of another tenner to Arthur who was unceremoniously told, '*Prends notre cachet, et va-t'en!*' (Take the cash and hop it!) and the acquisition of a British passport which was far more genuine than its owner.

Life for Marthe went on; she had acquired a flat in Duke Street where the rent was £6 per week. Indisputably, the landlord must have known her profession, since the average weekly rent at that time was 12s 0d.

One of Messinas' places of enjoyment was The Palm Beach Bottles Party Club, situated at 37 Wardour Street, W1, and it was whilst Eugenio – now calling himself Edward Marshall – was there with some of his brothers and their women, that on 3 April 1941, he and Marthe Watts (who had just returned from a continental trip) met.

Eugenio, sensing that he had a winner in Marthe, turned on a charm offensive, and she later accepted an invitation from him to dinner at the Ritz. The date for their assignation was 10 May 1941. This venue was chosen not only for its opulent surroundings but because The Palm Beach had been shut down nine days previously, due to gangster Eddie Fletcher being stabbed to death there by Antonio 'Babe' Mancini, who in turn departed this life following an appointment with Albert Pierrepoint in his capacity as hangman.

So that night, 10 May, there was a romantic full moon to herald Marthe and Eugenio's relationship, but had they only known it, the date was to be an ominous one indeed for Londoners.

Since September 1940, Britain – and especially London – had been enduring German air raids; it was known as the Blitz (an abbreviation of *Blitzkrieg* or 'lightning war'), when, over a period of eight months, 1,000 high explosive bombs, 55 heavy oil canister fire bombs, 11 parachute mines and thousands of incendiary bombs rained down on London. In the first four months of the Blitz alone, more than 13,000 people were killed, and the wounded numbered tens of thousands.

But it was the last night of the Blitz – 10 May – that was the most frightful.

It was then that *Luftwaffe Generalfeldmarschall* Hugo Sperrie ordered 505 bombers to fly to London, and as the Heinkel He 111s, Junkers Ju-88s and Messerschmitt Bf 110s made their way down the Thames, helpfully aided by that romantic full moon, they dropped 711 tons of high explosive bombs and 86,173 incendiaries, starting at 11.02 pm and not finishing until almost 6 o'clock the following morning. Many of the bombers carried out two or three sorties; having dropped their bombs, they flew back to base, refuelled, rearmed and returned for another go. It was one of the most destructive raids of the war. The District Line railway was badly damaged, as was Hallam Street, the House of Commons, New Bond Street, the Queen's Hall, St Clement Danes, the Turner Buildings and Westminster Abbey. A bomb struck the north-west corner of the Old Bailey, completely demolishing the court of the Recorder of London; as well as the top judge's court being destroyed, so was the top cop's office. A bomb struck the south-east turret of Scotland Yard, penetrating several floors and putting fifteen rooms out of action, one of them being General Registry which contained the Yard's correspondence. In turn, the contents of the registry crashed down on to the Commissioner's desk – fortunately, he was absent, out checking the damage in London – and the following morning, as Londoners crunched their way, ankle-deep, through streets full of broken glass, two women clerks were found searching the Embankment for the one million index cards which were strewn in and amongst the rubble. The Secretary – the man in charge of that department – noted, with unintentional humour that 'the index did need overhauling'.

The resultant 2,136 fires during that night covered 700 acres and were so intense that they actually set the roadways alight; the area affected was approximately double that burned in the Great Fire of London, and the damage – in 1941 values – amounted to £20 million. Although the Royal Air Force managed to shoot down 33 of the enemy bombers, 1,435 Londoners were killed and over 2,000 others seriously injured. Unfortunately, Eugenio Messina was not amongst the casualties.

Dodging Hitler's ordnance, he and Marthe managed to reach the sanctuary of the Hungaria Restaurant in Lower Regent Street and there they stayed, eating and drinking until the 'all-clear' sounded at 5.57 am.

Eugenio booked a room at the Ritz for her; at that date guests were permitted to stay at a hotel for four days without handing over their ration books.

Seven weeks after they first met, Marthe became one of 'The Messina Girls'. She later moved in to Eugenio's apartment in Berkeley Square with two other girls, Anita and Jeanne, both of whom were Belgian, and later shifted to Lansdowne Street.

Marthe Watts was certainly no newcomer to the world of prostitution (on the continent she had variously been known as 'Daisy' or 'Georgie', but now, in London, she had become 'Gina'), although she had never experienced the strict regimentation that was imposed by the brothers, particularly Eugenio. Neither she nor the other girls were permitted to wear clothing that was in any way provocative; not that that would have mattered, since they were never permitted to undress when they were with a client. Indeed, there would have been little time for the girls to disrobe, since 'The Ten Minute Rule' was imposed; the maximum amount of time the girls were permitted to spend with clients who, to use somewhat inelegant phraseology, often went before they came. Not unnaturally, this tended to cause differences of opinion; in the summer of 1942 alone, police were called to arbitrate between prostitutes and dissatisfied punters on thirty-three occasions. Often girls thought it more prudent to return the customer's money, rather than draw attention to themselves and the premises in which they were operating which could quite easily be identified and targeted by the police as a brothel. On one such occasion, after an unsatisfactory coupling with Marthe Watts, a young, good-looking pilot stayed behind when Marthe returned to her beat, and had sex with her 60-year-old, mixed-race maid, claiming that she was far more sympathetic than her employer had been.

In addition, the girls were not permitted to stray beyond the boundaries of their own beat, nor was the equivalent of the Metropolitan Police's discipline offence of 'idling and gossiping' allowed, either with acquaintances or fellow prostitutes. But despite this rigid regime, the girls had clothes, shoes and jewellery lavished on them. Their 'pocket money' could also be as much as £50 per week. Not only that, but as far as they were concerned, rationing of all saleable items might not have existed. Rationing orders came into force in January 1940, and by 1942, sugar, bacon, butter and meat were all on ration; the following year, margarine, jam, syrup and treacle followed. However, there was never any shortage of these commodities for the Messinas or their girls who, given their punishing workload, needed to keep their strength up. Additionally, the price of petrol rose – not that that bothered the Messinas – but then, in 1942, the petrol allowance was abolished. This was intolerable; they needed their cars to patrol the streets to ensure that their girls were working (no pun intended) flat out. The girls would cadge petrol coupons from their clients and immediately handed them over to the brothers.

The girls' working hours were from 4.00 pm to 6.00 am. If any of them was five minutes late arriving at her 'beat', that five minutes would be added on at the end of her shift. Most of their spare time was spent sleeping; no time for reading, especially not glossy magazines which depicted glamorous Hollywood film stars – they were expressly forbidden. Italians and Frenchmen were not allowed to be clients and, initially at least, neither were Americans. Each girl was allocated a 'maid', who was employed not only to strictly observe that 'The Ten Minute Rule' was meticulously observed, but also to collect the fees and to report directly to the brothers.

So it can be seen that whilst discipline was as strict as King's Regulations in the British Army – not that the Messina brothers would have known anything about that – their generosity was equally forthcoming.

However, it took very little to turn Eugenio into a sadistic monster. When one of Salvatore's girls asked Marthe, '*Vous n'avez encore goûté le fil electrique?*' ('You have not yet tasted the electric wire?'), she had no idea what the girl was talking about. But she soon found out. Following a furious row, Eugenio took a length of electric flex and beat Marthe black and blue with it.

Exhibiting the sort of allegiance that many girls in that situation do, Marthe had her left breast tattooed with the inscription,

'L'homme de ma vie, Gino le Maltais' ('The man of my life, Gino the Maltese').

Devoted to the man of her life or not, Marthe (just like the other girls) was not allowed any holidays; they were permitted one day off on their birthday and a kind of a Bank Holiday to celebrate the anniversary of the day that they and Eugenio had met.

Many ponces reserved their violence for the girls in their charge, but Eugenio's temper was highly unpredictable; in 1940 when a War Reserve constable politely pointed out that Eugenio's Cadillac was parked in a 'no parking' area, the officer had his spectacles broken and bled copiously after Eugenio punched him in the face. Apart from any other punishment which might have been dished out at the local police station, Eugenio was also sentenced to 6 weeks' imprisonment. He became a minor statistic among those who increased the prison population by 40 per cent during the war years. Precisely why he was not immediately conscripted into the armed forces is unclear; perhaps – since this was his first conviction – he used one of his many aliases.

When conscription was introduced in December 1941 under the National Service Acts for unmarried women aged between twenty and thirty, it did not really present a problem to the working girls; they simply (and accurately) inserted 'prostitute' as their occupation and were excluded from being called up since the authorities feared that including them in the ranks of the women's services could lead to contamination, demoralization and possibly recruitment of girls into prostitution. Not that that bothered the Messina girls; weren't they legally married, with British marriage certificates and passports to prove it? It led to a scathing article in the *Sunday Times* in 1942 under the heading, 'Reserved Occupation'.

And so their activities continued: being bombed out of their opulent addresses, the beatings, awkward customers, the arrests, and all the while the brothers meticulously entering details of their revenue into old fashioned ledgers. It was just as well; it was estimated that whilst there had been approximately 3,000 prostitutes in London in 1931, by the end of the war there were 6,700, so there was a great deal of competition. The beats were now becoming crowded, with the newcomers jostling the more established prostitutes for space; two men employed by the Public Morality Council reported to their employers that one evening in Soho, as the clocks struck midnight, they were approached by no fewer than thirty-five women over a distance of 100 yards (it was referred to as 'A Guard of Dishonour'); and that four hours later, seven of the original thirty-five women were still working.

The girls were colloquially known as 'The Hyde Park Rangers' and 'The Piccadilly Commandos'. At the behest of the Public Morality Council, and to deal with lascivious behaviour which often occurred in public air raid shelters, 'The Girl Protection Patrol' was formed, consisting of a woman inspector, eight sergeants and thirty-one constables.

By now, the Messinas were permitting American servicemen to become customers; it was hard to ignore them since in the week before D-Day their numbers in England had swollen to 1,526,965. Because US army sergeants were paid at four times the rate of their British counterparts, it was quite acceptable for the prostitutes to charge them £5 for 'a short time', and a combination of the Americans and the Messina girls unpatriotically priced the British troops right out of the market. Sometimes the girls pushed their luck a little too far and the Americans decided that the price suggested to them was exorbitant; in that eventuality the GI's usual response was, 'Honey, I want to rent it, not buy it.'

The American critic and broadcaster, Alexander Woolcott, who visited Bow Street Court, remarked upon 'The old-world courtesy with which your magistrates treat your whores'. It was true, with some magistrates calling for social reports before sentencing, and others, like the genial St John Bernard Vyvyan Harmsworth at Marlborough Street Court who tended to impose only minimal fines. He also caused unintentional humour when he gently told one prostitute, 'Young women who stop men in cars in Hyde Park often come to a sticky end.'

In August 1942 a cautionary piece appeared in the *Sunday Pictorial*:

> War has dimmed the bright lights of Piccadilly. The worst kind of war profiteers have turned a place that was once gay into a den of organized vice in which no one may walk with safety.

With such startling headlines, and amid the growing number of American service personnel, the Assistant Commissioner 'A' Department demanded an overview of prostitution in London; on 27 August 1942 Superintendent Cole delivered one to him:

> The advent of war has made the problem more complex but its nature remains fundamentally the same – effective control of prostitution within the scope of our limited legislation, the object of such control being to keep within bounds the crimes that prostitution engenders and the

degree of offence to the public sense of propriety. Right in the centre of Mayfair is Shepherd Market which for years has been notorious as one of the localities frequented by prostitutes . . .

It is emphasised that these streets have always been used by the Shepherd Market prostitutes and their sphere of solicitation has not been varied or extended by the arrival of the American troops. Other favourite haunts are Burlington Gardens area: a type of prostitute similar to that in Shepherd Market – rather expensive and using fairly clean premises for their trade but occasionally dishonest if given the opportunity. Some of these women are French by birth. Maddox Street area: French prostitutes, a colony amongst themselves, clean and business-like who, although persistent in their soliciting, rarely cause trouble by committing larcenies or getting involved in disputes.

It appeared that the area of Maddox Street – where the prostitutes employed by the Messinas habitually congregated – was given a fairly clean bill of health by Superintendent Cole.

But irrespective of the soothing report which had landed on the AC(A)'s desk, American GIs had been writing home and excitedly reporting their carnal encounters in London. These stories found their way into American newspapers, and with the *New York Times* stating that incidents of venereal disease were 25 per cent higher in London than in the United States and that half of these infections could be traced back to the Piccadilly area, the salacious stories were picked up by the *Daily Express* and the *Daily Mirror*. The Allied leaders feared, with some justification, that this would represent a publicity triumph to the Axis powers.

The popular First World War hero, Admiral Sir Edward Evans KCB, DSO, SGM (later 1st Baron Mountevans), was the London Regional Commissioner for Civil Defence and he took a hard line on the matter. In a letter to the police commissioner, Sir Philip Game, he wrote:

Leicester Square at night is the resort of the worst type of women and girls consorting with men of the British and American forces, in which the latter seem to predominate. Of course, the American soldiers are encouraged by these young sluts, many of whom should be serving in the forces. At night, the Square is apparently given over to a vicious debauchery.

The Times picked up on Sir Edward's leaked memo and reported that 'GIs in the West End were led astray by "young sluts and vicious debauchery"'; the commissioner of police was hopping mad and demanded a response from the senior officer whose policing covered Leicester Square. Back again to the apprehensive Superintendent Coles, apparently still as fearful for his employment halfway through the war as he was prior to its commencement, who played down the scale of organized prostitution when he reported:

> The West End of London is an acknowledged 'Mecca' of service personnel and visitors to London and there are undoubtedly unsavoury individuals ready and waiting to make easy money out of them, but police are always on the alert . . . The path of the servicemen on leave in the West End of London is not such a grim, sordid and sensational area as the newspapers would have the more unsophisticated of their readers believe.

Cole added the corollary that there was a problem with 'the good-time girls', as opposed to the battle-hardened women of – for example – the Messina clan, and suggested that it was the Americans who caused the current problems, rather than the prostitutes.

But there was more to it than Cole simply papering over the cracks to keep his tenure secure, because with memoranda flying between the Civil Defence, the police and the Home Secretary, in April 1943 a Home Office committee was formed which included the police, various governmental departments and American military personnel, as well as a US judge. This covered everything from 'West End promiscuity to venereal disease and bastardy'.

The American contingent was concerned about the effect that venereal disease would have upon US personnel, although Major General Paul Ramsey Hawley, the Chief Surgeon to the United States Army Forces in the British Isles, stated that 'There is no more moral laxity in this country than in the US.'

Knee-jerk measures were suggested, including reducing the GIs' wages by making them bank a certain percentage of their pay, and also banning prostitutes from certain streets where they were likely to meet American servicemen. Of course, withholding pay would have led to an upsurge in gambling amongst the GIs in an effort to bolster their pay in order to satisfy their lustful desires. That, in turn, could have resulted in accusations of cheating when they won, leading to violence, or instances of rape, when they didn't. As to prohibiting prostitutes from named areas, one wonders how this would have been enforced in the blackout.

Sir Philip Game was certainly having a hard time of it, with the American contingent suggesting that London's 'Thin Blue Line' was doing too little; and after a rather abrasive consultation with a US judge and a major, he wrote to the Home Secretary, saying:

> I told them frankly, it was our view the problem was best tackled from the other end, i.e. by getting at the men and that, whilst it was a waste of time to talk to 'a hard case', it was not a waste of time to talk to a decent boy. The Judge is very persistent in his idea that the boys should be able to write home saying that they never saw a doubtful lady of the streets of London. I pointed out that in these days it was quite impossible to distinguish many over-painted, possibly respectable persons from the professionals and that to me, at any rate, they all looked the same.

It is difficult, if not impossible to envisage a modern-day Commissioner of Police penning such a forthright memo to the Home Secretary.

★

Over-painted or not, the girls often displayed exemplary courage in the exercise of their profession; when air-raid sirens sounded and sensible citizens raced for the shelters, the Messina girls braved the bombs and the shrapnel and kept right on soliciting.

Eugenio failed to show the same representative pluck. He was living in a seventh floor apartment at Porchester Gate, W2 with four bedrooms and three bathrooms (where three-bedroom, two-bathroom flats currently sell for £2 million); there was also a balcony in the lounge which overlooked Hyde Park, not that he spent much time admiring the view; he was terrified of air raids and particularly of the V1 flying bombs. Of these, 9,521 were launched against south-east England, travelling at 400 mph and known as 'doodlebugs' because of the noise they made just before their engines cut out and crashed, whereupon their 1,870lb explosive load detonated. Their successor was the V2 rocket, which many Londoners found more frightening because it was noiseless, travelling at supersonic speed, with even more destructive power. Eugenio had his own personal shelter specially manufactured out of reinforced concrete and placed in the building's basement where other shelters were situated. Consequently, when raids were imminent, he could take shelter within a shelter. He was more fortunate than he knew; many specially commissioned shelters were made of sub-standard materials, and when their worthlessness was demonstrated during an air raid, charges of manslaughter were proffered.

The girls were not so lucky. On Sunday, 18 March 1945, having spent the night in the shelter, they went upstairs and at 9.31 am – when Eugenio was out, visiting his wife – one of Hitler's 1,402 V2 rockets which had visited Britain since October 1944, travelling at 3,580 mph and packed with 2,200 lbs of high explosive, crashed and exploded on Speakers' Corner at the north-east end of Hyde Park, close to Marble Arch. Three civilians were killed, eighty-one were injured and the explosion shredded trees, burst a water main and blew in the windows of the nearby Cumberland Hotel.

The blast also caught Eugenio's apartment; windows were blown in and the doors ripped off, but fortunately the girls were in their rooms at the back of the building. Nevertheless, the concussion was considerable; they were disorientated and dazed, and when the rescue squad arrived they found three very stunned prostitutes with most of their clothes ripped off, staggering about in a state of terror and bewilderment. Stan Poole of the Auxiliary Fire Service gave an interview to the Imperial War Museum in 2001 in which he stated, 'Up the stairs and at the back, there were three women. They didn't have any clothes on. Whether they'd been blown off them or they'd got up in a panic, I'll never know.' Now, if Mr Poole's reading this, he does.

Giuseppe Messina came round to take charge. He had by now reached state retirement age and was certainly claiming an undeserved pension, although not for too long; less than a year later, he would succumb to a well-deserved heart attack. The premises were no longer structurally sound enough for Eugenio's large safe to repose on the seventh floor, so with the assistance of half a dozen workmen under Giuseppe's supervision, it was transported down to the sanctuary of his reinforced shelter. There was no question, of course, of the concussed girls being allowed time off. They were sent back to their already bomb-damaged apartment at St James' Place – they had been obliged to move there after their previous apartment in Duke Street had been raided for being a brothel – and there on the second and third floors they would sleep, as well as entertain clients.

*

D-Day eventually arrived, the Allies surged victoriously forward, the last V2 rocket landed on 27 March 1945 and then six weeks later, the war in Europe was all over.

Londoners sat back and licked their wounds; 29,890 of them had been killed – including 2,754 by the V2 rockets – and 50,000 had been injured. London was a mess; 116,000 homes had been totally destroyed by enemy bombing, another 288,000 required major repairs and a further million needed smaller repairs.

The country had gone to the polls, Churchill and his coalition Government were kicked out of office and Attlee's Labour, with a massive majority of 393 seats, was in.

VE Day – 8 May 1945 – was deliriously celebrated by Londoners everywhere, especially the forty-nine who became Marthe Watt's customers on the busiest night of her life. By the time she staggered into bed at gone six the following morning, she must have felt like a rather old boxer who had unwisely strayed outside his or her weight division.

CHAPTER 4

Threats, Lies, Bribes, Prison

During 1945 there had been 1,983 arrests for soliciting prostitution; however, with the ending of the blackout prostitutes became rather more visible, and in 1946 the number increased to 4,289.

Not that that really mattered; after all, what was a piddling £2 fine to the brothers? If the war had been good to the Messinas, the post-war years were even better. Eugenio acquired his first Rolls-Royce, bought the lease of 7 Stafford Street and he, Marthe, Anita and Jeanne moved in. The girls acquired a maid – inevitably, a retired prostitute – and even though the population of London had dropped to 3,245,000, a decrease of 20 per cent from 1938, business was booming. The brothers also rented flats at Cork Street, St James' Place and Duke of York Street; they could well afford to pay a £500 bribe to obtain the tenancies. Due to the bombing of London during the war, accommodation was scarce; it made good sense for the Messinas to buy a share in an estate agent's business, and in fact they had already done so in the 1930s. In this way they avoided any problems when leasing flats, and the business also provided them with a convenient front.

There was a hiccup when Marthe was charged, for a second time, with keeping a brothel – on this occasion she was fined £110 (and was exceedingly fortunate, bearing in mind that a second offence merited a fine of £250 or six months' imprisonment, or both) – but with England in the grip of austerity (plus one of the fiercest winters ever recorded) Eugenio made good his half-hearted promises of a continental holiday and Marthe joined him and his brother Carmelo at the Hotel Plaza in Brussels. From there they travelled south, to France and Spain, then back to Paris, before returning to London, fortunately just in time; within a few months, motoring holidays, both at home and abroad, were banned by the Government.

There was a further problem – but not really a serious one – when the 26 January 1947 edition of the *Sunday Pictorial* ran a featured entitled 'Vice in the Capital' in which it mentioned the 'brutal control of a group of Maltese brothers' but added, 'The police have not been able to pin a single thing on them'. So whilst it drew attention to the Messinas (without actually naming them), it also suggested their invulnerability which was an added and essential ego-boost to the brothers.

The next glitch appeared almost as soon as the girls returned to their respective 'beats' in March 1947; Marthe Watts, together with two more of the Messina harem, was intimidated by a five-man gang led by another Maltese, Carmelo 'Charles' Vassalo, who threatened the girls with violence if a payment of £1 per day from each of them was not forthcoming.

On the face of it, a total of £3 per day for a five-way split could not be considered a venture into the realms of high finance, but that was the substance of the allegation. There followed a confrontation between Vassalo's gang and the Messinas – they were old enemies – on 11 March at Winchester Court, South Kensington, and during the ensuing fracas Vassalo had the tips of three of his fingers sliced off, courtesy of Eugenio.

Knowing that retribution would be coming his way, Eugenio offered £25,000 to anybody who could smuggle him out of the country; but if that happened, the girls concerned would be in a parlous, unprotected position indeed. So they complained to Scotland Yard – and, for good measure, to West End Central police station as well, where the Divisional Detective Inspector was my friend, the late Bob Higgins, a tough veteran of the 1930s Flying Squad. He had no time for prostitutes, whom he referred to as 'these painted, ravaged harlots', but even less time for the men ('riff-raff' as he described them to me) who exploited them.

He detailed Detective Inspector Leslie Watts, Detective Sergeant Victor Massey and a team of detectives to keep watch on Saturday, 15 March at the girls' beat in Burlington Gardens, and just after 10.00 pm a car drew up containing five Maltese thugs. When Watts heard one of the gangsters shout to the girls, 'It's better for you to give us the money, otherwise I'll cut your face!' this was quite sufficient for the men to be arrested. One of the gang had a large, closed knife in his pocket, and there was a heavy hammer in the car. A later search of their addresses revealed a lead-loaded cosh, a knuckleduster and an automatic pistol with six rounds of ammunition.

Vassalo and his gang stood trial at the Old Bailey before Mr Justice Singleton, charged with demanding money with menaces from two of the women and conspiring with each other to do so.

All of the prostitutes – Marthe Watts, Blanche Costaki and Janine Gilson – nobly lied their heads off, denying that they were 'Messina girls'.

Marthe Watts told the court, 'In February, I was with a lady and gentleman whose names I do not wish to reveal, staying at the Hotel Plaza, in Brussels. We met the two Messina brothers there by chance. The five of us drove with a gentleman from the Spanish Embassy in two cars from Brussels, through Belgium to Spain and back to Paris.'

Quite apart from the obvious lie about meeting the Messinas 'by chance', it did seem a bit rich for Marthe to dictate to the court whom she would or would not name, without getting banged-up for contempt, but nevertheless, it appears she got away with it.

Billy Rees-Davies (and we shall hear more about him, later on) appeared for two of the defendants and put it to Marthe, 'You have called Eugene Messina in your evidence, "a perfect gentleman". I suggest he is a brutal man?'

'No', she replied, conveniently forgetting about her punishing encounter with the length of electric flex wielded by Eugenio.

'Have you ever heard of his branding anybody with an iron?' asked Rees-Davies, and again Marthe replied, 'No'.

When Rees-Davies asked, 'I suggest you arranged a plot to catch these men for the protection of the Messinas?' unsurprisingly, and for the third time, Marthe answered, 'No'.

Janine Gilson was asked, 'Do any of these Messina men look after you in your profession?' and she replied, 'No. I don't have anybody to look after me. If I want protection, I go to the police.'

For courtroom purposes this did have the ring of authenticity about it, since Detective Inspector Watts was just about to inform the jury that she had done just that. She and the other girls were on a bit of a sticky wicket because the addresses which they gave to the court were those in which the brothers had an interest. However, the defence appeared unaware of that, and so, quite possibly were the police.

'I arrested the five men after I heard threats and demands for money coming from inside the motor car where they were', said Detective Inspector Watts. 'They were making the demands from the women who have already given evidence.'

He went on to say that he knew the brothers, 'not personally but by reputation' and said that there was gang warfare between the defendants and the Messina brothers.

'Their reputation is that they are men who keep women on the streets on London?' asked the defence, and Watts replied, 'They are reputed to be so.'

The defendants' case was that they were out in a car in Bond Street looking for the Messinas who, they said, had chopped the tops off Vassalo's fingers. A girl – simply referred to as 'Gladys' –

had told them that the Messinas would be in that vicinity on what
turned out to be the day of their arrest.

In his closing speech for the prosecution, Mr Anthony Hawke
(later Sir Edward Anthony Hawke, Common Serjeant of London
and subsequently Recorder of London) told the court:

> This is not an enquiry into gang warfare. However much
> one may dislike the idea of a collection of people like
> this, getting themselves into a gang and cruising about
> London, looking for another gang, quite prepared to use
> weapons if necessary, that is nothing to do with this case.

Representing Romeo Saliba, Mr Leonard Caplan delivered his
final speech with unerring accuracy when he told the jury:

> We say there exists in London a powerful gang of men
> known to the police as the Messina brothers, who are
> living on the immoral earnings of women of the streets –
> powerful and rich, on the evidence of one of the women
> called, who said they had two Rolls-Royces, and who are
> able to make journeys for what purpose you may surmise
> to Brussels, Paris and Barcelona. This rich and powerful
> group of men is connected with the vice racket. There
> may be something behind and beneath the obvious facts
> that have come out in this case.

Summing up to the jury, Mr Justice Singleton (who might well
have been dubbed 'Mr Justice Simpleton') told them:

> You may think it is a pity that a gang should be going
> out for revenge or to fight the Messina brothers in the
> West End in the year 1947. If this is a plot got up by the
> Messinas to get the girls to give false evidence in the dock,
> and if into that plot by mistake the police have fallen, then
> I should think you would say the accused are not guilty . . .
>
> For most of today, you have heard these girls discussed
> again and again. They knew when they came to this court
> what would be said about them. I confess I became almost
> a little sorry for them. They are not natives of this country
> I gather, but are living on the streets in the West End of
> London.

Of course, rather than suggesting that they lived 'on the streets', it
would have been more accurate to have said that they resided in

the opulent surroundings of a four-storey town house in Berkeley Square which Eugenio had purchased for cash – but no matter.

The men were found guilty on 24 April 1947 and, to the usual accompaniment of cries, screams and wails from ladies in the public gallery, Carmelo Vassalo, a 29-year-old seaman, Anthony Paul Mangion, aged 38 and also a seaman, Paul Anthony Borg, a 41-year-old agent and Romeo Saliba, a caterer aged 29 were each sentenced to four years' penal servitude, while 32-year-old Michael Sultana, a seaman, received two years' imprisonment. With the immediate danger thus out of the way, Mmes Watts, Gilson and Costaki resumed their roles as 'The Queens of Maddox Street'.

In fact, following the convictions, reports reached the police that this gang had been successful in blackmailing other prostitutes, who had paid up rather than run the risk of disfigurement.

Two months later, it was Eugenio's turn to appear as a defendant at the Old Bailey, having been committed there from West London Magistrates' Court. He was represented by three heavyweights of the legal profession: Sir Patrick Gardiner Hastings KC, then aged sixty-seven; he had been a fairly disastrous Attorney General during 1924, a job which he described as 'my idea of hell'. Next was Derek Curtis-Bennett QC, who specialized in defence cases. Among his less successful clients were William Joyce aka 'Lord Haw-Haw' (hanged), the serial murderer, John Reginald Halliday Christie (also hanged) and the atom spy, Klaus Fuchs (fourteen years' imprisonment). Bringing up the rear was Victor Durand QC, also a specialist in defence work. He was later suspended from the Bar for three years, having been found guilty of professional misconduct, a sentence which on appeal was reduced to twelve months' suspension.

During the trial, Vassalo was produced from prison and, with the three fingers of his left hand still bandaged, gave his account of the night of 11 March at 11.30, when he and three companions were driving along Jermyn Street.

'I noticed three men coming out of a restaurant', he told the jury. 'Messina [Eugenio] was one, the others were his brothers. They were round their car and made some remarks. Messina spat at our car.'

After Vassalo & Co. had followed the Messinas in their car to Winchester Court there was a confrontation, during which a knife was thrust at Vassalo's stomach; when he instinctively grabbed at it, off came the tips of three of his fingers.

'You are a dangerous gang?' asked Sir Patrick Hastings, to which Vassalo perhaps rather unwisely replied, 'That is what they call us.'

The prosecution repeatedly (and accurately) described Eugenio's mode of living – during the trial it was suggested that his own personal fortune amounted to £500,000 – but he stated adamantly that he was a diamond merchant; indeed, in the previous trial, hadn't Janine Gilson told the court when asked about the brothers' profession, 'I know them as diamond merchants and I know them as very wealthy people'?

Eugenio told the court that on the night in question he had been dining at a restaurant with two of his brothers and that upon leaving they appeared to have been followed.

'A large black car drove up and four men jumped out', he said. 'I did not use a knife, nor did I have one in my possession. I was not in any way responsible for the injury to Vassalo and I have no idea how he got the tops of his fingers cut off. There is no feud or vendetta between us.'

On 24 April 1947 Eugenio got half a result; he was found not guilty of inflicting grievous bodily harm with intent, for which the maximum punishment was life imprisonment. However, he was found guilty of unlawful wounding, for which the maximum penalty was five years. The Recorder of London, Sir Gerald Dodson MA, LLM, QC, weighed him off with three years' penal servitude – Eugenio was the first of three of the brothers to be sentenced by the Recorder – and he was packed off to Wandsworth prison.

He appealed; and whilst he waited for the result, brother Carmelo, when visiting his brother in prison, rashly tried to bribe a prison officer with £5 to show favour to Eugenio. When the two began to speak in what Warder Vincent James Johnson described as 'a foreign language', he threatened to terminate the visit unless they spoke English.

Carmelo produced a £5 note and Johnson told him, 'Put that thing away or else you'll get into trouble.'

But Carmelo didn't; and at the end of the conversation, he touched the warder, who saw that he still had the note in his hand.

'Put it away', said Johnson, adding, 'I don't want it.'

'Yes', said Carmelo. 'You take this, sir.'

He then put the note in Johnson's hand and he saw that there was writing on it.

Eugenio Messina, when Johnson took back to his cell, said, 'Try to get me on your landing, sir.'

Johnson reported the matter, and consequently on 8 October 1947 detectives from the Yard knocked on the door of Winchester Court, Vicarage Gate. When Carmelo answered, they plonked a summons in his hands alleging attempted bribery, which was returnable to South-Western police court on 20 October.

Carmelo pleaded not guilty. He was represented by no less a personage than Mr J. D. Casswell KC, who in 1913 had acted against the Oceanic Steam Navigation Company, owned by the White Star Line, and managed to obtain £100 compensation for several of the relatives of those drowned on the RMS *Titanic*, after the jury found that the Captain, Edward John Smith RD, RNR, had been negligent. A decorated veteran of the First World War, by the end of his career Casswell had defended forty people accused of murder and had saved all but five from the gallows. Carmelo must have felt that he was in a reasonably safe pair of hands.

Warder Johnson – he was also known as 'Jungle Joe' – told the court, 'I took the note because the man was very persistent. I thought I had evidence in my hand.'

In an attempt to show that there were dodgy goings-on at the prison, Casswell asked, 'There was some trouble at Wandsworth prison in August, cases in which duplicate keys were being smuggled in?'

Johnson was up to that one and rather smartly replied, 'According to rather lurid newspaper accounts, yes.'

'Did a smuggled £5 note come into your possession by any chance?' suavely asked Casswell, to which Johnson firmly replied, 'No'.

Carmelo was seriously disbelieved, and on 7 November the Magistrate, Mr T. F. Davis, sentenced him to two months' imprisonment with £50 costs. Casswell asked for bail, pending an appeal, and got it – £250 in Carmelo's own recognizance plus a surety in a similar amount – but the appeal was as unsuccessful as Eugenio's had been and Carmelo served the sentence of imprisonment.

Following Eugenio's conviction, there was some political sabre-rattling; not much, just a little. James Chuter Ede (later The Right Honourable the Lord Chuter-Ede CH, PC, JP, DL) had been appointed Home Secretary at the commencement of the Clement Attlee government two years previously; before that, he had been a teacher.

Now, as a result of the evidence which had emerged during Eugenio's trial, these questions were raised in the House: would the Home Secretary appoint a committee to investigate organized prostitution in the capital with a view to suppressing it? Would he appoint a commission with the power to examine the bank accounts of suspected ponces? Was he aware that the Messina brothers had allegedly already made £500,000 out of organized prostitution? That they reputedly had no fewer than twenty prostitutes working for them – and that during the war, one of those girls had earned

£3,000 for them? Because if he had not previously been aware of it, he was now – and what in heaven's name was he going to do about it?

The short answer was 'nothing'. Chuter Ede's full answer was:

> I do not think that the appointment of a commission of enquiry would be of assistance in this matter. It is a criminal offence knowingly to live on the earnings of a prostitute and the police exercise all possible vigilance with a view to the suppression of activities of this kind. Any enquiry would not help the police because their difficulties arise from the fact that they are sometimes unable to obtain evidence upon which criminal proceedings could be based.

Well, that was that. It was good enough for Sir Harold Scott GCVO, KCB, KBE, who had been appointed Commissioner of the Metropolitan Police at the same time that Chuter Ede had become Home Secretary; prior to that, Sir Harold had been a civil servant for all of his working life. His appointment by the Labour Government was seen as a change from former police commissioners, who were mainly from a military background.

He was aware that the law was far from satisfactory, but as he said, in a neat bit of buck-passing, 'Any attempt to amend it arouses so much controversy that governments are not anxious to burn their fingers in the attempt.'

His words were echoed, rather more forcefully, by Bob Higgins, who said, 'Now is the time for us to act, and perhaps one day there will be a government courageous enough to reform our out-of-date laws on the subject and make them much less hypocritical.'

However, Sir Harold had done his bit. 'More than once, however', he said, 'I have put forward the proposal that the law should be amended to enable us to send back to their own countries certain classes of British subjects who are consistent and flagrant law-breakers. Cypriots, Maltese and coloured British subjects are responsible for a disproportionately large part of the offences connected with gaming, living on the immoral earnings of prostitutes and the sale of drugs and liquor. If they could be sent home on conviction, there would be a distinct improvement in those areas where they are active.'

But they couldn't, so there wasn't.

CHAPTER 5

Enter Duncan Webb

L ife was obviously hard for Eugenio in Wandsworth, deprived as he was of his gold knick-knacks, any of his fifteen £45 hand-made Saville Row suits, his Rolls-Royce and, of course, feminine company. But he had money, which bought him sufficient treats and a certain amount of protection from the other cons; this was necessary because ponces were just about as far down the list from armed robbers in the prison pecking order of respect as it was possible to be; in fact, they were only slightly more admired than child molesters.

Nevertheless, affluent or not, it was advisable for ponces to keep a still tongue in their heads. It was a lesson that Eugenio should have learnt when a prison van was about to convey him to Wandsworth. A kindly uniform sergeant had taken him by the arm to assist him into the van, whereupon Eugenio rebuked him, saying, 'Take your hands off me. I buy and sell people like you in the West End.'

It was an ill-advised remark for a tubby little ponce to make, because he suddenly found himself propelled down the central aisle of the van on his stomach, coming to an abrupt halt with a sickening thud.

'Look here, mister', he was told. 'You may have bought people in the West End, but you haven't bought me. You keep a civil tongue in your head, because you'll come through here several times.'

As a serving prisoner, Eugenio might have profited from that exchange; but on one occasion when he clearly did not, he suffered the consequences in the form of a ferocious pasting from a South London villain.

Apart from that bit of injudicious behaviour, Eugenio was no fool; he still had a business to run, and the key to this was communication. His handwriting had been poor; in fact he was almost illiterate. Now, he wrote to his girls and encouraged them to reply; and in the process his handwriting improved and so did his ability to issue written directions. To the prison censors it appeared that those missives were nothing more than amorous, over-the-top, indeed rather soppy love letters, but they were all posted in the same name to Carmelo's address, marked with a special sign for each girl to whom instructions were issued. Carmelo would then pass the letters on to the girl in question, and the girls would visit Eugenio once a month, in the company of two of his brothers.

The girls worked harder than ever before and the money they earned was handed on a weekly basis to the brothers, one of whom kept Eugenio's large safe, which had been rescued from the basement of Porchester Gate. Each brother had a key, and one key could not be used without the other – family they might have been, but Eugenio was not *that* trusting!

Eugenio was well behaved during his sentence and achieved the maximum remission, being released after twenty-six months on 1 August 1949. Four days later, he acquired a fresh passport. He had, of course, completely missed the 1948 Olympics held in London – no television sets in prisoners' cells in those days! – but when the 4,104 athletes arrived from all over the globe to participate in the two-week long games, which commenced on 29 July, so did a lot of spectators. Consequently, the number of prostitutes' arrests shot up to 5,363 that year; and even though the pound had been devalued by 30 per cent against the dollar, the brothers' takings went through the roof.

Upon Eugenio's release, Marthe Watts would later say that she handed over £22,000; not, certainly, purely as a result of her own labours but earned by the girls who worked exclusively for Eugenio. By now it was estimated that the brothers ran 30 brothels in Mayfair and had a total of 200 girls.

Eugenio's release was a time for celebration; and he did it in grand style. First, there was the purchase of another Rolls-Royce, this one yellow, at a cost of £8,000. Next, a flat in South Street using his alias of Edward Marshall. Then there were gifts: for Carmelo, a diamond ring valued at £700 to thank him for looking after the girls and attempting at bribing the prison officer, and in commiseration for copping two months' imprisonment. Marthe received a mink coat, earrings and a brooch, and the other girls received costly presents which they proudly and ostentatiously displayed on the streets to the amazement of the poorly dressed passers-by, most of whom were wondering when their next tin of Spam would materialize. Although the Messinas were well able to afford this beneficence, the expensive stores and jewellers they patronized were only too pleased to offer substantial discounts to these, their best customers. Since all their purchases were made in cash, no receipts were given, thereby circumventing the huge rate of Purchase Tax which had been placed on jewellery. And Eugenio toured the girls' beats in his opulent Rolls-Royce, both keeping an eye on them and openly flaunting his wealth, his power and his utter indifference to and contempt for the honest police, the corrupt police who received his backhanders and the blustering, impotent Home Secretary.

It was hardly surprising that upon hearing Chuter Ede's simpering comments, Attilio openly boasted to óne of the prostitutes, 'We Messinas are more powerful than the British Government', adding, 'We do as we like in England.'

In modern day parlance, those remarks went viral, and in all fairness they weren't too far from the truth.

Then this happened.

★

Thomas Duncan Webb was a newspaperman who came with a rather odd back story. Having served as a cub reporter during the 1930s with the *South London Press*, he became a war correspondent and, having been invalided out aged twenty-seven, he had come to notice after being arrested on 18 January 1944. The charge was 'communicating to certain persons information with regards to certain of His Majesty's ships', contrary to the Defence (General) Regulations, 1939. He pleaded not guilty, but a week later at Plymouth Police Court he was found guilty and was fined £50 with ten guineas costs, the Magistrate remarking that his guilt 'arose from carelessness, rather than intent'. The 'certain persons' to whom the information was communicated by telephone, so loudly that he was overheard, were his employers, the *Daily Express*, which was reprimanded.

Two years later, there was another encounter with the law. After using and paying for the services of a prostitute named Jean Crews, he refused to leave her flat. When Herbert Gardner Wadham, a passer-by, came to her aid, Webb punched him in the face and, pretending that his press card was a Metropolitan Police warrant card, tried to arrest him. It's fair to say that this offence (like the previous one) was probably fuelled by drink, because at Tottenham Court Road police station Webb denied ever having seen Wadham before. He was fortunate to be convicted only of common assault, as opposed to unlawful wounding and impersonating a police officer. At Marlborough Street Police Court on 8 August 1946 he was bound over and ordered to pay two guineas costs; he was nevertheless sacked by the *Daily Express*.

Following a row with the editor of the *Evening Standard* he left this paper too, and he fared no better with the *Daily Graphic*; after eight days as news editor in 1948 he was sacked by them as well, when his unorthodox methods of procuring information came to light.

He had busied himself with the 1947 murder of Alec d'Antiquis and retired, hurt, when the senior investigating officer, Detective Superintendent Bob Fabian ('of the Yard') refused to accept his phone calls. During the widely publicized murder case involving John George Haigh, who dissolved his victims' bodies in acid, Webb discovered that Haigh's wife was living in a bigamous marriage; immediately after Haigh's execution, Webb persuaded her to legitimately remarry her consort. Webb acted as best man and was photographed with the happy couple; the picture appeared in the following Sunday's edition of the *People*. That, too, was thought to be rather unconventional.

Undeniably, Webb was unorthodox; in January 1950 his presence was demanded at No. 1 Court at the Old Bailey by Mr Justice Sellers, who was presiding over the trial of Donald Hume for murder. Webb had sent a telegram to Hume's wife Cynthia which, on the face of it, asked her not to appear as a witness in her husband's defence. When the judge pointed out that to interfere with a witness was a misdemeanour at common law, Webb replied that Mrs Hume's mother had told him that her daughter intended to sell her story to a newspaper and that this was the reason for the telegram: purely to advise her not to sell her story, but not, of course, to stop her appearing as a witness.

'I was given to understand that she was not coming to this trial', Webb told the judge. 'Had I dreamed that she was going to give evidence I should not have dreamed of writing to her in any way. I have had too much experience to dream of doing such a thing.'

And on that dreamy, wistful note, Webb was once more off the hook. What he failed to tell the court was that his association with Cynthia Hume was rather more amorous than professional; after Hume was acquitted of murder but convicted of being an accessory after the fact to murder and sentenced to twelve years' imprisonment, Cynthia and Hume were divorced and she and Webb were married.

With Cynthia's exclusive scoop under Webb's belt and published by the *People*, the managing editor, Renton Stuart Campbell, gave him the job of chief crime reporter. To justify the editor's faith in him, Webb now needed a 'spectacular'. When Campbell, referring to the Messinas, told him, 'Smash this gang of ponces', he got one.

If it appears from the foregoing events that Webb (who was known to his friends as 'Tommy') was a rather sleazy, irregular reporter who took chances that others of his profession might not have, well, that is probably a fair assessment. His description – small, close-set eyes, ginger hair liberally plastered with Brylcreem, a pock-marked face inclined to puffiness, hinting that he was a serial imbiber – would only have added to that assessment. But two things were quite clear: first, Duncan Webb knew how to write a compelling newspaper column, and second, he had courage by the bucket-load; that was just as well, because he was going to need it.

CHAPTER 6

'Smash this Gang of Ponces!'

Webb started his quest in mid-May 1950 with a completely blank canvas. He did not know the Messinas, or any of their women. He spent several weeks reading what he could about them in various newspaper files, scouring the streets, meeting members of the underworld in pubs and clubs, and asking, asking all the time about the brothers. He even spoke to Carmelo Vassalo, newly released from his 4-year 'lagging';[1] but at the end of the day he had as much information as when he had started his enquiries – nothing.

What Webb did know was that practically all of the Messina women came from lands beyond our shores; and so, walking around certain areas of Mayfair, he noted who the foreign prostitutes were. On the evening of 6 June 1950 he allowed himself to be picked up by seven such women and taken back to their addresses. Four of them were not interested in his quest for material, two provided some sparse information but one in particular told Webb a little about the Messina women and revealed that their protectors, practically nightly, patrolled areas of Mayfair, supervising them. It was a start.

Consequently, Webb allowed himself to be taken by a French prostitute to an opulently furnished apartment at 4 Queen Street. Later, another took him to 49a Hertford Street; before the act of consummation at either address could take place, as he would later virtuously (and possibly untruthfully) inform his readers, 'I made my excuses and left', amidst a torrent of abuse.

During the next few nights he entered both 5 and 7 Stafford Street in the company of prostitutes; again, he left – he said – with his virtue intact and having received some hard punches and virulent insults.

In two weeks he had made the acquaintance of possibly 100 prostitutes, some of them Messina girls, others not. He also had a

---

1 Sentences of penal servitude were referred to as 'laggings', a distortion of 'leg-irons' which referred to the days when recipients of that form of punishment were obliged to wear these encumbrances, rather like a present day electronic tag, only weightier and more difficult to remove.

list of addresses, but none of them appeared to have any association
with the Messina brothers.

Webb went back to where his enquiries had commenced – 4
Queen Street. He discovered that the property was managed by a
Philip Faith, a partner in an estate agents, Foster & Faith, situated
at 10 Queen Street, Mayfair. Using the name 'Taylor', Webb told
Faith that he was interested in purchasing a property, especially
the one sited three doors away, at 4 Queen Street. Alas, replied
Mr Faith, that property was not for sale; indeed, it was already
occupied. But Webb discovered that the person who occupied the
ground floor flat was a Mr Marshall and that a Mr Maitland was
considering renting the flat on the first floor. This was a partial
breakthrough for Webb; he knew from his own enquiries that
Marshall was Eugenio and that Maitland was Carmelo.

But that was all. Webb made further enquiries in respect of
some fifty other addresses. Some had no connection with the
Messinas; in the case of others, there was no direct link with them
– until he researched 5 Stafford Street. The rated occupier was
a Mr Raymond Maynard – and although that was Attilio's alias,
Webb was unaware of it at the time. But when he next researched
74 New Bond Street, he discovered that the rated occupier was Mr
C. Maitland – Carmelo – and there was a common denominator
between the two addresses. The rates of both properties were paid
to the council by the same firm of solicitors, Webb, Justice & Co.,
of 24 Haymarket, W1.

Why should this be? Two – no, three men – using aliases and also
getting a firm of solicitors to pay their rates. It certainly appeared
that the occupiers of those properties were trying to distance
themselves from any provable connection with them.

The solicitor's company merited further investigation. Its
principal, William Percy Webb, had originally been a partner in
the firm of H. S. Wright and Webb, Solicitors of 18 Bloomsbury
Square, London. On 5 October 1935 the company was dissolved –
at least, as far as Webb was concerned. It was decreed that money
due to and owing by the firm would be received or paid by the two
remaining partners, who would carry on the business in Mr Webb's
absence.

But even odder was the fact that the solicitor's address at the
Haymarket was not run by William Webb at all. His home address
was Croxted Road, Dulwich, his business address was 5 Verulam
Buildings, Grays Inn Road, WC1; the Haymarket office was run
by a Mr H. Watson, a solicitor's clerk. So there was one firm of
solicitors with two different offices at two different locations with
two different telephone numbers and two different letter headings

– why? It was as though – just like Messrs Maynard alias Attilio, Marshall alias Eugenio and Maitland alias Carmelo – the two addresses of the same firm of solicitors were trying to distance themselves from each other; which of course was nothing more than the plain unvarnished truth.

Mr Webb and Mr Watson were two crooked pieces of work. Since February 1948 William Percy Webb had acted for Mr Edward Marshall, whose name, he later admitted to the Law Society, he had known to be Eugenio Messina. He was aware that Messina had assaulted a police officer in 1940 and that he had been sent to penal servitude for three years in 1947 for grievous bodily harm.

On 16 March 1950 Messrs Keith Cardale, Groves & Co., Estate Agents of 43 North Audley Street, wrote to Webb at the Haymarket address, asking if Mr Edward Marshall 'was likely to prove a desirable and responsible tenant for certain premises belonging to our clients'.

The very next day, the reply read, 'Mr Marshall has been known to us for some time and he should prove a responsible tenant and in our opinion is well able to pay the rental named.' The letter was signed by Watson in the name of the firm.

When it came to light that a similar reference had been written by Watson for a prostitute named Mrs Hermione Hindin – and we shall be hearing a great deal more of both Hindin and Watson in the very near future – the Law Society took a very dim view of matters. Webb piteously told the committee that whilst Watson was authorized to give references, he had no idea of the details which he had provided or of the actual transactions he had had with the other Messina brothers, but the Law Society believed that the buck stopped with Webb. Declaring that these two references 'had provoked a national scandal', the Law Society's Disciplinary Committee told Webb, 'The public are entitled to expect that a solicitor who is asked for a reference will reply with candour and honesty', and on 1 August 1953 he was suspended from practising for a period of three years for 'conduct unbecoming a solicitor' and was ordered to pay costs.

Back now to the other Webb – Duncan's – endeavours.

★

When good detectives reach an impasse in their investigations, it never does any harm for them to stop, take a break, retrace their steps and consider what evidence they've accrued. What have they missed? What has been staring them in the face all the time but has been overlooked?

Duncan Webb was of that mindset. He thought back to his chat with Carmelo Vassalo, who had been phlegmatic regarding his confrontation with Eugene Messina. True, he disliked Messina, but he bore him no ill will. Vassalo did add that he had been fitted up by the three prostitutes who, he said, had perjured themselves; but, as Webb knew, most convicted criminals claim they have been fitted up, if not by the police, then by someone else. However, could it be true in this case?

Now, Webb went back through his newspaper files. One of the chief witnesses in the Vassalo case had been Marthe Watts. At the trial she had given her address as Stafford Street, W1. However, Webb had already been to all of the flats at 5 and 7 Stafford Street and she had not been among the prostitutes working there, although that had been her address three years previously; obviously, she must have moved on.

Or had she? Webb looked up the last volume (S–Z) of the London telephone directory and found what he was looking for: 'M. Watts, 7 Stafford Street, W1'. Just above that entry was the same name, with an address at 2 Winchester Court, W8. Back, once again, to his files; at the time of his trial, Eugenio Messina had given 2 Winchester Court as his address, and when Webb telephoned the number at that address, it was Eugenio Messina who answered. Next, Webb dialled the Stafford Street number, spoke to a maid and asked if Mrs Watts was at Winchester Court; she replied that she believed Mrs Watts was on her way to Stafford Street.

Now Webb had made a breakthrough. Watts had stated she was not connected with the Messinas; who else had said that? Janine Gilson, that's who. Webb traced her husband, who admitted that he had been approached in the south of France by associates of the Messina gang who persuaded him, for a decent bursary, to marry one Henrietta Janine Moret in Gibraltar; having obtained a marriage certificate and later, a British passport, the latter went straight to London and received her first conviction for soliciting. Like Watts, Janine Gilson had been a participant with an Englishman in an arranged marriage, was a prostitute and a perjurer. Webb eventually ran her to ground at 5 Stafford Street, the property run by Raymond Maynard – alias Attilio.

Webb needed more assistance so he enlisted the help of Jack Robinson, a former Scotland Yard detective, and also of Bert Linfoot; he briefed both of them to set up an observation outside Winchester Court and, when Eugenio Messina appeared, to follow him to see whom he met and where they went.

Eugenio and Carmelo Messina and two of their women were seen getting into a car and driving off. Checking the registered owner of a car revealed that it belonged to Charles Maitland (Carmelo) of 3 Lancaster Lodge, Lancaster Road, W11. A check carried out on another car seen in suspicious circumstances showed the owner to be Raymond Maynard (Attilio) – who was shown as living at the same Lancaster Lodge address.

Webb checked out that premises; the telephone had been rented in the name of Harvey but the flat was let to a Mr Eugenio Messina. He also discovered that a Mr Martin allegedly lived there; this was the alias of Alfredo Messina.

All this information was an absolute windfall. Now Webb consulted the Bow Street and Marlborough Street Court lists every morning to check the addresses of the arrested prostitutes appearing there.

He discovered that Marthe Watts and Blanche Costaki gave 7 Stafford Street as their address, and Janine Gilson gave No. 5, next door, as hers. Violet Carter worked from 4 Queen Street, and at 74 New Bond Street Robina Dickson Torrance and Edna Kallman plied their trade. Jeanne Connolly gave 49a Hertford Street, Shepherd Market as one of several addresses; Duke Street was another, but she actually lived at The Lodge, Kensington Palace Gardens, W11. Coincidentally, Marie Sanderson, whose address for court purposes was given as 5 Stafford Street, lived just a short distance away from Jeanne Connolly, at the upmarket No. 8 Kensington Palace Gardens.

Andrée Messina was the wife of Eugenio; she gave 24 Bruton Place, W1 as her address. This was the same address as that occupied by Eugenio, who paid the property's rates and who spent some weekends there. But then Webb also discovered that the rates of the adjoining properties, Nos. 26 and 28, were paid for by Edward Marshall – alias Eugenio – via Webb, Justice & Company, solicitors of 24 Haymarket; and oddly enough, it was those addresses which were additionally given by Andrée Messina, as an alternative to No. 24.

A lady named Charpentier, who originally hailed from Brussels, had married a man named Evans – that was the name she now used – and stated that she lived at 52 Shepherd Market. Coincidentally, so did Mrs Ida Messina and Mrs Marie Messina. However, that was not her – or their – permanent address. Followed one night, Charpentier took her watchers to a block of flats at King's Court, Hammersmith. Salvatore Messina – also known as Arthur Evans – had four flats there. Of these, he occupied one, and Ida Messina née Poumirou, who had gone through a travesty of a marriage with Carmelo Messina, occupied another. Marie Messina née Burratti who, like Mrs Evans, had been part of a dubious marriage ceremony, was also an alleged wife of Salvatore, and the two women occupied flats three and four.

Are you keeping up at the back, there? It's rather confusing, I know.

Webb had flown to Paris where he discovered the details of the arranged marriages for the Messina women which had been carried out at the British consulates in France, Spain and North Africa.

Collating all that evidence, he now had a total of twenty-eight addresses linked to the Messinas and all of their aliases, plus details of twenty prostitutes, *their* aliases and addresses; plus a firm of very dodgy solicitors.

*

Undeniably, Webb had carried out a superb piece of investigation. Now, like any good detective, he wrote up a log of events, plus the information that he and his associates had accrued, looking all the time for corroborative evidence, meeting informants, making telephone calls and carrying out searches on properties. In addition, he now enlisted the services of another former Scotland Yard detective, Tom Grosvenor, and he, together with Jack Robinson, Bert Linfoot and every available reporter from the *People*, carried out observations on the properties owned by the Messinas as well as on the men themselves.

Often the observers were switched from one location to another; they used a variety of hire cars, taxis and buses – fortunately, due to its healthy circulation, the pockets of the *People* were deep – and wore out a great deal of ordinary shoe-leather.

But it was inevitable that the Messinas would get to hear of Webb's activities; quite apart from innocent remarks made by those from whom Webb was seeking information, some of the Messinas' women became suspicious, and there were crooked newspaper men, as well as venal serving and former cops, who pointed out Webb and his associates. Messina thugs would use 'leap-frog' tailing tactics when following Webb; consequently, Webb's men would also shadow Webb's followers, to act as back-up in the eventuality of physical confrontation.

Webb now used his flat simply as a place to change his clothes; the Messinas knew where he lived, and Webb slept at different locations, at friends' houses or in hotels. When followed he would take one taxi, then change to another, before going to a location which had a rear exit, through which he could escape before taking a third.

Now, to add the finishing touches to his investigation, Webb needed photographs of the prostitutes soliciting and also the premises they used.

Initially, when Marthe Watts and the other prostitutes had seen Webb, they had believed him to be a police officer; their earnings started to tail off, because they were nervously keeping an eye on Webb and also on vehicles whose occupants appeared to be keeping them under observation. Once the truth was known, the brothers marshalled Marthe Watts to take care of Webb and the photographers busily snapping the Messina girls – who had been unequivocally told they were *not* to be photographed.

Let's pause here for a moment and let's be clear about the women that Webb had in his sights. Dispel any notions you might have that any of them was the archetypal 'Tart with a Heart', as so lovingly portrayed by the late Dora Bryan OBE in grainy old black and white post-war British films. This lot – apart from being as hard as nails – were personable, attractive and, most of all, believable; remember the words of the simple-minded Mr Justice Singleton after they had lied their heads off at the Vassalo trial? 'I confess I became almost a little sorry for them.' Certainly, the jury believed them when the five-man gang went down for blackmail.

Yes, they definitely were believable when they were put to the test and were certainly not found wanting. Shrieking, 'Help! Murder! Police!' the likes of Marthe Watts, Jeanne Connolly and Blanche Costaki would launch a violent attack on the photographers. This resulted in bystanders, doormen from clubs, even householders, as well as pimps and members of the Messina gang, joining in this sham 'hue and cry' as the men were chased down the street. The photographers would be punched, kicked and thrashed with the umbrellas wielded by their pursuers; even when they reached the sanctuary of a waiting car and drove off, it was not unknown for taxis – the drivers believing them to be fugitives from justice – to join in the chase.

Bill Breeze was one of Webb's photographers, and after chasing him from Stafford Street into the adjoining Dover Street, Marthe Watts ('He was a little man, but he ran just fast enough to escape me') was disappointed when he jumped into a waiting car. Webb enlisted help; Charles Rowe, the *People*'s news editor, and another reporter, Stanley Buchanan, were brought in to mind Breeze, but on a later occasion he was not so fortunate, when he was knocked down by a duo of harpies – Marthe Watts and Blanche Costaki. And when he was chased down the street by a small mob of frenzied prostitutes headed by Violet Carter and Jeanne Connolly, he forsook his profession for one with less immediate dangers.

Stan Jaanus took his place; and much to their fury, the Messina girls were snapped when they least expected it.

Nor was Webb immune from the Messina girls' attentions. Marthe Watts, Blanche Costaki and Marie Sanderson waited outside a pub in Stafford Street for almost two hours, forgoing the custom of any possible punters, before Webb, having ordered a taxi, emerged. It was only two and a half yards from pub to taxi, but this was quite sufficient for Webb to be insulted, slapped and punched, his pipe knocked out of his mouth and his spectacles to go flying, before he made it to the taxi door; and not before Watts had done her utmost to rip the lapel from his jacket.

The Messinas had a good intelligence service. The girls had noted the registration numbers of cars used by the photographers and reporters, and the Messinas used their crooked police contacts to find out to whom they belonged. No sooner did a hire car containing Webb and his associates draw up than it would be surrounded by a gang of screaming prostitutes, who would often break their umbrellas as they lashed out at the vehicle. Marthe Watts would later say that the umbrellas were opened to coyly protect their identities when being photographed; so they were, but those umbrellas were also handy weapons to attack Webb & Co.

When a car mounted the pavement, narrowly missing Webb, one of the prostitutes remarked, 'That was meant for you, dearie.'

This, as can well be imagined, was a pretty tough way to earn a living. Webb had to flee his flat in Brunswick Square when it was surrounded by heavies employed by the Messinas. He managed to board a train which was just pulling out from Euston station, destination unknown. Alighting at the first stop, Webb spent several hours, walking the deserted streets of Luton, before in the early hours of the following morning getting a train back to London.

Webb became aware – through a highly-placed contact within the Messina organization – of a conspiracy to negate, if not him, then his investigation. The most serious suggestion (especially since it involved not only the Messinas but a solicitor, a police officer and a Fleet Street reporter) was that he should be killed. That was rejected, possibly as being too extreme; the next plan (similarly vetoed) was that he should be blinded. Then the idea was floated of appropriating the evidence which Webb had accrued to see exactly what he had found out and to feed him disinformation, in the hope that he would accept it as genuine and publish, which in turn would open him to legal action. The final idea was to have Webb framed for a criminal offence – and this was later attempted.

By now, Eugenio was urging Marthe Watts & Co. to attack Webb at every available opportunity, but he knew that something – exposure or arrest – was in the air and he had stopped ostentatiously patrolling in his yellow Rolls-Royce to supervise the girls. The Messina women carried out Eugenio's instructions with fervour; they knew that if he and the rest of the brothers fell, they would lose their source of fine living, smart clothes, jewellery and accommodation – plus their income.

Despite all this intimidation, Webb found himself crowned with success in a way that the arrogant brothers would never have thought possible.

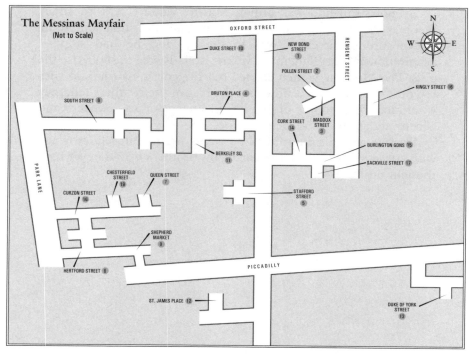

The Messinas Mayfair
(Not to Scale)

OXFORD STREET

DUKE STREET ⑩

NEW BOND STREET ①

POLLEN STREET ②

REGENT STREET

KINGLY STREET ⑱

SOUTH STREET ⑥

BRUTON PLACE ④

CORK STREET ⑭

MADDOX STREET ③

BURLINGTON GDNS ⑮

SACKVILLE STREET ⑰

BERKELEY SQ. ⑪

PARK LANE

CHESTERFIELD STREET ⑲

QUEEN STREET ⑦

CURZON STREET ⑯

STAFFORD STREET ⑤

SHEPHERD MARKET ⑧

HERTFORD STREET ⑨

PICCADILLY

ST. JAMES PLACE ⑫

DUKE OF YORK STREET ⑬

1. New Bond Street. No. 74 rented by Carmelo and Attilio. Used by Roberta Torrance and Edna Kallman.
2. Pollen Street. No. 3 used by Hermione Hindin and also Giuseppe Messina. No. 4 used by 'Marcelle' (Alfredo's wife). Rented by Eugenio Messina
3. Maddox Street. This thoroughfare was a 'beat' used by the Messina women. No. 30 was used by Hindin.
4. Bruton Place. Nos. 24, 26, 28 had the rates paid by Eugenio Messina. Andrée Messina used No. 24.
5. Stafford Street. No. 5 rented by Carmelo, Attilio and Janine Gilson. Nos. 5 and 7 used as brothels by Marthe Watts, Marie Sanderson and Blanche Costaki. The lease of No. 7 was purchased by Eugenio Messina.
6. South Street. Apartment purchased by Eugenio following prison release.
7. Queen Street. No. 4 rented by Eugenio and Carmelo and used as a brothel by Violet Carter.
8. Shepherd Market. No. 36 purchased by Eugenio. No. 52 acquired by Salvatore for Mme Charpentier/Evans, plus Ida and Marie Messina. A further property (number unknown) acquired by Attilio for Edna Kallman.
9. Hertford Street. No. 49a used as a brothel by Jeanne Connolly.
10. Duke Street used as a brothel by Marthe Watts and Jeanne Connolly.
11. Berkeley Square, where Eugenio had an apartment.
12. St. James' Place. Rented by the brothers and used as a brothel by Marthe Watts & Co.
13. Duke of York Street, flat rented by the brothers as a brothel.
14. Cork Street, flat rented by the brothers as a brothel.
15. Burlington Gardens, a 'beat' used by Marthe Watts & Co.
16. Kingly Street. No. 7, used by Hermione Hindin and Georgette Borg.
17. Sackville Street, where Cissy Cohen was seen to pass an envelope to Alfredo Messina.
18. Curzon Street. No. 39 was owned by Eugenio and used as a brothel, as was No. 49 and used by Marie Smith.
19. Chesterfield Street. No. 12 owned by Eugenio Messina.

CHAPTER 7

'Arrest These Four Men!'

On the morning of Sunday, 3 September 1950, the jaws of the 4½ million readers of the *People* collectively dropped. So did the mandibles of the Home Secretary Chuter Ede, the Commissioner of the Metropolitan Police, and not a few dodgy coppers. The Messina brothers undoubtedly headed for their respective lavatories in haste, since with the arrival of the Sunday newspaper they experienced a sudden a lack of pressure in their lower bowels.

The reason for this nationwide agitation was the headline of that edition of the *People* which roared, 'ARREST THESE FOUR MEN', above the sub-heading 'They are the emperors of a vice empire in the heart of London.'

This was accompanied by photographs of four of the Messinas – Alfredo was the exception – with the caption, 'Four despicable brothers'. There was also a photograph of Janine Gilson, plus one of her husband and details of their arranged marriage.

That, as far as the Messina brothers were concerned, was bad enough, but far worse was to come. Apart from naming and shaming them, plus giving details of their convictions, Webb went further and published accurate details of their addresses.

Eugenio was shown as living in a mews cottage at 24 Bruton Place under the name of Edward Marshall; Attilio was living in a block of flats at Kensington Park Gardens, W11, where he was known as Raymond Maynard; Carmelo was the resident of 3 Lancaster Lodge in North Kensington, where letters addressed to 'Charles Maitland' popped through the letterbox; and Salvatore lived at King's Court, Hammersmith, using his alias of Arthur Evans.

Details of the other addresses used by both the brothers and the prostitutes were revealed to the readers of the newspaper, who were enthralled by the whole business. Amidst the austerity of the post-war years, this was something to brighten up their grey lives; nothing since the salacious and well publicized details of King Edward VIII's affair with Mrs Wallace Simpson, some fifteen years previously, could compare. They thronged to see where the girls plied their trade, to see what they looked like in 'real life'; they

longed to gaze at the opulent homes of those whom they presumed
to be 'the filthy foreign Johnnies' who grew rich on their pickings.

And that was just a start. Going into explicit detail, this was just
a part of what Webb told his readers:

> Going to gaol did not do any harm to the business Eugenio
> Messina had built up. His brother looked after his side of
> it, and Carmelo even went so far as to bribe a warder in
> Wormwood Scrubs gaol to provide certain favours for his
> elder brother while he was inside. For this Carmelo got
> three months' [sic] imprisonment.
>
> But nothing was done by the police to book any of the
> gang for organising vice, and by the time Eugenio Messina
> had done one year in prison, his brothers were openly
> boasting how they had defeated the law in running their
> vice business. They were laughing at the Home Secretary's
> answer in Parliament, and chuckling when one Member
> of Parliament suggested that the gang had coined millions
> from their proceeds from prostitution.
>
> So brazen did the Messinas become that when someone
> got in their way, they no longer exposed themselves to
> the fate of Eugenio by indulging in knife and gun play;
> they framed false charges against them, usually with some
> success. There was a succession of cases in the courts
> in which accused persons pleaded that they had been
> framed by the Messina gang. Magistrates expressed their
> annoyance with this, what they thought to be empty pleas
> and only increased the sentence.
>
> In fact, by 1949 the Messinas had become so much of
> a legend in London that they were accepted as part of the
> London scene. So many fantastic stories were told about
> them that persons in authority attributed such stories to
> mere gossip, multiplicated anecdotes, and in some cases
> romantic and wishful thinking. I am sure from some of
> the remarks passed by some magistrates, that they did not
> believe that there was such a thing as the Messina gang.
> They certainly did not when Sally Wright was charged
> in court by Robina Dixon Torrance with assaulting her
> with a knife. Sally Wright pleaded in court that Torrance
> was a Messina woman, that the whole charge had been
> framed by the Messina gang, and that she was innocent.
> She should have known what she was talking about, for
> she had been a Messina woman herself for some years,
> and knew more about the gang than most people.

She was by no means the first person who had not been believed after pleading that she had been victimised by the Messina gang. It seemed that when anyone upset the Messinas all they had to do was enlist the aid of the courts, apparently with police assistance, and that someone was conveniently imprisoned, and incidentally discredited for life.

The *People's* weekly circulation was already high; with the publication of Webb's scoop, sales soared. The paper's managing editor, Stuart Campbell, capitalized on it as weekly editions brought more and more revelations of the disgusting brothers' activities. They had supposedly engaged contract killers from Corsica to assassinate Webb, and the editor gave maximum publicity to the bulletproof glass which now allegedly surrounded his desk.

*

Meanwhile, Webb was attacked in the street by a thug who told him, 'The Messinas are pals of mine; it's about time you journalists were done proper.' And then the brothers hit back, after a fashion. They broke cover when they rushed into the Brunswick Arms, Webb's local pub, to confront him – but that was all. Webb was in company with the much feared gang leader, Billy Hill, whose expertise with a razor was legendary. He was not long out of Wandsworth prison, having served three years, and with the exception of Jackie Sangers, whom he had cut to ribbons, hadn't striped anyone for ages. Surrounded by some of the toughest ne'er-do-wells of North London, the Messinas realized that they could well become his next victims. Slicing the tips off a fellow ponce's fingers was one thing; risking having their faces hacked to shreds was quite another, and they beat a hasty retreat.

Webb's star was in the ascendant; and so were the sales of the *People*. Between 10 September and 22 October 1950 the Messinas provided headlines for eight consecutive weeks. A piece in the edition dated 8 October read:

The public is entitled to ask when the courts are going to send these women to prison and when police intend to take steps to close down the premises from which they operate – and to arrest the four Messina brothers who run this vile gang.

In response to the Home Secretary's comments in the House of Commons, following the jailing of Eugenio and the Vassalo gang in 1947, a piece in the *People*, dated 22 October 1950, read:

> If Mr Ede believes that the people are as tolerant as he is, he should glance through the hundreds of indignant readers' letters that reach the *People*. They represent a rising tide of public opinion that will not be quietened by anything short of a full-scale warfare against the masters of London's vice empire.

This was a prescient piece of reporting, because the Messinas had capitalized on the publicity given to the Home Secretary's remarks; as Webb had stated in his report, with the help of corrupt police officers the brothers had had people framed for offences, knowing that although the victims would say it was the Messinas who were responsible, they would be disbelieved by the courts, since police officers, in the mould of the fictional PC George Dixon, always told the truth.

This was especially true when Sally Wright, who had originally been one of Attilio's flock, had tried to break from the family; as Webb had reported, Robina Dickson Torrance stated that Wright had attacked her with a knife. In vain, Wright desperately pleaded that she had been framed by the Messinas, but the magistrates obviously thought that this excuse was wearing a bit thin and sentenced her to three months' imprisonment.

But with Webb's revelations, this disbelief went out of the window. Now, everybody believed *everything* said about the brothers. In 1951, when 11-year-old Ron Feldman's family moved to Stoke Newington, it was said that the brothers owned a large Victorian house in Evering Road. It may or may not have been true, but as Feldman told me, 'If the street door opened whilst we were in the vicinity, we would run for our lives, such was their fearful, violent reputation.'

Marthe Watts set up rearguard actions with the aid of Blanche Costaki, who alleged that on 21 November Webb had blackmailed them, saying that unless they coughed up £50 each, photographs of them would be published in the *People*. Afraid of being thus shamed, the girls offered Webb £7, but this was contemptuously rejected, they said. The authorities refused to take tosh like that seriously, especially since the two women's accounts contradicted each other.

When two of the Messina girls complained to the Home Office that Webb had tried to bribe them to say that the Messinas were their ponces, this was given maximum publicity in the newspaper, which informed its readers that the matter had been passed to 'Inspector Mahon of the Vice Squad' for investigation.

Two matters arose out of this. First, there was no 'Vice Squad'. True, the newspapers liked to suggest there was, and former Detective Superintendent Bob Fabian was keen to inform the readers of his memoirs that he was 'the head of Scotland Yard's Vice Squad'; but in fact, it was a seedy office which had opened in 1937 at 'C' Division's Vine Street police station, nothing more.

Second, 'Inspector Mahon' was Detective Superintendent Guy Mahon. He was then attached to C1 Department at the Yard which, apart from representing what was inaccurately referred to as 'The Murder Squad', also housed a number of miscellaneous departments of which Mahon was now a member. It was Mahon's third such posting to C1; he had lasted there for three months in 1937, then rather longer, for six months, during 1944. He was what was known as a 'high-flyer', never stopping in one department for long, spending time in such unexciting postings as the Information Room, the Detective Training School, C2 Department, which dealt with case papers and correspondence, and the Research and Planning Department (twice); when he was later appointed the head of the Flying Squad he lasted just four months.

At the time of receiving these complaints the investigating officers at the Yard found there was no substance in them (certainly because they were palpably untrue), and there the matter rested. A little later, Mahon would achieve success in what was probably the biggest case of his career.

CHAPTER 8

The Messinas in Europe

Scotland Yard was now obliged to act; they were faced with Hobson's choice – in other words, no choice at all. A conference was held with the managerial staff of the *People*, their barrister, the Assistant Commissioner (Crime) and the Director of Public Prosecutions.

Webb's dossier had initially been passed to Bob Higgins, who since 18 July 1949 had been promoted to detective chief inspector and, like Mahon, had been posted to C1 Department at the Yard. In fact, given his trenchant views on prostitutes and their pimps, he was the ideal officer to investigate this long overdue matter, especially since he had supervised the arrest of Eugenio and Vassalo in 1947. He had also investigated the murders of two prostitutes, Rita Barratt aka 'Black Rita' and Rachel Fenwick, also known as 'Ginger Rae', and in consequence had made many contacts in the world of prostitution.

But for whatever reason, Ronald Martin Howe CVO, MC, the Assistant Commissioner (Crime), decided that the Messinas should be investigated by Guy Mahon. Perhaps he felt that since Mahon was regarded as a high-flyer, success in this case might push him even further up the promotional ladder, or maybe he thought that such a high profile case ought to be handled by an officer with the rank of superintendent.

As well as sending his dossier to the Yard, Webb had also sent a copy to Westminster City Council, but they complained to the Home Secretary that the existing laws were insufficient for them to take legal action, and they requested new legislation to enable them to launch successful prosecutions. However, introducing a new law takes a great deal of time; and now, in November 1950, Howe simply said, 'Mahon will do the job. He will have all the men and other assistance he needs. If the Messinas can be brought to justice, he will have my full backing in trying to do so.'

In sending Mahon out on to the field of battle, Howe, as a former barrister, might have chosen his words more carefully and given a tad more encouragement: 'if' and 'trying' did not suggest that he was anticipating a swift conclusion from the man appointed to investigate these matters which had gripped the attention of the British public. Rather, it appeared that he was hedging his bets.

Additionally, his rank of superintendent meant that Mahon was 'in the frame' at C1 – as a senior investigating officer he would be one of three superintendents liable to be despatched, often at very short notice, to investigate murders and other serious crimes, not only in the United Kingdom but also on board British ships and anywhere else within the British Empire.

No doubt Mahon was a competent officer; but Higgins would have been the better choice.

*

Could this matter have been better handled, to sweep up all of the Messinas before they fled? Well, yes and no.

Prior to Webb's sensational exposé in September, his enquiries had been complete and well documented – in other words, all the evidence was there. Would it not have been better to have called a meeting with the Yard one week – or perhaps even a matter of days – prior to publication? In this way, an investigating officer could have been appointed and detectives briefed, and there could have been an impressive round-up of the Messinas, their girls and their dodgy briefs, to coincide with copies of the *People* popping though the public's letterboxes. The Flying Squad approach of 'Nick 'em, first – get the evidence later' is certainly not necessarily the best in every investigation; but in this one, I believe it would have been justified, especially since the evidence was all there. This would have made sense; the police and Webb knew about the brothers' frequent trips abroad, and to delay arresting them would give them the opportunity to flee the country – which, of course, they did.

However, two considerations were against this, the first of which would have come from Webb and his employers. They were aware that some very dodgy characters – among them, venal police officers – were in the Messinas' pockets. To involve the Yard prior to publication could have resulted in leaks and ruined the whole operation, with documentation being destroyed and witnesses vanishing.

The second of these considerations was the character of a key police officer. As the Assistant Commissioner (Crime), Ronald Howe was a very fine administrator with an acute grasp of criminal matters. But he was not a career policeman; in 1924, he had been called to the Bar and two years later he had joined the staff of the office of the Director of Public Prosecutions. It was not until 1932 that he joined the Metropolitan Police as Chief Constable of the CID, and twenty-one months later, he was appointed Deputy Assistant Commissioner, a post he held for the next twelve years. He soaked up the workings of the CID like a sponge and when he succeeded Sir Norman Kendall CBE as the Assistant Commissioner (Crime), everybody agreed it was a move in the right direction, since Sir Norman was regarded by the rank and file as fussy, schoolmasterish and obstructive.

But Howe still retained his lawyer's ways; they like to have everything laid out in front of them in black and white before making a decision. This became evident when the Chief Constable of the CID, Percy Worth MBE, submitted his report, ten days after the end of the Second World War, proposing the formation of what would become known as the Ghost Squad to tackle what was sure to be an upsurge in post-war crime. It required the appointment of just four officers, a car and an office; that was all. However, it took Howe seven months to make up his mind and, with the commissioner's tentative approval, to implement the idea.

It was a pity. With trust on the side of the press and initiative on the side of the police, action against the Messinas could have been so very different.

I have already mentioned that Bob Higgins would have been a better choice than Mahon, but if Howe wanted an officer of superintendent rank to carry out the investigation, he need have looked no further than Jack Capstick. After successfully running the Ghost Squad as a detective inspector (first class), he was already known to Howe as an officer of unimpeachable integrity; in fact, it was Howe who emphatically demanded to the commissioner that Capstick should head the Ghost Squad. Capstick had been retained on C1 Department after his promotion to detective chief inspector in 1947, and two years later, still at C1, he had been promoted again, to the rank of detective superintendent.

Capstick would have been ideal in every way. Vastly knowledgeable, with an army of informants and his Flying Squad and Ghost Squad background, and used to making snap decisions, he also was known – and respected – by prostitutes in the West End of London because of a particular case: a ponce had slashed the face of a prostitute in his charge but believed himself immune from prosecution because of the control he exercised over her. However, Capstick ran him to ground in a Covent Garden pub; drawing his truncheon, he effected the ponce's arrest by hitting him across the face, left and right, fracturing both his cheekbones. Believing that a little more humiliation was then necessary, Capstick eschewed the use of a police van for transportation and instead dragged his prisoner all the way to Bow Street police station, through lines of cheering prostitutes.

That was the calibre of the 1925 police constable who – initially, at least – the market porters at Covent Garden dubbed 'Baby Face'; in later years, the villains spoke with considerably more respect of the detective known as 'Charlie Artful'. A supremely capable thief-taker, he was commended by the commissioner on forty occasions.

But of course, Howe did not appoint Capstick to the Messina enquiry; who knows how different things might have been, if he had?

*

Mahon got to work studying Webb's well-crafted documentation, which really had done most of his work for him. He had a number of officers to assist him, including Detective Sergeants Bert Foster and Leslie Rouse and Detective Constable David Fenton. The press reported that the officers travelled all over England and interviewed 300 witnesses. If that was so, the operation turned up very few witnesses for the first prosecution – they numbered just eleven, all from the London area, of whom five were police officers. It was just as well those enquiries were made, because Mahon was indeed called away on other investigations. But the first question to be answered was: where were the Messinas?

The public were informed that when the first stunning exposé appeared in the *People* full details of the revelations had immediately been passed to Scotland Yard. Although this was not strictly true, the Messinas were not to know that. What they did know, without any doubt whatsoever, was that everything written in that initial newspaper report was absolutely accurate. With their solicitor, William Webb, advising them to stay out of England 'until the fuss has blown over', at 10.30 am on Sunday, 10 September, just seven days after the initial publication, Eugenio climbed into his Rolls-Royce, pointed it in the direction of Dover and left England. Apart from what he perceived to be his imminent arrest, revenue from the girls was falling appallingly.

As a measure of his panic, he had abandoned his latest property, an apartment in South Street. It had just been decorated, including the hanging of some rather costly wallpaper, and some very expensive furniture had been delivered. The curtains – equally expensive – had not been hung, but that was the least of Eugenio's problems; that could be left to the likes of Marthe Watts, who could extend her expertise as a milliner (which is how she described her occupation in the telephone directory) to embrace curtain-hanging.

Eugenio was joined by Carmelo and, a few weeks later, Salvatore, and then Attilio. Meanwhile, the brothers' interests were looked after by Anthony Micallef (variously described as their brother-in-law or their cousin), himself a ponce and brothel keeper as well as being the Messinas' private secretary and accountant.

The disappearance of the brothers produced a strange effect for the Messina girls. Now that their names, addresses and photographs had been published, they were visited by or received letters from a number of men entreating them to abandon their shameful lifestyle and sometimes providing money to assist them in doing so. It was a noble effort on the part of these well-meaning gentleman, but it appears unlikely than any of the ladies who received their beneficence were persuaded to pursue a more modest existence.

One suspects that Duncan Webb would have wanted to set off in hot pursuit of the brothers, and so he did, but not immediately. His health over the past three months had suffered badly; he had worked excessive hours, had had very little sleep and had eaten at irregular hours; moreover, his alcohol intake had increased immeasurably. All that, as well as constant stress as a result of actual and threatened attacks, had left its mark on him, and matters were not improved by the effects of wartime injuries he had received following a bad landing from a parachute jump after the plane he had been travelling in to cover the 1944 Battle of the Bulge was shot down. He had suffered a broken arm and two crushed vertebrae, and his lung had been punctured as the result of several ribs being broken. Snow had fallen at his landing site in the Ardennes, and before he was rescued, his feet had become frostbitten.

So, with his health in tatters, Webb was admitted to hospital for an operation. Not that he gave up the fight entirely; he continued to pursue his enquiries from his hospital bed on the telephone with his contacts on the Continent.

It seemed as though Eugenio and Carmelo were running scared; they went first to Paris, then to the Pyrenees, to Switzerland, back to France, to Brussels and then Amsterdam. The two brothers invariably travelled together. Salvatore was staying in Marseilles and from time to time he met his siblings, as did Attilio. Marthe Watts visited Eugenio in Paris, as did other Messina girls who brought money, jewellery and furs out to the brothers. Jeanne Connolly brought two silver fox capes, worth thousands; when she made a return journey to London, the furs did not accompany her.

It seemed that wherever Webb went he missed the brothers by days, sometimes by just a few hours. This was the case when he arrived at the Hôtel de Paris in Pau – the hometown of Ida Poumirou, otherwise known as Ida Messina. She had stayed there two days previously together with Salvatore, using one of his *noms de guerre*, Arturo Evans. The hotel registration cards had been completed in those names and as usual they had been collected by the police. Although the hotel management agreed that the couple had indeed stayed there, when Webb made further enquiries, the head of Pau's *Sûreté National* denied that the couple had ever been there; indeed, he asserted, nobody with the name Poumirou lived, or in fact had ever lived, in the region of Pau.

It appeared that the brothers had a strong pull with the police in most places they visited.

However, the police chief's declaration was effectively nullified after Webb spoke to Ernest Poumirou, the brother of Ida, who lived in a flat seven minutes walk away from the *préfecture*. He confirmed that Salvatore had been in Pau for two weeks, let alone two days, and had visited him practically every day. Webb also met a young woman in Poumirou's second-floor flat who described herself as Salvatore's 'niece' and stated that her 'uncle' had promised her 'a very good job' in London. Five months later, Webb was able to observe the selfsame girl working hard at that 'very good job', soliciting prostitution in Shepherd Market.

Webb discovered that the brothers had gone to San Remo, and so they had; in the Miramar Hotel on the Corso Matuzia, with its swimming pool surrounded by a palm tree-lined park, they thought they were safe from Webb's attentions. Not so. Jeanne Connolly and Janine Gilson had met them there, and every night they had phoned 24 Bruton Place, where Eugenio's wife was living; they also placed calls to Switzerland and locations all over France, but they left in a hurry.

They next sought sanctuary in the Bristol Hotel, in Genoa's Via XX Settembre, where since 1905 guests have been greeted by the sight of a sweeping grand central staircase which leads on to elegant high-ceilinged rooms. When Webb arrived there he discovered that they had left that morning for Milan, telling the management that Carmelo, Jeanne Connolly and Janine Gilson would be returning in three days' time. During the brothers' absence, Webb managed to gain entry to one of the three rooms they had booked (details of how this was accomplished are unclear), took a pair of Carmelo's trousers and posted them back to him with Webb's business card attached.

The brothers took a suite at the splendid Duomo Hotel, in Milan's Via Alberico Albricci, and when they telephoned Marthe Watts and Marie Messina in London, Webb managed to listen in.

Webb telephoned Eugenio and gave the impression that he was speaking from London; Eugenio suggested a meet in Rome and gave him an address there. Webb returned to London, where he made himself conspicuous by walking around the Messina girls' beats in Stafford Street and Shepherd Market, knowing that his presence there would be reported to Eugenio.

Meanwhile, Mahon had established that Eugenio, Attilio and Carmelo had been born in Egypt and had their births recorded by the Italian authorities. Once their falsely obtained British passports could be seized, their wives, too, could be stripped of their bogus nationality and deported. When Carmelo's passport needed to be renewed in 1951, he visited the British Consul General's office in Rome. Pinned to the wall was a notice requesting contributions towards a charity; he made a handsome donation and, handing over his passport, smilingly asked the Vice-Consul, Mr B. Nuttall, to renew it. Nuttall saw that it was out of date, made some enquiries and when he discovered that Carmelo was on the 'stop list', promptly confiscated the passport.

Eugenio, meanwhile, moved from one apartment to another in Paris, visited tea dances and dance halls, met enchanting and probably naïve young women and, with Marthe Watts' assistance, shipped them over to England.

Since the South Street apartment had been let, the girls retired to their former, rather less salubrious habitats; and one of the Rolls-Royces was sold. Eugenio did, however, acquire a new Parisian apartment, together with a chauffeur for his Rolls whose wife acted as housekeeper. It was whilst Marthe Watts was visiting him there that he received a call from the *Police Judiciare*. This was at the instigation of Scotland Yard, but Eugenio, his initial panic now dissipated, was savvy enough to know that if the French police had anything on him, if they possessed a warrant for his arrest, they would have come straight to his apartment and claimed him there and then. They would not have telephoned beforehand, requesting his attendance at the local *préfecture*.

That being so, Eugenio reacted true to type. He and Marthe Watts took their time dressing themselves up to the nines, he in one of his handmade Savile Row suits, she in mink and glittering with jewels, and thus attired they haughtily strolled down the staircase to the entrance hall to be greeted by the goggling police officers. The officers' esteem intensified after Eugenio dismissed his chauffeur, whom he had instructed to bring the Rolls to the front door of the apartments. He then drove himself to the *préfecture* where, during the following two hours, he and Marthe untruthfully answered all of the innocuous questions put to them; the questions and answers were typed on the *Procès-Verbal* forms as required by the *Ministère de l'Interieur* which were then stamped with the official stamp and signed by the witnesses and the questioners – and that was that. Once again, Eugenio had ostentatiously displayed his contempt for the forces of law and order and no charges had been preferred; indeed, the glamorous couple had received a number of deferential salutes. The forms were forwarded to Scotland Yard, via Interpol, and when they arrived, probably several months later, they were as much use as if they had never been obtained in the first place.

Within a few days, Marthe returned to England. Her exit from France and her arrival in London failed to excite the attention of customs officers on either side of the Channel, nor did she receive a visit from the British police. It was, in fact, business as usual.

The same applied to Eugenio; he met a young woman named Augustine Verlet and rented an apartment in her name in the fashionable (and extremely expensive) Rue de la Faisanderie, where his Rolls-Royce was parked next to a car owned by the Duke and Duchess of Windsor. Augustine received the usual amount of Messina flattery, and it was not too long before she, too, arrived in London to become part of the brothers' harem; in common with others of that assemblage, Mlle Verlet will be making a further appearance later on, in a sensational court case.

As 1950 came to a close, Marthe Watts and the girls continued to greet the new imports, work the streets and take their clients back to the addresses which were still retained in London; the finances were being taken care of, and Westminster council were as powerless as the Home Secretary to do anything. The four brothers were living the life of Riley on the Continent. That left the fifth brother, Alfredo who had not even been named in Webb's revelations. What was he up to?

The answer was, plenty.

CHAPTER 9

'A Lovely Lunch'

Alfredo let it be known that now he was no longer a carpenter; he was a diamond merchant. That explained his frequent visits to North Africa, Spain and Belgium. When war broke out in 1939, despite Belgium's declaration of neutrality, it was widely expected that Germany would attack France through northern Belgium. In fact, when that attack came, the Wehrmacht's Lieutenant General Erich von Manstein decided instead to launch it through the Ardennes in the south of the country. However, he failed to communicate this to Alfredo Messina in Brussels, and on 10 November 1939 Alfredo beat a hasty retreat and arrived in Britain. He would have arrived sooner but he had to wait for the British Consul in Brussels to provide him with a permit allowing him to take £360 out of the country. In fact, what he would later say to explain away his wealth was that due to foreign banks closing with the advent of war, he had brought £30,000 out of Belgium as the proceeds of his, er, diamond business. When the crunch came – as it soon would – he would thus be able to explain away the large sums of money he had in accounts at various banks. At least, that was the idea.

Whatever Alfredo's business was, it appeared to be thriving; in 1934 he had opened an account at Barclays Bank, Newgate Street and during 1936 he made five deposits by bank transfer from his account at the Bank de Commerce, Brussels which amounted to £1,645 and in 1938, one transfer of £199 14s 0d from his account at Barclays Bank, Paris; altogether, £1,844 14s 0d. However, into the same account at the Newgate Street Branch of Barclays, between 1936 and 1940 Alfredo was regularly paying cash amounts of approximately £100 a time on fourteen occasions: the total came to £1,820. Of course, there was also the £1,659 which, as previously mentioned, he had deposited with the Egyptian banks between 1928 and 1932.

But in addition to the Bank de Commerce account in Brussels, plus the Barclays Bank accounts in London and Paris, he also had accounts at banks in Casablanca, Tangier, Spain, Gibraltar, Malta and the London branch of the Crédit Lyonnais, Charles II Street, SW1. Oh yes, and also at the United Bank of Scotland, High

Street, Kensington, where during six weeks in 1948 he deposited £500, £800 and £200, all in £1 notes; in April and June he further deposited cash sums of £100, £400 and £200. In 1944 he had paid in a total of £3,100 at the same branch.

Due to his thriving jewellery business, he was compelled to open safety deposit accounts at Selfridges, the first on 7 August 1937 and another on 8 September 1941, as well as a further one at the London Safe Deposit, also in 1941 ('Where all the diamond merchants go', as he would later say). So why two safety deposit boxes in the same building? The two boxes measured respectively 6" x 7½" x 17½" and 4¼" x 4¾" x 17½", and diamonds don't take up a great deal of space; but of course, currency (especially in £5 notes) does. There were no diamonds in either box at the time of his arrest; there was £300 in the smaller box and £1,050 in the other. Of course, matters weren't helped when, prior to the boxes' discovery, he was asked if he possessed a safe deposit and denied it.

There was another anomaly. When he had withdrawn £1,000 from the Bank of British West Africa at 37 Gracechurch Street, EC1 on 5 July 1947, £825 of that money comprised 165 £5 notes and, as was common in those days, a record was kept by the bank of the numbers of those notes. But when his safety deposit box was opened in 1951, 108 of the £5 notes in the box containing £1,050 were those original notes; it was an early form of money laundering.

So that, plus the contents of his safe at the time of his arrest, amounted to £1,972; then there were the deposits in the British West Africa Bank, the United Bank of Scotland and Barclays Bank, Hatton Garden, which again at the time of his arrest amounted to a total of £8,960. It was not bad going for a man who claimed that he was an invalid, a diabetic with high blood pressure and a weak heart who had been unable to work since 1939, but nevertheless, with a reckless disregard for his well-being, had been able to pay £400 to a wine merchant at the Railway Hotel, Wembley during the space of one year.

In 1935 Alfredo had married a woman named Mary – she was also known as 'Marcelle' – in Spain's capital, Madrid. He claimed not to know her maiden name, but that was of little consequence because she arrived in London (with British nationality, once again) and settled into 4 Pollen Street, W1. This was a short thoroughfare thoughtfully situated right in the middle of a triangulation of Oxford Street, Bond Street and Regent Street. It was also convenient for Marlborough Street Police Court, because between September 1935 and June 1936 Marcelle was convicted there for soliciting prostitution on fifteen occasions;

and during the following fifteen years that number of convictions swelled to 122.

According to Alfredo, as soon as the first fifteen convictions came to light, he was so appalled that he piously dumped her, and serve her right. It was fortunate that his father, Giuseppe, was living at the same address in Pollen Street to keep an eye on her. Giuseppe was also in a position to keep an eye on the person who lived next door, at No. 3.

This was Hermione Hindin. She also called herself Barbara Trent and Barbara Harvey and she had been known to the police since 1938.

She had been born in 1909, the daughter of Isaac Jacobs, a London bookmaker, and in 1929 she had married a man named Isaac Hindin. Two sons were born, the marriage broke up and after she started working as a prostitute she became part of the Messina harem. As well as the Pollen Street address, she also had use of an apartment at 7 Kingly Street; the lease had been purchased by one Charles Maitland, who in his other identity as Carmelo Messina had made an abrupt exit to France when the going got hot.

But Alfredo stayed put. Why shouldn't he? He had not been named in Webb's exposé so there was no reason for him to leave. Short, dumpy Alfredo was not ostentatious like his brothers, nor did he live in the opulent surroundings of Mayfair. He drove a Ford 8 saloon, which at £585 was not cheap but considerably less expensive than brother Eugenio's £8,000 Rolls-Royce. His address was a detached house at 45 Harrowdene Road, Wembley, situated in an ultra respectable neighbourhood, which he purchased – with cash – in March 1942 for £1,400 12s 10d. At the time of writing it is valued at £1 million. Furnishing it cost a further £2,500; again, mainly paid for in cash. Hindin moved in with Alfredo and with one of her sons (until a period of Borstal training intervened), and by the time Detective Superintendent Mahon commenced his investigations, Hindin had been convicted of soliciting prostitution on 106 occasions.

Now – before we go any further, this was the law regarding living on immoral earnings, as it stood at the time of the investigation:

> The Vagrancy Act of 1898, section 1, provides that it is an offence for any male person knowingly to live wholly or in part on the earnings of prostitution; and by section 3 of the same Act, together with an amendment to the Act which was made in 1912, the law provides where a male person is proved to live with, or to be habitually in the company of a prostitute, or is proved

> to have exercised control, direction or influence over the movements of a prostitute in such a manner as to show that he is aiding, abetting or compelling her prostitution with any other person, or generally, he shall, unless he can satisfy the court to the contrary, be deemed to be knowingly living upon the earnings of prostitution.

Therefore, the onus was on a person charged with such an offence to prove that he was unaware that the person he was living with was a prostitute, or that he was not living on her earnings from prostitution.

Undeniably, being a ponce could be a tricky business. Of course, the profits could be huge, but so were the pitfalls. Between 1913 and 1925 221 men were convicted of living on prostitutes' immoral earnings, and a subsequent conviction could mean being committed to the Quarter Sessions for punishment. This included corporal punishment; between 1926 and 1935 nine convictions resulted in sentences of between nine and twenty-two months' imprisonment, some with hard labour and 'bashings' – between 12 and 18 strokes of the cat o'nine tails. Fortunately for Alfredo, by the time he had his collar felt, the Criminal Justice Act 1948 had abolished 'bashings', penal servitude and hard labour. Some might think that in Alfredo's case that was a pity.

However, his case seemed straightforward enough. Alfredo had been seen on numerous occasions driving Hindin from Wembley at about 6.30 in the evening to the West End and then collecting her during the early hours of the following morning. Hindin had been seen in the company of other prostitutes as well as soliciting prostitution; it looked like an open and shut case.

On 15 March 1951 Mahon and Detective Sergeant Albert Foster were in the vicinity of Harrowdene Road when they saw Alfredo drive past them, twice, in his Ford 8, registration number JVD 15, before disappearing. An hour later, they went to the house, where they saw Hindin; apparently Alfredo was not there. They returned the following day and this time they made an appointment with Hindin to see Alfredo at 12 noon on 19 March.

In fact, it was 12.30 pm when the officers arrived and saw Alfredo; this – according to the police – was the conversation which followed.

After introducing himself, Mahon said, 'I think you know we are making enquiries into allegations that for some years past you have been living on the earnings of a prostitute', to which Alfredo replied, 'I know that.'

London's West End: Messina territory.

Above left :Alfredo Messina.

Above right: Salvatore Messina.

Above left: Carmelo Messina.

Above right: Attilio Messina.

Above left: Eugenio Messina taken to court in Belgium.

Above right: Marthe Watts and Eugenio Messina.

The Hunters

Above left: John Du Rose.

Above right: Duncan Webb.

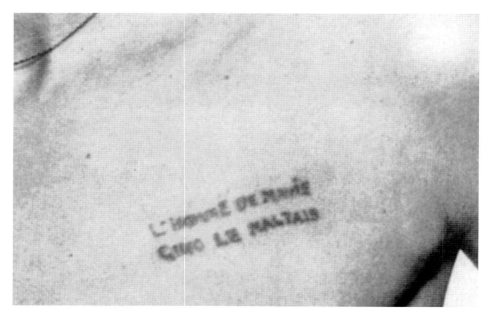

Marthe Watts' tattoo: 'Gino the Maltese: The Man of my Life'.

Above: Sir Gerald Dodson, the Recorder of London, who at different times sentenced Eugenio, Carmelo and Attilio.

Left: Marie Smith: The other woman in 'Gino the Maltese's' life.

Eugenio
Messina
arriving
at court in
Belgium,
handcuffed.

Eugenio
(left) and
Carmelo
(right)
during
a court
adjournment
in Belgium.

L-R: Marthe
Watts,
Eugenio and
Carmelo
Messina.

Folio No.	Name
C.R.O. Name and No.	Nickname
Corres. No.	Nationality Claimed
Passport Particulars	Nationality at Birth
Alien Identity Book	Address
Deportation Order	From :—
Gating Order	To :—
Marriage Particulars	
Maiden Name, etc., of Woman	
Nearest Relative Abroad	Photo.
Motor Car Particulars	
Previous Convictions	
Division Where Known	Born Height Build
	Eyes Hair Marks

A sample sheet from Scotland Yard's Secret Foreign Prostitutes' and Associates' Album.

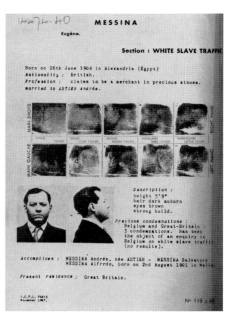

Above left: A prostitute's licence, Cairo, 1885.

Above right: Eugenio Messina's descriptive form.

THE PEOPLE

SUNDAY, SEPTEMBER 3, 1950 · No. 3591—69th Year · 2d

OVER 4,500,000 SALE

ARREST THESE FOUR MEN

ey are the emperors of a vice mpire in the heart of London

day 'The People' has found the facts about a vice ring he heart of London that is a national scandal.

● This is an unsavoury story but we believe it is our duty to the public to reveal it so that swift action can be taken.

THE MESSINA GANG EXPOSED

By Duncan Webb

YESTERDAY I made the final entry in a dossier that uncovers the activities of a vice gang operating in the West End of London on a scale that will appal every decent man and woman.

Today I offer Scotland Yard evidence from my dossier that should enable them to arrest four men who are battening on women of the streets and profiting from their shameful trade.

And, to support that demand, I intend to expose in detail the way in which this gang operates—a story so sordid that I am certain public opinion will now demand that this state of affairs should not be tolerated a moment longer.

The four men I am accusing are brothers, members of what is openly known to the police—and even to Parliament—as The Messina Gang.

Let there be no doubt as to whom I am naming as the members of this gang on these grave charges. The four men are:—

EUGENE MESSINA, who normally calls himself Edward Marshall and who lives at 24, Bruton-place, a mews flat off New Bond-st., Mayfair.

ATTILIO MESSINA, who is usually known as Raymond Maynard and who has been living in a block of flats in Kensington Park Gardens, London, W.11.

CARMELO MESSINA, who has changed his name to Charles Maitland and who lives at 3, Lancaster Lodge, a respectable block of flats in North Kensington.

SALVATORE MESSINA, who has changed his name to Arthur Evans and who lives at Kings Court, Hammersmith, London.

These four brothers are Maltese, and therefore have British nationality. They have been in London for some years and they are now wealthy men.

"Lives of shame"

They are engaged in business as dealers and merchants, and undoubtedly they have made some of their money legitimately.

But, by the most detailed investigation which has taken me and my assistants three months to complete, I have proved that in fact they are controlling a chain of flats used for immoral purposes.

They are emperors of an empire of vice in London's West End.

There are women of the streets who are virtually in their power. Many of these women have come from the Continent to carry on their disgusting business.

And these four men know full well that the wives of some of them are openly taking part in this life of shame.

It is a state of affairs that would disgrace one of the licentious ports of the Middle East. That it should exist in London on this scale is almost incredible.

This newspaper commissioned me to uncover the operations of the Messina Gang as a public duty.

For too long the Messinas have been talked about in high places. But for too long nothing has been done to round them up and put the leaders in a place where they can no longer defame the good name of the capital.

There have been mentions of the Messinas in Parliamentary debates. Their names have cropped up in police court proceedings.

Yet they have gone on battening on the proceeds of vice to the point when they have built up a virtual sense of fear among women of the streets.

Three of these Messina brothers have been in trouble with the police before.

EUGENE MESSINA was born on June 26, 1908, in Alexandria, Egypt.

He was convicted in London in 1947, and sentenced to three years' penal servitude for unlawful wounding.

CARMELO MESSINA has been convicted for bribing a warder while visiting his brother in prison. He got two months.

SALVATORE MESSINA was convicted in Egypt in 1932 for living on immoral earnings, and was sentenced to six months imprisonment.

Let me now put on record some of the facts I have uncovered about the despicable side of these men's business interests. I have no intention of affronting public decency by printing in detail the way in which their women conduct their hideous business.

It is enough to say that I have records of what has been observed over long periods to have taken place at flats and other residential premises in the West End of London—places that are owned, rented or leased by one or other of these Messinas.

They are able to flout the law in this way partly because they have operated on the grand scale—strange as that may seem—but also because they have been expert at covering up their tracks.

Take first Eugene Messina. He is a man of many addresses, official and otherwise, and he has built around himself a smoke-screen that is not easy to penetrate.

"I watched"

When he was released from prison some months ago, he gave his official address as 3, Lancaster Lodge, London, W.11, which is also the official address of his brother Carmelo.

But, for rating purposes, he gives to the Westminster City Council the address of 24, Bruton-place, W.1. There he occupies a flat under his real name of Eugene Messina.

Next door is No. 26, Bruton-place, which is rated with No. 28. And the name of the rated occupier of this house is E. Marshall, the second name he commonly employs.

And I can prove that 28, Bruton-place is a house used for immoral purposes. It is frequently

Turn to Page 2

FOUR DESPICABLE BROTHERS

HERE are the four Messina brothers we accuse today.

Top left is Eugene Messina, who calls himself Edward Marshall.

Top right is Carmelo Messina, who has changed his name to Charles Maitland.

Below him is Attilio Messina, who is usually known as Raymond Maynard.

Last of the four in this gallery of despicable brothers is Salvatore Messina, who has changed his name to Arthur Evans.

WAS AN ARRIAGE

Jean Gilson, of the women with the Mes-

her husband, who declares ve her British —she was born —by marrying altar.

ys he was paid the wedding wife left him, ealised it was a f convenience.

RED TROOPS HALTED IN 'BULGE,' ROUTED IN SOUTH

AFTER two days of furious fighting on a 50-mile front, the Communists in Korea have failed to achieve a decisive break-through. Last night their troops had been brought to a halt at the foothills rising from the plains that form the Naktong River "bulge."

This was their only major penetration—and American reserves, held back until the general picture became clearer, were expected to be hurled into the battle at any moment.

"The position is still fluid but on the way to being stabilised," was the report from General MacArthur's headquarters.

In this central sector the Reds had advanced eight to ten miles, over flat country that could only have been held by trench warfare.

But last night their attacks were weakening, and their forward units were believed to have lost touch with divisional headquarters.

American tanks and combat engineers yesterday recaptured **YONGSAN,** pivotal town twenty miles north of Masan, and fanned out along the road to Changnyong. This counter-attack may turn out to be the decisive action of the battle.

Further north, the Americans were attacking hills above **WAEGWAN,** and in the extreme south they had pushed two miles beyond battered **HAMAN** in the struggle to protect Masan, main coastal town on the road to Pusan.

Heavy casualties

Light Communist forces got to within five miles of Masan before they were forced back by the U.S. 25th Division, which estimated enemy losses in the southern battle as 10,000 killed and wounded.

The latest U.S. tanks, the 48-ton Pattons, with 90 m.m. guns, went into action for the first time.

"We have retaken all our old positions—Masan has been saved," said a divisional spokesman.

On the east coast Pohang front, the Communists were reported to have captured **KIGYE,** but there was no evidence that the main weight of the Red offensive was likely to be switched to this area. Later, the Americans made rapid progress in a two-pronged attack.

Everywhere the North Koreans suffered heavy casualties. Allied aircraft knocked out twenty-seven tanks.

Jellied petrol bombs and rockets loosed by 200 Navy planes blasted the Red troops. The Nam and Naktong rivers ran red with blood at points where the enemy attempted daylight crossings.

THEY HELD BRITISH WIFE AS 'SPY'

A BRITISH housewife, mother of a seven-years-old boy, has returned to her home, after spending ten days in a cell in the Soviet sector of Germany, and being "grilled" by the Russians, who accused her of being a spy.

She is Mrs. Joan Brennan, of Gipsy-lane, Grays, Essex. She said last night:

"I was in Germany sightseeing and quite innocently went walking in a wood. I suppose I wandered into the Soviet zone. Suddenly I stumbled on a party of Russian troops.

"I was frightened and began to run. I heard one of them call to me to stop, but I ran on through the trees. Then I saw him raise his rifle to his shoulder and aim. I thought he might be a good shot so I stopped."

She was taken by car to Soviet headquarters, stripped and searched by a German policewoman, who even looked in her hair and ears. Later, she was taken for interrogation for hours at a time. Once she was taken from her cell at midnight to be questioned.

Hunger strike

"They said I was an American spy and that I was wearing an American dress," Mrs. Brennan went on. "I bought it in Grays before I left. They asked me my grandmother's name and how much military transport went from England to Germany. I said I didn't know.

"They also asked me: 'Will you be punished when you get back?' and I told them 'No.'"

After five days Mrs. Brennan went on hunger strike. The following day she was told she would be released, but a Russian officer had taken her passport and she would have to wait until it was recovered.

A few days later she was driven, under escort, to the frontier of the American sector and freed.

"I was worried at times," she said. "I thought anything might happen. I was very lucky to get back."

KILLED BY COW

Arthur Partridge, sixty-six, Langdon Hills (Essex) farmer, was killed by a kick from a cow he was trying to rescue from a ditch.

Good Morning People!

IN spite of the rebuff he received last week from President Truman, General MacArthur is still up to his trouble-making tricks. Now he has thought up a new dodge to force the American Government to claim Formosa as a defence bastion in the Far East. He has been trying to convince Washington that Red China was about to intervene in the Korean War. From his headquarters reports were spread that Chinese Communist troops had already crossed the Yalu River, which forms the frontier between China and North Korea.

These reports are untrue. The British Government's latest and most reliable information is that, far from crossing the Yalu, the Chinese are building fortifications on their own side of it! They are simply digging in against a possible backwash of the war.

THIS supports our Foreign Office's confident belief that Red China is, in fact, most anxious to keep the peace. Her internal problems are so urgent that nothing short of open provocation would induce her to give battle.

MacArthur, unchecked, might supply that provocation. That is why Mr. Ernest Bevin, our Foreign Secretary, is eager to meet Mr. Acheson in Washington next week to discuss a plan for the settlement of the whole Formosa question.

Attlee attacks 'Dictator' Churchill

MR. ATTLEE, in a party political broadcast, last night replied to the "peremptory demand" of Mr. Churchill for an earlier recall of Parliament, and outlined the reasons he had given the Tory leader for fixing the date for September 12.

"He described my attitude as sullen," said the Prime Minister. "I should describe him as dictatorial.

"For the last 30 years Mr. Churchill seems to me to have regarded Parliament mainly as a place where he makes speeches.

"He comes down like a prima donna, delivers his oration and then, except for an occasional appearance at question time, is seen no more until the next occasion.

"The real work of the House proceeds without his assistance.

"His constant running down of Britain is injurious to the national interest."

Turning to Korea, Mr. Attlee said: "There was no muddle or hesitation. Mr. Churchill knows this quite well, but apparently it's not much good giving him information.

"The same old charges and the same old phrases come out time after time."

Russian trade

On Craven Brothers' contract with Russia for supplying machine tools, Mr. Attlee said:

"It has never been our policy to set up an iron curtain in trading matters.

"We made a trade agreement with Russia to our mutual benefit. We have since received feeding stuffs and timber in exchange for machinery. They have carried out their side of the bargain and we are carrying out ours."

Neither Mr. Churchill nor his colleagues made any protest at the time the agreement was made, went on the Premier.

"Eighteen months ago we took steps to ensure that equipment and tools regarded as of key importance for strategic purposes should not be exported except in the case of contracts already concluded.

"We shall not allow such exports to damage essential defence needs.

"As to inspection, which is not unreasonable in the manufacture of goods of this kind, specific instructions have been given to ensure that it is made in conditions which prevent any disclosure of secrets."

ANGELA says: "Thank goodness it's still only September; at least I've got a warm seat."

MORE RAIN

Lighting-up time tonight 8.44

DON'T be deceived by a bright start to the day: more rain is on its way—and it will not be long in coming.

The new wet-weather spell will come in from the West, and by this afternoon it will be cloudy in most parts. Heavy showers will follow, but the South may escape with light drizzle.

WILL SUE FRANKLIN

NEIL FRANKLIN, Stoke City and England centre-half, is threatened with an action for damages by the Santa Fe football club following his decision not to go back there but to seek reinstatement in English football.

A spokesman for the Bogota club said yesterday: "An Englishman's word is regarded as being as good as his bond, and we are determined to go all out to get our redress."

Franklin has already cost Santa Fe £2,800, and that is the sum the club is out to recover as damages.

FATAL BALLOON

James Doolittle, aged three, of Ohio, collected toy balloons. He sucked one into his throat yesterday and choked to death.

Thought reading

It's not hard to guess what the other man's thinking when you've both taken a lot out of yourselves . . . a deep cool Guinness for strength

You'll feel better when you have a

GUINNESS

ballito Stockings

The Messina brothers exposed.

The gravestone of Giuseppe Messina.

'Who told you that we had been to see Mr Roper about yourself?' asked Mahon; this was a reference to Charles Roper, a former police constable who was in Alfredo's employ.

He replied, 'I get to know these things. I know many people and they tell me what is going on.'

'Did Mr Roper tell you we had been to see him?' asked Mahon, and Alfredo replied, 'No, but I knew he was worried about something'. He then continued, 'Let's be friends. We are men of the world and can't afford to fall out. I'm going to give you a lovely lunch with turkey and champagne.'

Mahon asked, 'Do you do any work?' and Alfredo replied, 'No, I'm an invalid; I don't do anything.'

Having established that Hermione Hindin lived with him, and referring to her, Mahon asked, 'Do you know that she's a prostitute and that she's worked the streets of the West End for many years?'

'You seem to know all about us', replied Alfredo, adding, 'Between men of the world, I don't deny it.'

Pressing home the point, Mahon said, 'You know, then, that she has many convictions for prostitution offences?' to which Alfredo replied, 'Oh yes'.

'As you are living with a prostitute, the onus is on you to prove that you are not living on the earnings of her prostitution', said Mahon; to this Alfredo made no comment but invited the two officers to have a drink, which they did.

'I believe you take Mrs Hindin by car to her pitch or beat in Maddox Street, Mayfair, almost every evening,' said Mahon, 'and bring her back here in the early hours of the morning after she has been working as a prostitute.'

The conversation was obviously not heading in the direction which Alfredo had intended; it was becoming clear that the friendship which had been extended to Mahon was not being reciprocated, and it was doubtful if Mahon could be considered to be among 'men of the world', because Alfredo's next comment was, 'I would like to speak to you on your own.'

As Sergeant Foster left the room, Alfredo shut the door behind him and said, 'Now we are on our own, I can talk. I have got a lot of money and can help you. Will you take £200 to square up this matter?'

'What do you mean?' asked Mahon, to which Alfredo replied, 'I will go and get the money' and left the room.

He returned a minute later, shut the door behind him and produced two bundles of notes, one from his trouser pocket, the other from inside his jacket, saying, 'There you are, Mr Mahon. There is £200 for you to square up the matter and do nothing more against me.'

Taking the money, Mahon opened the door and said to Foster, who was still there in the hallway, 'He has just given me this money and requested me to take no further action against him.'

'I did not give it to him', expostulated Alfredo. 'He must have found them somewhere in this room.'

In fact, it was later established that the two rolls of notes and the notes later found in the safe were tied with exactly the same type of string.

Mahon then arrested Alfredo for living on the immoral earnings of a prostitute and told him he would be reported – since there was no power of arrest – for attempted bribery. He also established from Hindin that she was a prostitute with many convictions, and then Foster suggested going into the kitchen – the room that Alfredo had entered after he had momentarily left Mahon before reappearing with the money. In there were two items of interest. The first was a 15 cwt. safe concealed by a curtain. Opening it with a key which Alfredo had in his possession, Foster found Alfredo's and Hindin's passports and some jewellery, plus £222 in £1 and ten shilling notes; Alfredo declined to say where the money had come from.

The second item of interest was a freshly cooked turkey on the oven; in the nearby dining room lunch had been set for four people, just as had been promised.

Taken to Wembley police station, Alfredo was charged with living on immoral earnings and, a fortnight later, with attempting to bribe a police officer. To both charges, he replied, 'I will answer before the magistrates.'

So that was that; and remember, £200 was a hefty sum in 1951 – the equivalent of about three months' wages for Mahon. An appointment had been made for Alfredo and his solicitor to be present when the safety deposit boxes at Selfridges were opened in the presence of the police on 22 March – but Sergeant Foster went to Selfridges on the day prior to the formal inspection, to make enquiries regarding the boxes. He was in the company of Arthur Sydney Little, who was in charge of the safe deposits, when suddenly both men saw Alfredo appear; seeing Foster, he turned and ran. Why had he come – to abstract the £1,350 contained in those boxes? Difficult to say, since when questioned about the incident he denied ever being there.

CHAPTER 10

Alfredo's Trial

After Mr Ian Smith outlined the case for the prosecution at Wealdstone Magistrates' Court, Alfredo was committed in custody to stand his trial at the Old Bailey. However, he was soon free on bail with sureties totalling £1,200, and the trial (case No. 30 in the calendar) commenced on 3 May 1951 before Mr Justice Cassels, then aged seventy-four, a decorated veteran of the First World War and said to be 'brusque'. Christmas Humphreys, surely one of the most unpleasant barristers who ever graced the stage at the Old Bailey (and later, one of the most despised judges) appeared for the prosecution, with Mervyn Griffiths-Jones as his junior, and the defence was represented by Mr John Scott-Henderson KC, supported by Raymond Stock. To the two charges Alfredo pleaded not guilty.

On the face of it, the charges were strong ones, supported with a great deal of compelling evidence.

There was the preliminary questioning of Alfredo by Mahon regarding his association with a known prostitute in which deeply incriminating remarks were made, plus the attempt at bribery. Convincing though that evidence was, the detectives' testimony would be robustly challenged.

However, what would not be challenged was that Hermione Hindin, who possessed 106 convictions, was a common prostitute, nor would it be disputed that she lived with Alfredo.

Neither would it be disputed that Alfredo's wife was also a common prostitute with 122 convictions who lived with Alfredo's father; it would be proved beyond doubt that during the time that Alfredo and Hindin had lived together, large sums had been paid into his bank accounts, he had impressive amounts of cash in three safe deposits and, since 1939, he had had no known legitimate income in England.

But impressive though that evidence was, experienced detectives, wise in the ways of the Old Bailey, know that nothing is done and dusted until that jury foreman says the magic word, 'Guilty' – and on that note, the trial got underway.

The first witness was Police Constable 602 'C' Leonard Teale, who told the jury that he had known Hermione Hindin to be a prostitute for thirteen years, had personally arrested her on five occasions for soliciting prostitution (the last occasion being three months previously, when she was fined thirty shillings) and had been present at Bow Street and Marlborough Street Courts 'on numerous occasions' when she had been convicted. He had arrested her in Maddox Street and, in answer to a question put by the judge, said he had seen her take men into No. 3 Pollen Street. None of this was disputed by the defence.

Police Constable 460 'C' Bernard Raby had known Hindin for ten years and had arrested her twice, once in Maddox Street, and furthermore had seen her in the company of Alfredo on three occasions, in the area of Pollen Street – but not since the middle of March – and that was not disputed, either.

However, there was sloppiness on the part of the prosecution; for PC Teale to say that she had appeared at court on 'numerous occasions' was not good enough. It was pointed out by the defence that these convictions should be proved; the judge agreed, and they were later produced to the court. Similarly, PC Raby was unable to provide the dates when he had arrested Hindin. These were perhaps minor points, but given that they were vital pieces of evidence they should have been rock solid. In fact, they were the subject of criticism by the judge during his summing-up. In addition, a map of the area surrounding Maddox Street, showing the proximity of other Messina-related addresses to it, would have been helpful. It was not until the last day of the prosecution's case that one – hand-drawn by a detective and prepared that very morning at the judge's request – was produced.

John Stuart Buston, who had been the licensee since October 1950 of The Running Horse public house, situated at 50 Davis Street, approximately one-quarter of a mile from Maddox Street, told the court that he had seen Alfredo and Hindin together in his premises on at least half a dozen occasions, always in the evenings. He was the third witness whose evidence was not challenged.

But what was strongly disputed was Mahon's version of events in the house. Scott-Henderson led up to his disagreement with the facts in a very shrewd way. When Mahon was doing his best to win the confidence of Alfredo and Hindin by discussing things not associated with the case, he mentioned personal matters to them; if he had been as astute a crime-buster as his rank suggested he would never have done so. You see, this type of thing is ammunition to wily criminals; they file it away for use later on. Mahon had mentioned the Haigh murder case and said that he had been the officer in charge – as he was. When Mahon learnt that Alfredo was a diabetic, he told him that he, too, was diabetic and had been for twelve years – and that was correct, too. When Scott-Henderson asked if Mahon had said, 'I am only six months younger than you are', Mahon denied using those exact words; but the fact was that Mahon was born on 8 October 1901 and Alfredo on 6 February 1901.

It was by putting these – and many similar – questions to Mahon, knowing that he would have to agree with them, that when Scott-Henderson alleged that Mahon was present when Alfredo opened the safe and it was he – Mahon – who took out the money, which was strongly denied, that denial did not sound particularly convincing. It was also suggested that at that time Sergeant Foster was upstairs – that too was disputed – and when it was put to Mahon that he called out, 'Bert! Come down, I want you!' although he denied saying that, since Foster had not gone upstairs, it did sound exactly like the kind of words that a senior officer might have used to a subordinate.

Mahon denied that Alfredo had said, 'It is 2 o'clock, Superintendent Mahon, my lunch is ready. Will you join us?' and similarly denied replying, 'Really? It is 2 o'clock and I am hungry.'

Mahon agreed that he was not in possession of a warrant for Alfredo's arrest; and much was made of this by the defence, although it was not an illegal arrest – a power of arrest existed without a warrant. He also agreed that he was not in possession of a search warrant but had asked Alfredo if there were any firearms in the house.

Scott-Henderson asked, 'And you told him you were going to search him and search the house?'

'He had told me previously that I could search the house', replied Mahon. 'I told him I was going to take advantage of his invitation to search the house.'

'It is very convenient for a police officer who has not got a warrant to search to turn round and say, "This man told me to search the house", is it not?' sarcastically enquired Scott-Henderson, to which Mahon gave the only possible answer when he replied, 'Yes'.

The officers had drunk whisky with Alfredo prior to his arrest, although the police and the defence claimed very different amounts had been consumed. Scott-Henderson suggested that three quarters of a freshly opened bottle had been drunk; Mahon stated that he and Foster had 'Two small whiskies, about two tablespoons each, and each of us had it reluctantly.'

'If you were reluctant to have a drink, why have a drink?' asked Scott-Henderson, which just goes to show you shouldn't pose a question in court if you don't know the answer.

'Because I wanted to keep on good terms with him', replied Mahon, 'because the object of my visit was to find out something from him about the leakage which has been mentioned. I had been sent there by senior officers.'

'I am not asking about that', said Scott-Henderson rather hastily, because the answer suggested that Alfredo was in cahoots with one or more crooked police officers, but Humphreys intervened, saying, 'He is entitled to answer the question.'

'It does not let in a long explanation, though', said Scott-Henderson and then, turning to Mahon, attempted to obfuscate matters by saying, 'I quite agree, you wanted to keep on good terms with him.'

Fortunately, Mahon was having none of it, because he replied, 'Only to get information from him.'

From a promising start with his cross-examination, Scott-Henderson was not having matters all his own way. Another setback came when he suggested that during the search of Alfredo Mahon had pushed him around, which Mahon denied.

'Did he say, "I am not very strong. You will push me on the floor"?' asked Scott-Henderson.

'No, sir', replied Mahon.

'And having done that, did you then call in another police officer from outside?'

This was a common defence barrister's trick: to smoothly gloss over a witness's denial, turning the answer completely around, and then in the same sentence proceed with a further question. However, it was not a ploy which worked on this occasion, because Mr Justice Cassels intervened.

'It is not quite right to say, "Having done that",' he said, 'because he said he did not do it.'

'My Lord, I am sorry', replied Scott-Henderson but then, with bare-faced effrontery, he said to Mahon, 'I thought you told me you did.'

'I did not say I pushed him around', replied Mahon, but the matter did not end there, because the judge had now got the bit between his teeth.

'He says he did not make any remark about pushing him around and he did not say, "I am not very strong. You will push me on the floor",' said the judge. 'And then you start your remark by saying, "Having done that . . . "'

By this time Scott-Henderson was floundering badly and quickly interjected, 'My Lord, I was going back to the searching . . . '

Mr Scott-Henderson KC was learning the hard way not to trifle with the judge, who had been described (much to his own amusement) as 'the second rudest man at the bar'.

It happened again after Scott-Henderson had questioned Mahon about what he had found in Alfredo's safe deposit boxes at Selfridges. But when Humphreys re-examined Mahon to describe the conversation he had had with Alfredo regarding the boxes, this was something which Scott-Henderson did not want the jury to hear, telling the judge that the matter had arisen out of cross-examination and that it was not material.

'Oh, but if you ask about this witness going to the safe deposit, the defendant's safe deposit at Selfridges', said the Judge, 'surely questions in re-examination will arise out of that cross-examination as to what was discovered?'

'I asked about that because I know my friend is going to give evidence about bank accounts and that was in the nature of a banking account', replied Scott-Henderson, adding, 'I have not asked about any conversation about safe deposits.'

'No, but surely that is not against you,' said the Judge. 'The information about the existence of a safe deposit at Selfridges has come from the defendant. That is not against you, surely?'

Scott-Henderson was now floundering badly, and he knew it. 'I don't know whether it is, my Lord' he replied, rather helplessly. 'He told me he got a search warrant to go to Selfridges.'

'Well, that may be', replied the judge, who by now appeared to be getting rather fed up with this pointless argument. 'It is no good going into Selfridges and looking at every deposit. You want to know what is inside.'

'You have got to get the key', said Scott-Henderson, but again Mr Justice Cassels was against him, saying, 'Well, the search warrant might assist to open it. I cannot stop this re-examination. It seems to me to arise out of cross-examination and that is the rule with regard to re-examination.'

'What did he say, or what did you say to him and what did he say to you about the safe deposit?' Humphreys asked Mahon.

'I said to him, "Have you a safe deposit anywhere?"' replied Mahon. 'And he replied, "No, I have not got one",' – and with that, the cat was well and truly out of the bag.

Detective Sergeant Bert Foster was next; it was suggested to him (as it had been to Mahon) that on the first occasion that they went to the house and Hindin had told them Alfredo was not at home, Mahon had said to her, 'You're a liar – I know he's in the house!' and this was denied.

However, Foster was able to give crucial evidence on another matter; when, at Mahon's request, he had been waiting in the hallway, he saw Alfredo emerge from the room where he and Mahon had been talking and go into the kitchen, where Hindin was and where, as he told the court, 'I heard the rattle of keys. I heard a key in a lock, followed immediately by a noise which appeared to be a safe door opening, slammed and locked. The defendant appeared in the doorway of the kitchen and I noticed him put a bundle of £1 notes in his left-hand trouser pocket. He crossed the hallway and entered the room where Mr Mahon was and closed the door.'

There was a brisk exchange regarding the opening of the safe following Alfredo's arrest. Alfredo had been told to turn out his pockets, and when he had done so, the officers personally searched him. Among the contents of his pockets were two sets of keys, but when Foster went to the safe in the kitchen, none of those keys fitted the lock. Mahon had told the court that Alfredo produced the safe key.

'Where from?' asked Scott-Henderson.

'That I do not know', replied Mahon. 'It may have been hanging behind the door.'

'He was not a conjuror!' sneered Scott-Henderson, to which Mahon replied, 'It may have been hanging on a peg, or hook, or somewhere in the kitchen, but he produced the key and handed it to Sergeant Foster, who then unlocked the door of the safe.'

'When he was asked if he had the key, did he not say, "You have it"?' asked Scott-Henderson.

Mahon replied, 'He did not, sir.'

'You ought to have had it if you had conducted your search properly', commented Scott-Henderson, to which Mahon smartly replied, 'Not if the key was not on him.'

Matters were finally brought to a close when Foster (referring to Alfredo) emphatically told the court, 'The key was in his hand, sir.'

The next witness was a retired police officer, Charles Samuel Roper, who had given the Yard serious concern, since it was thought that he was the conduit feeding information, gleaned from a serving, crooked police officer, to Alfredo. He was not the most impressive or the most believable witness. Telling the court that he had carried out 'odd jobs' for Alfredo, he mentioned that he had been a police officer from 1920 to 1946 and that he had known the defendant for eight years. He added that he had 'a good opinion of him', that he regarded him as 'respectable' and that he had never seen anything to indicate the contrary.

That being the case, even though they were undermanned at the time, the Metropolitan Police must be congratulated for their tolerance and diversity in hiring an officer who was both deaf and blind.

CHAPTER 11

Lies and Arrogance

Alfredo now took the stand. He was described (quite accurately) by an onlooker as follows: 'On the short side, bald and rather stout, he dresses in a semi-flashy style and oozes a lubricious self-satisfaction.' He stated that his wealth came from his diamond business, as a result of which he had brought £30,000 in cash to England from Belgium in 1939. He stated he was allowed to bring any amount of cash into the country – 'even a million'. Asked why the money was not converted into a banker's draft to guard against the possibility of being robbed of such a large amount of cash, he replied that 'you cannot have £1,000 and bring it into the country'. It was the first of a number of contradictory, barely coherent statements which he would make during his testimony.

He stated he had difficulty in writing cheques and did not pay income tax. Asked repeatedly why he had so many bank accounts, his response was, 'Because I like to.' This was an answer he often repeated, as were the very arrogant, 'Exactly!' and 'It is in order.'

However, it was established that although he had never invested his alleged £30,000 into safe, gilt-edged securities, which during the war would have paid him £900 per annum in interest, he had nevertheless paid more money in cash into his accounts than he had ever drawn out. In addition, it was not satisfactorily explained why he had to make a 22-mile round trip from Wembley to frequently pay cash into any of those banks. It was almost as though – like his brothers' property dealings – he was trying to distance himself from them, especially since he stated that his address was 3 Lancaster Lodge.

Dealing with Mahon's visit, he stated that when he had pulled a carton of cigarettes from his pocket out popped a key, and he had remarked, 'That is my safe key.' Taking Mahon into the kitchen he said, 'I show it to you', and opened the safe whereupon, laughing, Mahon took the two rolls of notes. Alfredo then said that he told Mahon, 'Don't be silly – put that back', but that Mahon called out to Foster and he was arrested.

The allegation that he had come in for some rough treatment from the police was too good to miss. It had already been put to

Mahon; now, it came out in detail: 'Then he grabbed me like this from the jacket, he put himself, his back against my piano . . . then he say to me, "Have you got a firearm?" . . . with that, he pulled me again by my shoulder. I say to him, "Please don't pull me because I am not very strong. You will drag me to the floor" . . . When he say, "I go to charge you with bribery", I say "Put it back" and then I say to Mrs Hindin, "Phone to Mr Watson, the solicitor and tell him to come quickly here".'

Finally, when Watson did arrive, Alfredo stated that Mahon refused to let them speak to each other; nor did Mahon tell him why he was being arrested.

In cross-examination he fared quite badly. It transpired that on 7 June 1950 he had obtained an identity card, No. PC 1854, in the name of Alfred Martin and gave his address as 3 Lancaster Lodge. This was three months prior to Duncan Webb's exposé in the *People*, but by then the brothers were well aware that Webb was making enquiries about them. However, Alfredo said that he had done so because 'people kept looking at him' due to a 1947 newspaper article which referred to his brother Eugenio's arrest, although he was hard pressed to explain why it had taken him three years to change his name. The truth of that matter may have been a little different. The day before he obtained his identity card – 6 June 1950 – was when Duncan Webb started making his enquiries with seven prostitutes, and it is highly likely that it was this information that was passed on to Alfredo and precipitated his actions.

It was suggested that the address, 3 Lancaster Lodge, was owned by brother Carmelo; Alfredo denied this and said it was occupied by Eugenio. But it was also given by Alfredo as his own address when he had to pay Schedule 'A' Tax on Harrowdene Road, and when he changed the registration of his car on 1 January 1951 he also changed his name to Alfred Martin and maintained he was living at Lancaster Lodge. When he applied for a passport on 21 March 1948 – this was to replace the one issued on 16 April 1939 in the name of Alfredo Messina – he gave his address as 'at present residing at 3 Lancaster Lodge, W11'. To questions on all these matters Alfredo's sullen reply was, 'It is in order.'

But there was another resident at the Lancaster Lodge address. Alfredo claimed that he had never heard of Cissy Cohen, or by her alias of Vera Johnson, or even as Vivienne. However, an observation had been carried out on 2 February 1951 at 7.15 pm outside 13 Sackville Street when Miss Cohen was seen to pass a bulky envelope to Alfredo, who was sitting alone in his car; and that, Alfredo *definitely* denied.

Did that envelope contain the proceeds of prostitution? Almost certainly. If so, what happened to it? It might have been some (or all) of the £1,000 which Alfredo paid into his account at Barclays Bank on 1 March that was made of £1 and £5 notes, or it might have been part of the £422 which was in his safe when he was arrested.

When Mahon was giving evidence, an attempt was made to introduce the fact that a prostitute named Georgette Borg also lived with Alfredo, and Mahon could certainly give evidence of Borg's domicile at Harrowdene Road. But when he was asked, 'Did you then ask him [Alfredo] about another prostitute [meaning Borg]?' Scott-Henderson smartly interrupted, 'I object'.

Mahon, in fairness, did his best, saying, 'Yes, sir, I spoke to him about . . . ' before Scott-Henderson, knowing precisely what was coming, interrupted once more: 'My Lord, this must be irrelevant. Apparently this is a conversation with many irrelevancies in it so far as this charge is concerned, and this is one of them, in my submission.'

'What do you say about it, Mr Humphreys?' asked the judge.

'My Lord, I say it is admissible because the whole relationship of the accused with women of a certain type is in issue', replied Humphreys. 'The officer has told you about what he was enquiring about and this is part of his enquiries and these are the answers. Surely the answer is relevant and therefore, presumably, the question.'

However, the question was not pressed, which was a pity; but little was lost because it was resurrected in cross-examination. The answers to questions which Scott-Henderson had wanted never to be asked and which could have been given by Mahon were certainly not corroborated by those given by Alfredo.

He was obliged to accept that he knew a prostitute named Georgette Borg. 'You knew her well enough to have several of her photographs taken with you, in your safe?' asked Humphreys, which elicited the startled reply, 'I beg your pardon?'

'Are these three photographs of Georgette Borg and yourself on one of them?' asked Humphreys, and it was time for another interruption from Scott-Henderson: 'My Lord, I do not want to take unnecessary objection, but my submission is that this cross-examination is quite irrelevant in this case. It goes to no issue. It does not even go to credit.'

'I am now upon the issue of this man's association with a prostitute', riposted Humphreys, to which Scott-Henderson replied, 'That is not an issue in this case.'

'One of the issues in this case is that the defence have to prove to the satisfaction of the jury where this money came from', replied Humphreys. 'That is what it amounts to. I am now going to ask this witness questions about association with prostitutes.'

'They have not got to prove where the money comes from', replied Scott-Henderson. 'They have got to prove that it did not come from Mrs Hindin.'

But once again, Mr Justice Cassels was against him: 'The question seems to me to be a proper question – association with prostitution.'

Alfredo admitted that the photographs of the two of them together had been taken in Belgium some seventeen years previously and that she had borrowed money from him – on one occasion, £550 – but he stated that he was unaware of where she lived.

This was seriously untrue. Until very recently, Borg (who possessed 104 convictions for soliciting) had not only been domiciled at 45 Harrowdene Road with Alfredo and Hindin; she also paid the rates and was the only person registered as being able to vote at that premises. Alfredo took both of them to work their beats in Mayfair and brought them home again in the morning. Because Mahon had given Alfredo and Hindin several days notice of his intended visit, this had given Borg the opportunity to clear out her possessions and vanish.

Now – time to pause. The envelope-passing transaction between Cissy Cohen and Alfredo had been witnessed not by the police but by Duncan Webb, as had Alfredo's taking Hindin and Borg to their Mayfair beats. However, for reasons which will shortly become clear, it was deemed inadvisable to call Webb as a witness.

When Alfredo's cleaner, Mrs Olive Garrish, gave evidence, Mr Mervyn Griffiths-Jones, the junior prosecuting counsel, should have been aware of these foregoing matters; and if he had, he could have asked about the possibility of there being a third party in the house. Since for the previous five years Mrs Garrish had arrived at the house at about 9.30 am and left at midday, she would have been aware of the presence of Georgette Borg. But for whatever reason, she was not asked those very pertinent questions; certainly, Mr Scott-Henderson failed to raise them in cross-examination, since it would have been ruinous to the defence if he had.

Alfredo stated that he certainly did not know that Borg lived at 7 Kingly Street; he had never visited that address and was unaware of who did live there. He expressed astonishment when he was told it was his brother Attilio's address and was flabbergasted to discover that when Hermione Hindin was convicted on a dozen occasions in 1948 for soliciting prostitution, that was the address that she gave to the authorities.

Although he now accepted that Hindin had been a prostitute, Alfredo stressed that he had been quite unaware of it at the time. It was rather strange then, that when on 24 July 1948 she met a man in Brewer Street and took him back to 7 Kingly Street, as she started to undress he grabbed her by the throat, produced a knife and shouted, 'I have no time for you bloody people, I'm going to do all prostitutes in!', she didn't inform Alfredo of this occurrence. After screaming the place down, causing the man to run off, she certainly did inform the police. She certainly didn't appear to have informed Alfredo's defence barrister, because this incident was not mentioned during his trial.

Since at one stage Hindin and Alfredo's wife 'Marcelle' had lived next door to each other in Pollen Street, Alfredo was asked if she and Hindin were close friends.

'She is a close friend of Mr Mahon and Mr Foster', he sneered, and although Alfredo's wife was never called to give evidence for the prosecution since in law she was neither competent nor compellable, it is conceivable that she had furnished information regarding her husband's activities; and that Alfredo, as his remarks suggest, had heard of it. Certainly, she was not called by the defence.

When an accused person makes allegations of impropriety or untruthfulness against a prosecution witness in court, the prosecution – subject to a ruling from the trial judge – can adduce evidence of the accused's bad character. Now, Alfredo had certainly impugned Mahon's and Foster's characters. Asked if he thought the officers would invent 'this very wicked charge against you without any evidence whatsoever . . . and support it here upon oath?' his reply was, 'They are used to that. If they lie – I saw them yesterday – I say they are used to witness on oath even if it is not true, because what they say before yesterday was all lies.'

Even allowing for his jumbled English, it was certainly a matter of calling into question the truthfulness of the two detectives' evidence.

However, as has already been said, Alfredo had no previous convictions; nevertheless, what could be proved was that he was an out-and-out liar. So when Humphreys questioned him about his giving of a false address, Scott-Henderson jumped into the breach. 'I object to this', he said. 'My friend is putting something that is quite immaterial to this charge. He is suggesting that he filled in a false address on an application for a passport. In my submission, he is not entitled to do that.'

'In the course of cross-examination (which will not be shortened by my friend's interruption), I propose to put a great many questions to this witness as to his credit', replied Humphreys. 'He has said virtually that the two police officers are telling lies in almost the whole of their evidence on 19 March. I now propose to put questions to this witness tending to show that he is a liar.'

'I'm not a liar!' bellowed Alfredo, but Humphreys continued, saying, 'His character is in issue. That question was asked in terms of the police officer.'

'I submit that my friend is not entitled to do this', Scott-Henderson told the judge and although he valiantly cited the 1944 appeal case of *Stirland v. The Director of Public Prosecutions*, Mr Justice Cassels wiped the floor with him, quoting instead the more persuasive case of *Rex v. Turner*; and although Alfredo had made a poor showing thus far, he now made a cracking fool of himself.

Just prior to the legal submissions being made, Alfredo had told the jury that he had not lived at Lancaster Lodge since 1946; now he said he had and endeavoured to validate this by saying, 'The law is, when you have got even fifty houses, that you can give any address you want; as far as you have the correspondence in your own house, you are in there. That is what they told me when I got this identity card – that this is in order.'

In his application for a passport on 21 March 1948, Alfredo put 'Belgium' in the section for 'Usual place of residence' – even though he had lived in Wembley since 1942. It brought the following exchange between Humphreys and Alfredo:

'Have you been in Belgium in 1948?'

'No'.

'Since 1939?'

'No'.

'And yet in 1948 you are saying "Usual place of residence – Belgium"?'

'Exactly. My usual residence in Belgium, yes'.

Duncan Webb, observing proceedings from the press box, was drawn into the matter in response to a question from Humphreys. Alfredo had been making some damaging remarks regarding Mahon at the time of his arrest when, out of the blue, Humphreys asked him, 'Did you discuss this with Mr Duncan Webb on 4 April, this year?'

Scott-Henderson shot to his feet. 'I object to that question', he snapped. 'It is hearsay even in cross-examination. What this witness discussed with somebody else is not a matter that should be put to him.'

'I was going to make a suggestion to him as to the explanation he made to Mr Webb', commented Humphreys mildly.

'Mr Henderson, I do not follow about it being hearsay evidence', said the Judge. 'The witness is making one statement. Any witness can be challenged in cross-examination that he has made a different statement to somebody else – in cross-examination. All that it means is that somebody else cannot be called unless certain steps are taken.'

'My submission is that in cross-examination he should not be asked about things he is alleged to have said other than to witnesses for the prosecution', protested Scott-Henderson and, wasting no further time on the matter, Mr Justice Cassels told him, 'I rule against you on that.'

The case proceeded, with Alfredo mentioning that a week before his committal, Webb had come to Alfredo's house. He said, 'We had a drink together – gin and vermouth. Then he said, "Look here, your case is in my hands". He said, "I have got the key to your case".' What Alfredo deduced from that remark was that 'it is up to him to let me go to prison or let me out'. He added that Webb had a criminal record, that he was very friendly with Mahon and that 'He can write in my favour or write against me.'

Alfredo then went on to say, 'He say, "Leave it to me. Tomorrow, I go with another man and we talk to Mrs Hindin and make a statement and everything will be all right." The next day I wait for him. He never came. I believe he must talk with Mr Mahon who told him not to come any more because I was under proceeding.'

By introducing Duncan Webb into the proceedings at all, Christmas Humphreys was playing a very dodgy hand indeed. There was, of course, a great deal of pertinent information Webb could give, but if he had been introduced into the witness box his own shady character would have been called into question; not only that, but the way – often doubtful – in which his information had been obtained would be revealed. Webb had two criminal convictions; Alfredo had none. Therefore with some very skilful cross-examination the whole validity of the prosecution case could be called into question and wrecked in very short order.

Of course, this would not have stopped the defence calling Webb, but that they certainly would not do. There was not only the evidence of the sightings of Alfredo, Hindin, Cohen and Borg that he could provide (and that would have been bad enough for the defence), but also the fact that when Webb visited Alfredo and Hindin at their Wembley address for a further, sensational story for the *People*, Alfredo had offered him a substantial amount of money if he would publish a piece stating that he was not a ponce;

moreover, Hindin asked him to name his price for helping Alfredo. All of this would have scuppered the defence case. Whichever way one looked at it, both sides were between a rock and a hard place. The solution? It was for both prosecution and defence to keep Webb out of it altogether.

Alfredo had not cut an impressive figure in the witness box; in turn, he was rude, contemptuous and arrogant. Asked why he needed to have three bank accounts in London, his reply was, 'Because I like to have three banking accounts in London . . . there is not a crime . . . what is wrong in that? . . . I can do what I like with my money . . . Why have to explain my money from where I bring it? What for? It is my money. I have not got to explain it to anybody, only to the judge.'

But now he had given an explanation to a judge – and had given the impression of being outrageously untruthful.

CHAPTER 12

Hindin's Account

D ark-haired Hermione Hindin also gave evidence, wearing a green dress, a gold bangle and gold earrings (which an onlooker described as 'penny-sized'). She vehemently denied that Alfredo knew she worked as a prostitute; he had never driven her to the West End for the purposes of prostitution; and she had never given him money. The words persistently and stridently used during her denials were 'Definitely!' and 'Never!' Indeed, she said, it was Alfredo who had given her money and presents as well, including a mink coat for which he paid £987 10s 0d to the National Fur Company in 1948.

She, too, had a safe deposit box at Selfridges which she had rented on 5 July 1947; when it was opened following Alfredo's arrest it was found to contain just five £1 notes. Like Alfredo, she had a bank account at the Crédit Lyonnais and between 1947 and 1951 she had paid in a total of £1,390; money which, she said, had been given to her by Alfredo.

In order to explain her absences from the Wembley home, she told the court: 'When I went to the West End, which was sometimes once, sometimes twice a week, I used to tell Mr Messina that I was going to see my mother or I was going to the pictures and he used to take me to my mother or to the pictures.'

Asked if he sometimes brought her home at night, the answer was a resounding, 'Never!'

She was obliged to admit that she had given 30 Maddox Street, 7 Kingly Street and 21 Frith Street – all Messina hideaways – as her address to the authorities but denied ever earning £200 per week as a prostitute, saying the most she ever earned was £15 per week.

With that money, she said, she supported her mother, her young son and 'her ailing brother'.

If that was to be believed, it meant that she was only earning two shillings for every conviction she acquired, and with the fines ranging from 30 to 40 shillings a time, and with rent at £18 per week (she stated it was, in fact, three guineas), she was definitely operating at a loss. And if that was the case, bearing in mind the beneficence that Alfredo was showering upon her, the money, the fur coat, the rings, the diamond and jade earrings (she produced the last two items from her crocodile-skin handbag), the jury may have come to the conclusion that to continue working the war-torn and often soaking wet London streets at night, running the risk of getting a dose of the clap, being bombed, throttled and stabbed by a lunatic, plus getting arrested and convicted on 106 occasions, she must have been simple-minded.

She was treading on very thin ice indeed when she answered questions regarding Georgette Borg. Humphreys asked her, 'Have you never seen Georgette Borg at 7 Kingly Street?'

'Never!' came the reply.

The questioning then continued:

'But she used to stay almost every weekend up in Wembley until about May 1950; is that right?'

'No'.

'No?'

'No.'

'How often did she stay there?'

'Never.'

'What?'

'Not whilst I was there.'

'You entirely disagree with Mr Messina?'

'She did not stay.'

'You say she has never stayed there any time while you have been there?'

'She has never slept there.'

All it required was for Duncan Webb or any of his team to come forward and disclose what they had seen during their observations to make matters very sticky for this witness, but fortunately for Hindin – as we know – none of them were called, by the prosecution or the defence.

She told the jury that when she had had a conversation with Mahon and he remarked that he could not always get cigarettes, she went upstairs, brought down a box of 50 Players and gave them to him, whereupon he remarked, 'You're a pal' – thereby giving the court the impression that Mahon was amenable to accepting free gifts; in fact, Mahon stated it was a box of 12 Players, of which he had smoked one and replaced it; he produced the box in court.

She strongly denied saying to Mahon, in a reference to Alfredo, 'You and he can get on all right together; he is very generous. He'll see you all right. Mr Messina is very wealthy and wants to be friendly with you.'

In fact, she backed up all of Alfredo's denials with regard to his interaction with the police and added a veiled assertion that Mahon had come to the house seeking a bribe and saying to her, 'I believe Mr Messina is a very wealthy man', to which she replied, 'I think he is' – and that was all.

Hindin had been asked by Mahon to produce her identity card. She went to get it but then suddenly realized that this card, which was issued on 24 April 1950, showed the address of 3 Pollen Street, and because she said that Alfredo had never seen it she pretended she had lost it.

Dr Edward Charles Sugden of 4 Half Moon Street, W1 was perhaps unwisely called by the defence to state that Alfredo had been diagnosed as being diabetic in 1949 – it rather negated his assertion that he had been an invalid since 1939 and therefore incapable of working. Dr Sugden was a noted psychiatrist and although he was also a Bachelor of Medicine, the actual diagnosis of Alfredo's diabetes was carried out by Dr Hancock of 73 Harley Street. In their examination in chief the defence did not ask Dr Sugden the circumstances of how he came to be a signatory to Alfredo's passport application in 1948 – the matter of Alfredo's address on the form could have been enlightening – nor was this picked up by the prosecution in cross-examination. Perhaps Humphreys thought he had done enough to secure a conviction; maybe it was a matter that was overlooked. Or perhaps Humphreys thought that 'it was not the done thing' to suggest that a respected member of the medical profession was just another pawn in a seedy little crook's pocket, thereby unnecessarily antagonizing the jury. It's possible that he thought by saying in cross-examination, 'What do you mean by "he should lessen his work?" He has told us he has never done any', he had scored sufficient points. But whatever the reasoning, that witness's testimony closed the case for the defence.

During his closing speech for the defence, Mr Scott-Henderson, referring perhaps unkindly to 42-year-old Hermione Hindin, said, 'It is a remarkable fact that a woman who has a son of twenty-one should (as the prosecution alleged) be able to earn £200 a week in the West End.'

Christmas Humphreys mentioned the attempt to bribe Mahon in his closing speech, saying, 'If the jury believes Messina, he gets off. What happens to the two police officers if they are found to be lying?'

Mahon and Foster were present in court, and as Humphreys made that remark, there was a power cut and the courtroom lights dimmed. Many a detective thus accused might have thought this was a warning from on high and swallowed noisily, but instead of celestial punishment the emergency lighting was switched on, and Humphreys continued, 'They go forthwith, with ignominy, their reputations and pensions lost. And be prosecuted for perjury.'

With some justification, Scott-Henderson muttered, 'Isn't that putting it a bit too high?'

CHAPTER 13

The Summing-up

Having heard the closing speeches to the jury by both prosecution and defence, Mr Justice Cassels started his summing-up. In part, he said this:

The defendant was cross-examined. After all, all those witnesses who go into the witness box have to have their evidence tested by what we call cross-examination, and there is no doubt that his case with regard to what happened on March 19th is a complete denial of the detective officers' account. Neither is there any doubt that his case is that the detective superintendent took these bundles of notes out of the safe and then trumped up this charge of bribery against the defendant. Neither is there any doubt that he is saying that he did not give these notes to the officer or attempt to bribe him. He calls it 'a dirty trick'. He says that the officers are telling lies.

One or two little things did emerge in the course of his cross-examination: That he has an address at 3 Lancaster Lodge, that he had not resided there since 1946. He gave that address when he applied for his passport in 1948 and you will remember what was said about that. He said if a man has got fifty houses he can give every one of them as an address. 'No law against it', he says, 'nothing at all', and he agrees that the tenant of 3 Lancaster Lodge is his brother, Eugene. The initials he has got upon his identity card are P.C. and the number is 1854, the surname is Martin (and the Christian name is Alfred) and the address, that false postal address, Lancaster Lodge, Lancaster Road, W11; holder's signature: A. Martin.

Well, that is how that emerged in the course of cross-examination. He also said in cross-examination that he did not know that Hermione Hindin was a prostitute, and that she had many convictions, until he heard it in this case, and it came as a great shock. Well, that is, of course, diametrically opposed to the evidence given by the police officers, who said that in the presence of both of them they

asked Mrs Hindin certain questions as to whether she was
a prostitute with many convictions and she said, 'Yes', so
if shock it was to the defendant, you may think that he
had an earlier shock than the one he speaks about now if
it was that he was hearing then for the first time that Mrs
Hindin, his housekeeper and mistress, was a prostitute.
He said that in the evening this woman either stayed at
home or went to the cinema or went to see her mother.
There she was, leading a model life, one might almost say,
in the evening, if they had a fire, sitting at the side of the
fire, perhaps she sitting on one side of the fire with the
defendant sitting on his side; and if that did not happen,
why, had she gone to such pictures as are available in the
neighbourhood or to see her mother! . . .

Mrs Hindin gave evidence, and you remember she spoke
of the telephone message she had received from the police
officer on March 15th when she said, upon being asked
whether Mr Martin was there, that Mr Martin was not in,
neither was Mr Messina in. Of course, we know that that
was the same person. And the police officer at the other end
called her a liar, and they came along and had whisky. Well,
she also spoke of the visit on March 16th when considerable
whisky was consumed and she agreed, you will remember,
that they talked about the Haigh case and she made
scrambled eggs for them. She gave them cigarettes, some
of which Mr Mahon took away. We had a discussion as
to whether there was a box of one hundred or a packet of
twelve and we even got as far as Mr Mahon in the witness
box saying that he had actually got the packet of twelve
still there, the one that he had smoked he had replaced.
Members of the jury, we do get into some funny places
when we come to have to discuss a person's case. This
case is not going to turn upon one of twelve cigarettes, you
know; this case has got to be considered upon the evidence
of much more important matters, you may think, than that.

When she came to deal with 19th March, which is the
important day, she said that she was preparing lunch for
herself and Messina when Messina and Mahon came into
the kitchen. I mentioned about the lunch being prepared
for two of them only because the suggestion was made by
the prosecution that this was almost a pre-arranged thing,
lunch for four being got ready. Turkey in March. For two,
you would scarcely think of it, but you might think of it for
four. And lunch set for four.

She has said she was preparing the lunch for herself and Messina. Now let me remind you of her own evidence that she gave in regard to this very important time.

She said with regard to the 19th March it was about 12.20 when they arrived. She showed them into Mr Messina and left them together.

'I took in a bottle of whisky – Black-and-White. I took it in as a new bottle which had not been opened before. I took in a siphon, three glasses and some ice.'

After the party on that day she said about *that* much was left. It had very nearly all gone. She said: 'I was cooking the lunch but I was preparing it originally for Messina and myself. Eventually, I prepared for more than two. The laundry came and I went and asked Mr Messina for the money for the laundry and he said they wished to have lunch and that I was to prepare for four. That was after one o'clock. Those two officers were in the sitting room. I did not see anybody come out of the sitting room. The next thing that happened was that Messina came out of the sitting room with Mahon. I do not remember the time. It was a good time after they arrived. Messina and Mahon came in. Messina asked me if the lunch was nearly ready. Mahon was on top of him. Mahon asked if the safe was big or small. Messina said, "Quite big, 15 cwt." Mahon said, "Is there plenty of room inside?" Messina said, "I shall show you." Messina got down and opened the safe and stepped back. Mahon knelt down and took some money out of the safe and went back into the sitting room. Messina said, "Don't be silly, Mahon! Put it back!" Mahon was laughing. Messina locked his safe and went after him and said, "Put it back; don't be silly." Mahon went into the hall and said, "Bert, Bert; come down; I'm going to charge him with bribery." Foster was upstairs and came down. I had not seen him go up.' And then she tells us about having telephoned to the defendant's solicitors.

Well, that is it. She denied that she had ever given the defendant money; she denies that absolutely. 'On the contrary', she says, 'He gave me money.' And I will deal a little later on, in a few moments I hope, with the money side of this case.

Under cross-examination she agreed that she had the address of 3 Pollen Street on her identity card but had never lived there, but had been living at Harrowdene Road for the last seven years; so here you have the case of a person going about with an identity card which had upon it an address where certainly she is not living. She has had many convictions for prostitution, but here let me say at once to you: do not accept the number which is put up here, which has been placed here somewhat irregularly. It is no good flourishing a piece of paper and saying, 'A hundred convictions for prostitution'; we are rather concerned in court like this about the word 'convictions'. We look to convictions being properly proved, and if you say to a man – I say 'a man' now, but in this case we are dealing with a woman – that he has got dozens of convictions, that is not regarded by us in this court as being the proper way to say it. If you're going to say a man has got convictions, prove them properly. A certified copy may be given by the Clerk of Assize or the Clerk of Sessions and a piece of paper produced which shows, if the identification is satisfactory, to that man and those convictions are closely related. And so here it was that with regard to this woman Mrs Hindin there was an officer who came forward and produced a certificate by a Clerk of the Magistrates' Court at Marlborough Street – and perhaps you might think that one of their specialities was dealing with prostitutes – that was produced, a police officer produced it and said that that related to Mrs Hindin, and Mrs Hindin does not deny it. She was shown a great bundle of convictions and she had a good look through it, and then she did not quite agree with some of the addresses. There you are. You need to be satisfied as to the exact number of convictions that she has had. She denies being out, night after night. She says she used to tell Messina she was going to the cinema or to her mother. She denied that Messina had taken her in the car to the West End and had brought her home later. She said that she knew Mrs Messina – that is the defendant's wife – as Marcelle. She did not know that she was the defendant's wife but she knew that Marcelle was a prostitute. So we have that funny little situation which was mentioned to you by the learned counsel for the defence, that with regard to the two persons what one was the other did not know and what one knew the other did not know, and it is a fairly good mix-up. But it is not to be put, you know, against the defendant. Neither is it to be considered against the defendant that he had a wife, or still has a wife with whom he has not lived since a very little time after he married her, and that she may be a prostitute now. That is nothing to do with him and he is not to be convicted of either of these offences because his wife, with whom he does not now live, happens to be a prostitute – assuming that she is – and whether he has nothing at all to do with her, one does not know. Comment has been made by learned counsel for the prosecution that there is this curious situation: the woman with whom the defendant was living is a prostitute and he did not know it; he did not know that his wife was a prostitute but the woman with whom he is living, who is a prostitute, did know it. And so you get that funny little situation. Do not be diverted too far away from the real issue which you are trying in this case, and that is the guilt or the innocence of this man upon either or both of these charges. The issue here at this stage of the case which I have reached is: did Mahon upon that occasion take £200 out of the safe and then turn round and make this serious accusation against the accused, or is his account, and the prostitute's account, a true account, or may it be true? If it is a true one, if you accept it as being true, then there is an end of this branch of the case. If you think it may be true, if it creates a doubt in your mind, why then, the defendant is entitled to be acquitted. If, on the other hand you are satisfied that the defendant did corruptly offer that £200 to Mahon to show a favour well then you will, of course, convict.

Let us now return for a few moments to the first account, the charge of knowingly living in part or wholly on the earnings of the prostitution of Hermione Hindin.

The evidence in this case commences, you will remember, with those two police officers – rather a long time ago but I daresay you will remember them going into the witness box and going out again – one with twenty-five years experience in the Police Force and the other with fifteen years experience. The first, Police Constable Teale, said that he has known this woman soliciting for thirteen years; he has himself arrested her on five occasions; the last time was February 6th of this year. So you are not to regard Mrs Hindin as merely a woman with a past: she is a woman with a present, as well. He says he has been present on numerous occasions in Marlborough Street Magistrates' Court when she has been convicted. That officer told us that Maddox Street, Mayfair, seems to have been the place concerned

and 3 Pollen Street (the address upon her identity card)
that is the house of ill-fame where this woman took her
men. You shall have a look at a plan, Exhibit 16, which
has been put in at a later stage in this case to show the
relationship between streets which are so well known and
this particular street, Pollen Street, you will remember,
Hanover Square, Maddox Street, Regent Street, all those
places, a neighbourhood which you may know or which
you may not know. It does not matter, but the evidence
would seem to disclose that it is frightfully respectable by
day and not frightfully respectable by night . . .

Then we come to another stage in this case. Hermione
Hindin does not hesitate to walk straight into that witness
box, stand up and take the oath and then proceed to
indicate that she is going, if she can, to tell the truth, the
whole truth and nothing but the truth. Learned counsel
for the prosecution says she does not look as though she
was dressed for the part that the prosecution has suggested
she filled in this case and what her life was – not flashily
dressed, no make-up, nothing of the kind. The £900 mink
coat she has not with her when she gives evidence. And
yet she steps into that witness box and almost the first
thing she said was, 'I admit that I am a prostitute,' and no
nonsense about it, either! 'I admit that I am a prostitute'.
And she also admitted that she had been convicted of
offences of prostitution. That is a fairly good start in this
case. She does not agree that she has been on the streets
every night; she said it was sometimes twice a week,
sometimes not for some weeks. She is a married woman.
She, too, has not lived with her husband for eleven years.
I suppose, seeing that her name is Hindin, it may well
be that her husband's name is Hindin as well. She has a
mother, whose sole support she is. She has two children,
one aged twenty-one and the other sixteen; the younger
son she helps, and she also has an ailing brother. She said
that Messina did not know that she was leading such a
life, and Messina said the same thing when he was in the
witness box. You will ask yourself whether that may be
true. They had been living together, you know, on their
own showing for seven or eight years. You may think it
strange, but then in these courts we get used to listening
to strange things. But you may think it strange. You may
think it very strange, strange that the man did not know
what the woman was doing. Well, of course, some women

are very clever and some men's eyes are very blind. You may also think it strange that a woman who is living as wife and mistress at his home with a man who can afford to buy her a £900 mink coat should have to be a prostitute in order to support her mother and her son and her ailing brother, with the safe in the kitchen all the time and everything provided for her.

Well, that is a strange story, and it is not a happening of a week, it is the happening of a seven or eight years and if you accept the evidence that has been given by those police constables – who are not in the gallery of detective superintendents and detective sergeants of Scotland Yard; I know they will forgive me for saying so. They are plain, ordinary police constables from a plain, ordinary police station – that they have seen her night after night for years soliciting prostitution ('I have arrested her myself five times', says one, and the other one said, 'I have arrested her twice. The last time was on February 6th. I have been present on many occasions when she has been convicted'), then you may well ask yourselves – and indeed it would be a reasonable and proper question for you to ask yourselves – when she had gone out one night, when she had departed upon her 'beat', whatever it was, when the police officer had interfered and she finished up next morning in Marlborough Street Magistrates' Court, how did she get away with it that time without her man knowing?

Well, all those are matters for you. If you think that he did not know, or may not have known, that Hermione Hindin was a prostitute, there is an end to this part of the case and he should be acquitted. The real question here is: was he, knowingly, wholly or in part, living upon her immoral earnings. The case for the prosecution is not made out, you know, merely because you are satisfied that he did know she was a prostitute. There is no law in this country which makes it an offence for a man to live with a prostitute so long as he does not live wholly or in part upon her immoral earnings. How often has it been said – aye, in this court, where so many sordid stories have to be unfolded – that this is not a court of morals. You may not approve of his conduct. No decent man, perhaps, would. But you are not here to say whether his was the conduct of a decent person; you are here to say whether he is guilty of living upon the immoral earnings of that prostitute . . .

You will remember that I told you that that burden
of proof is satisfied if he establishes a preponderance of
probability in that direction. It is for that reason that the
defence has put forward in great detail the defendant's
financial position.

According to him, he started his business life in Egypt,
in his father's furniture business. That, doubtless, is the
father whose address was 3 Lancaster Lodge that we have
heard about. He says that his father came back to London
– or came to London; whether it was 'back' or not, I do not
know – in 1932. Then he branched out into the diamond
business and went to Belgium, North Africa and Spain,
and lived in London only at weekends. Well, he seems to
have got about the country pretty quickly if he was able
to do that from Spain, but that is what he says he was
doing. In 1934 he opened an account at Barclays bank,
Newgate Street, and when, during the war, that bank was
destroyed he transferred the money to another bank. The
defendant had a safe at his father's abode. That is the same
safe that we have talked about in this case, the safe which
was moved to Harrowdene Road and which rested in the
cupboard behind the rubber material in the kitchen where
the turkey was cooking on the morning of the 19th March.
In 1939 the defendant claims to have had £30,000 with
which he left Brussels. Well, that is not a small amount
of money, £30,000; it is substantial. He might well be
described, if he had that amount of money, as a man of
means. He had three safe deposits, one at the London
Safe Deposit and two at Selfridges, and we have heard
about those at Selfridges, which, when the police opened
them, contained £1,350 in £5 notes. According to the
police evidence, the defendant denied that he had any
safe deposit when asked, and the defendant in his turn
denies that he was asked about safe deposits by the police,
so there is one denial followed by another denial, and the
prosecution suggests that he was denying the possession
of something that he turned out afterwards to possess and
the defendant says he was never even asked about it. In
the safe at Harrowdene Road there was a sum of £220
in pound notes and I think about £6 was in ten-shilling
notes. Three bank managers have been called. Large
round sums of money in £1 and £5 notes were being paid
into these accounts. On April 6th of this year his balance
at the Hatton Garden branch of Barclays was £3,390.

At the Union Bank of Scotland, High Street Kensington Branch, where the account was opened in August 1944, the balance on March 21st of this year was £4,514, and at the Bank of British West Africa, where the account was opened in 1946, the balance in July 1947 was £519; and in those banks the defendant had nearly £8,000. One other feature about them was the entry in the accounts that were produced of the large number of round sums which were paid into the banking accounts of round figures and consisting of £1 notes. That was a common feature as to the payment into these accounts. Well, that is all right. You are not to condemn a man because he happens to believe in cash. There is many a worse belief in this country than that. He rarely writes a cheque. Equally, I suppose, it can be said that he rarely receives one. He has done no work since 1939. He is diabetic. He draws attention to the fairly large sums of money paid into the banks when he was in Egypt twenty years ago to an account that he had at the Crédit Lyonais [sic]. He has had accounts in the past at Paris, Brussels, Casablanca, Tangier, in Morocco [sic] and Spain. He bought Hermione Hindin that fur coat which cost £980 10s 0d from the National Fur Company. He wrote a cheque for £900 but he could not write a hard figure. He could think and write in round figures, but when it comes to £280 2s 2½d it would completely bewilder him because he says English is the most difficult language in the world. That is how he says he paid for the fur coat.

Counsel for the prosecution says we have not seen the fur coat, and, what is more, we have not seen Hermione Hindin in the fur coat, and the suggestion made against the defendant is: 'Well, assuming that you ever did buy a fur coat, and assuming that it was for Hermione Hindin', well then, the reflection may pass through your minds that possibly it was for her to wear in Maddox Street when she was plying her trade.

He bought his house in 1942 and paid £1,400 for it in cash. His furniture cost £2,500 and was paid for mostly in cash although some payments were made by cheque. He claims to have been living on the money he brought to this country soon after the war started. He says that he gave Hermione Hindin a pair of diamond earrings which cost £200, two rings made out of his cuff-links, and that he opened an account for her at the Credit Lyonais in

Charles II Street with £900 in 1947, adding another £600 to it in that same year. The woman said that she has that money there still untouched, along with £90 that he gave her to dress herself in November of last year and £200 that he gave her on March 7th of this year.

According to him, he has not seen his wife for many years, and in reply to questions in cross-examination he said that he does not know where she lives, he does not know that she is known as 'Marcelle' and he does not know that she is a prostitute with convictions. And then he added a little touch which you will not forget. He added that his wife was a very close friend of Detective-Superintendent Mahon and Detective-Sergeant Foster. Hermione Hindin said that she has known Marcelle as a prostitute but did not know she was Mrs Messina. The woman by the name of Georgette Borg was put to the defendant in the witness box. Well, he says he knows her as a prostitute. She has visited his house to borrow money and he has lent it to her without knowing where she lives. I think, as he was being taken through his account, he picked upon one sum of money which was related to the Borg transaction . . .

You may say to yourselves – because the onus is upon him – if you are satisfied that he was living on a prostitute or had done any of those other things, accompanied her or had done anything in the way of controlling her, then where have all those £1 and £5 notes come from? The defendant said they represented what is left of his fortune in 1939, and that he has gradually transferred certain sums of money from his safe deposits to the banks. He says you cannot pay more than £1,000 at a time into the bank, not because there is any rule against it but because there is the face of the cashier and he does not like counting it, and if you have to count 1,000 pound notes, it is a bit of a task.

He denies that he has lived wholly or in part upon the earnings of this prostitute, Hermione Hindin. He denies that he has ever given her money. I have told you what the law is as to a male person who is living with a prostitute. He is deemed to be living on her earnings, wholly or in part. He is deemed to be. The defendant agrees that he has been with her in the Running Horse and occasionally at a restaurant, but not often. He denies that he has been in her company at the places mentioned by the police officer and he denies that he has taken her in his car in the early evening, or that he has collected her in the late evening. He says that he did not know until this case that she was a prostitute.

So there is this case for your good and careful consideration. You are quite entitled to look, so far as the second charge is concerned, at the evidence upon that as it is, the evidence supplied upon the one side by the police officers and upon the other side by the defendant and the woman. By all means. But when things like perjury are mentioned to you, when it is suggested you would convict these men of perjury upon the evidence of such people as the defendant and the woman, I would suggest to you that that is not quite the way in which you ought to look at this case. If there is one thing that is very difficult to do in the administration of the law it is to try two cases at the same time and no judge ever attempts it, and no jury ought to attempt it, either. You must remember you are trying this man, and only this man, and that you are trying him upon these two charges, and you are not to be diverted from giving what you consider to be the right verdict in this case merely because it is suggested to you that that particular verdict has the effect of condemning somebody whom you are not trying. You may make up your minds in this case. The officers have given their evidence. It may be that more good can be said about the two police officers than can be said about the defendant and the woman he was living with. That may be. But it is a perfectly proper and right reflection for you that you are considering the evidence of two police officers of high and substantial rank, particularly in the case of Superintendent Mahon, who has twenty-five years' experience in the police force. It is perfectly right and proper that you should be invited to let pass through your minds the reflection that it would be unlikely that a police officer, who could have no other interest in this case other than discharging his duty, would stoop so low (as well as stooping low to get money out of the safe) as to pull out of the safe £200 and then turn round and say to this man, 'Now I am going to charge you with bribery.' That is a thing, of course, which you are entitled to reflect on. But, when all is said and done, when you have put the police officers – of presumably highly respectable reputation and character – upon one side and the defendant, with his suburban house and an address in W.1, and the false name – well, I will not say 'false', but another name – upon his identity card and living with a woman for seven or eight years without knowing that for thirteen years she has been a prostitute, on the other side, you have those two opposing factors for your consideration when you have the evidence in your minds and it is a perfectly proper observation to make that you have to give your most careful consideration to the evidence which has been given upon both sides with those factors still in your minds.

Another observation was made: that we are not trying this man here for anything other than what is on the indictment. He was presented to you a little while ago as a man who did not pay any income tax. You may envy him over that; I do not know; but you are not to condemn him because he is not paying that. He is not charged with that here. That is one thing.

And suppose his application form for a passport was not all that it might be, that he said that his usual address was in Brussels whereas his usual address is the house in Harrowdene Road, for which he paid £1,400 (and that was a little matter that you would not think he would readily forget), that he said his usual address was Brussels and that he had lived there for so long, well, all those matters, of course, you will bear in mind but always reflect that he is not here for those. What you are asked to bear in mind is: here is a man who deals in pound notes. The observation was made to you that it is upon his word only that he has ever had a fortune of £30,000. Nobody else has ever said it. It is said these vast sums of money in pound notes have a taint about them. This so-called invalid who is diabetic, who has done no work for the last eleven or twelve years, has all these sums of money there, and who certainly has some association – it may not be criminal, but some association – with prostitutes; you are asked by the prosecution to say that those things cannot have happened unless this man was living wholly or in part upon the earnings of that woman, Hermione Hindin.

Now there, members of the jury, is all I have to say to you. You will bear in mind what I have told you about the onus of proof. You will give your most careful consideration to all the evidence which has been given in this case. You will now consider your verdict and say how you find, as to whether you find the defendant guilty or not guilty upon either or both of these charges.

CHAPTER 14

'An Evil Man'

The all-male jury (who now numbered eleven; a woman juror had been excused through illness) retired for 48 minutes before returning to ask that the detectives' evidence be read to them again. It was, after which they retired at 3.42 pm, returning twelve minutes later to find Alfredo guilty of both offences.

In passing sentence, Mr Justice Cassels said:

> Alfredo Messina, the jury have found you guilty of these two offences, the first one of living upon immoral earnings of that woman, she a prostitute, and the other of corruption of the police in attempting to bribe them with a sum of £200. You thought that so far as the police of this country were concerned money could do anything. You are an evil man. The jury have arrived at a proper verdict. The sentence of the court upon you is that upon count one and upon count two you will go, upon each count to imprisonment for two years, to run concurrently – two years in all – and upon count two, you will pay a fine, in addition to the imprisonment, of £500. In default of payment of the fine there will be five months' imprisonment.

Alfredo's counsel, Mr Scott-Henderson, said to the judge, 'My Lord, your Lordship heard my submission on the indictment. I would ask your Lordship to say there is something to argue in a court elsewhere and to give me a certificate of appeal.'

'No', replied the judge. 'I do not grant a certificate.'

Alfredo must have known that imprisonment was inevitable and simply shrugged the shoulders of his Savile Row suit, complete with a maroon silk tie and matching silk breast-pocket handkerchief from which a silver propelling pencil protruded, as he went down to the cells. That morning, he had arrived at the Old Bailey in a taxi; that evening, he left in a prison van, en route to Wormwood Scrubs.

★

The revelations at the Old Bailey regarding Alfredo's money had excited the attention of the Inland Revenue, who that evening stated, 'We are very interested in Messina in view of the disclosures in court. When the 1951 Finance Act becomes law, banks will have to disclose to income-tax investigators accounts on which interest has been paid.'

Cassandra was a figure in Greek mythology who had been given the gift of prophesy by Apollo but at the same time cursed, so that nobody would believe her predictions. It was also the pen-name of Sir William Neil Connor, who wrote a column in the *Daily Mirror* for thirty-two years, in which he aired his own, often controversial views. He picked up where the Inland Revenue had left off:

> It is unlikely that Alfredo Messina, who was sentenced to two years' imprisonment at the Old Bailey on Wednesday, ever heard of Clause 23 of the 1951 Finance Bill.
>
> But if he had he would have appreciated it.
>
> Messina was a particular, not to say a choosy, man about money. Not so much in the way he got it, but what he did with it when once he laid his hands on it.
>
> He wasn't satisfied with one banking account – he had to have two.
>
> And then, just to make sure, he crammed some of the takings away in safe deposits. The existence of three of these useful caches was revealed in court. The banking account, as the law stands at present, can conceal sums that have not been returned, and Clause 23 of the Finance Bill is a new measure that will empower income tax investigators full details of all interest that amounts to over £15 a year from which tax has not already been deducted.
>
> This clause has been hotly attacked.

Cassandra had often been sued for his contentious comments – but was not on this occasion.

★

The thrust of the defence case had been personally prepared by the Messinas' dodgy legal representatives, William Webb and Watson. Damaging allegations against certain persons had been made at Wealdstone Magistrates' Court by Alfredo's junior counsel, Mr Raymond Stock, and during the proceedings at the Old Bailey, Mahon in particular had been accused of perjury and planting money on Alfredo so that he might be convicted of bribery. Alfredo and Hindin had lied persistently, and when the jury found him guilty, it came as no surprise that Alfredo – a 50-year-old man with no previous convictions – received the maximum sentence.

But between conviction and appeal Mr Scott-Henderson personally visited the Home Office, where he persisted in his allegations again Mahon, with the result that senior figures at the Yard were instructed to carry out a detailed investigation into Mahon's conduct; their findings were forwarded to the Director of Public Prosecutions, Sir Theobald Mathew KBE, MC. When the Director came to the irrevocable conclusion that there was no basis whatsoever for criminal proceedings to be brought against Mahon, he sent the docket back to the Yard, where it landed on the desk of the Deputy Commissioner, Sir John Reginald Hornby Nott-Bower KPM. This was so that Sir John might determine what grounds there might be to bring disciplinary proceedings in respect of Mahon. Of course, there were none. Sir John informed the Commissioner of his findings and the rather lacklustre deputy breathed a sigh of relief and turned his attention to his usual pursuit of inveigling his colleagues into playing rubbers of bridge.

Mr Scott-Henderson had even less luck when he appeared at the Royal Courts of Justice on 9 July 1951, because in addition to the presence of Mr Justice Hilbery and Mr Justice Ormerod, the Court of Criminal Appeal was presided over by the Lord Chief Justice of England, Rayner Goddard, probably the toughest judge that the law courts had seen for many a long year. In April 1948 Parliament had voted that the death penalty be put in abeyance; that was smartly kicked into touch after Goddard's maiden speech in the House of Lords on 10 June, by 181 votes to 28. In cracking down on the wave of post-war crime, Goddard sentenced two 14-year-old boys who admitted knocking a woman unconscious during a robbery to seven years each, and also controversially sentenced Derek Bentley (unkindly referred to by Reginald Paget MP, QC as 'a three-quarter witted boy') to death for the murder of a police officer, even though the fatal shooting had actually been committed by a youth, one Christopher Craig, who was too young to hang.

Now, dealing with Alfredo's appeal, the Lord Chief Justice was not one to mince words or waste them, saying:

> This appellant whose appeal has been listed as an appeal but he has not obtained leave to appeal though it is alleged that certain questions of law arise, appeals against a conviction before Mr Justice Cassels at the Central

Criminal Court, firstly in respect of an offence of living on immoral earnings of a woman and secondly for offering a bribe to police officers.

A variety of points have been taken on his behalf, in none of which the court thinks there is any substance at all.

Lord Goddard then went on to demolish those points one by one, but that was by no means that, because he finished with the words 'We think that this is quite a groundless appeal and we dismiss it and order that the sentence shall date from today.'

Thanks to his profound arrogance in appealing in the first place, Alfredo received three months longer than he might have done. It was one calamity after another: being convicted in the first place, then having his appeal brusquely dismissed and now, by his conviction, being deemed – under the auspices of the Vagrancy Act 1824 – to be 'an incorrigible rogue'. That must have been the unkindest cut of all.

Little more was heard of Alfredo; the Harrowdene Road address was sold, and in 1961 he moved to Bridge House South, a block of flats in Boston Manor Road, Brentford, Middlesex, close to the Boston Manor tube station. There he was known to the other tenants as Alfred Martin – not that he maintained any appreciable level of conversation with them – and none knew him to have been one of the top vice kings of Mayfair.

He had a seizure at the age of sixty-two, and by the time his body was found in the hallway of his second-floor flat, he was quite dead.

He was buried at Gunnersbury Cemetery on 20 August 1963; his parents, who had died in 1946 and 1947, were already interred in the family grave.

Instead of showing his year of birth as 1901, the dates on Alfredo's tombstone were 1900–1963.

Even in death, the Messinas were incapable of telling the truth.

CHAPTER 15

Attilio's Return

Back now to 1951, and with Alfredo banged up and the other four brothers living it up in some of the more fashionable parts of Europe, it might be thought that their vice empire in Mayfair had collapsed. Was it possible that their girls, wide-eyed and lost, were wandering the streets in a pathetic daze, financially as well as morally bankrupt and asking passers-by how they could sign on to claim the forty shillings due to them as married women under the provisions of the newly established National Assistance Act, 1948?

Don't you believe it. They carried on just as before, each of them having their own ledger to enter the amounts which they'd earned; and since they were driven either by fear or devotion – or a mixture of both – those records were immaculately kept.

In fact, although all of the brothers were conspicuous by their absence, business was booming. The Festival of Britain, designed by the Labour Government to cheer up the population now that the post-war austerity years were coming to an end, had got underway on 3 May 1951. It was celebrated all over England but especially on London's South Bank. The crowds marvelled at the Dome of Discovery and the Royal Festival Hall became a Grade I listed building, although the futuristic 300ft tall Skylon which pointed its way to the stars was not so fortunate, since it later toppled into the Thames and was sold for scrap. Nevertheless, the South Bank alone attracted 8,455,863 visitors, a number of whom also sought the delights of 'The Queens of Maddox Street'.

Although those girls who were bonded to Eugenio visited him in Paris when their earnings reached £1,000, they were not entrusted with the money; that was kept hidden at various locations in London, to be taken out by couriers.

Eugenio was still recruiting girls and sending them over to London but, as Marthe Watts observed, they were getting younger and younger and less responsive to the code of discipline which the older women had observed. Having been enamoured of one young 23-year-old and lavished clothes, including a Persian Lamb coat, and other goodies, on her, Eugenio took umbrage when she was cheeky to him and he beat her up. That was a mistake, because the following day, she left, taking all of those prized possessions with her; and despite promises of jewellery and furs if she returned, ultimately to ensconce herself in Stafford Street, it was all to no avail. He had to console himself with her friend, a large, clumsy girl but one who, as Watts said, 'made up for this by the enthusiasm with which she worked'.

We can leave those matters ticking over quite nicely for the absent brothers and concentrate now on Attilio Francesco Messina, who had been born on 24 March 1910 in Alexandria. He had evaded National Service during the war; a warrant for his arrest had been issued but he had absconded and could not be found. In 1947 the warrant was withdrawn. He was the best educated of the family, and Mahon, fresh from his triumph over Alfredo's conviction, was keen to ensnare Attilio after he received information that he was periodically returning to England, as indeed he was.

However, he had sold his house at Woodlands Road, New Malden, Surrey (where the prestigious properties currently sell for anything between £2 and £8 million) and had gone to ground.

Mahon discovered that Watson, the clerk of the Messina brothers' solicitors, had been making frequent trips to Europe, especially Rome and Paris, at exactly the same time that others of the Messina brotherhood were visiting those cities. Could he have been one of the respectable looking couriers who had been ferrying funds, directions or information for the brothers, both in and out of England? Given his previous conduct, this was a possibility. But possibilities are not evidence, and so Mahon recalled the AC(C)'s dictum: 'He will have all the men and other assistance he needs.'

Mahon took him at his word, especially when it came to 'other assistance', and applied to the Home Secretary for a warrant to intercept calls on a certain telephone exchange's number. Chuter Ede had just bowed out of office; his replacement was Sir David Patrick Maxwell Fyfe (later 1st Earl of Kilmuir GCVO, PC, QC), a completely different kettle of fish from his predecessor. He had previously served with the Scots Guards in the First World War and, following the Second, had been both Solicitor General and Attorney General.

In September 1951 the Home office issued guidelines to the Metropolitan Police and Customs and Excise which laid out the conditions to be satisfied before a warrant for interception of communications could be authorized by the Secretary of State. They were:

(a) The offence must be really serious.

(b) Normal methods of investigation must have been tried and failed, or must, by the nature of things, be unlikely to succeed if tried.

(c) There must be good reason to think that an interception would result in a conviction.

As a result, this was one of the 177 warrants which were granted for telephone interception during 1951; and when Watson's plane landed at Northolt Aerodrome in October 1951, he was put under surveillance. The girl who occupied the same train carriage as Watson was, in fact, a police officer. She followed him to his home at Chalfont St Giles, Buckinghamshire, whereupon Detective Constable David Fenton took over. After a short while, Watson emerged from the house and got into another car which was parked nearby. Fenton joined Mahon in a taxi (borrowed from the Flying Squad for the occasion) and followed the car to a hotel at Amersham. When the car stopped, two men got out, whereupon they were surrounded by detectives. 'Are you Attilio Messina?' Mahon asked one of the occupants of the car, and when he admitted that he was, Mahon arrested him. Watson attempted to intervene; Mahon brusquely reminded him that he was not a solicitor and told him not to interfere.

Watson was very fortunate. No matter how deeply a person may be immersed in crime, what they say on a telephone is not, and never has been, evidence; it cannot be produced in a court of law. He was, of course, involved up to his armpits with the Messinas – so was his employer, William Webb. Just two months earlier, on 29 August 1951, the assistant secretary of the Law Society had written to Webb, pointing out that in the 5 August 1951 edition of the *People*, an article had been published in which Hermione Hindin had been described as 'one of London's worst prostitutes'.

But Watson had supplied a reference for her, saying:

> Mrs Hindin has been a client of ours for the past two or three years and we have always found her a respectable and responsible person and are quite sure that she is in a position to pay the rent.

Webb replied that the company's dealing with Mrs Hindin had been restricted to advice about divorce proceedings, advice and information about emigrating to the United States and a phone conversation about furniture valuation.

However, there was no account on the company's books for Mrs Hindin, and the disciplinary committee stated:

The only entries bearing this name appeared in an account headed 'A. Martin (Messina)' under dates in January and August 1951.

The respondent acted for one Alfredo Messina (later known as Alfred Martin) when he appeared at the Central Criminal Court on May 3, 1951 on a charge of knowingly lived wholly or in part upon the earnings of the prostitution of Hermione Hindin, and was convicted.

Webb would later tell the Law Society that he did not know of the references given by Watson and had asked him for an explanation of his conduct; for now, he busied himself with more legitimate enterprises, such as settling the estate of Minnie Eliza Cobb of 10 Croxted Road, Dulwich on 30 September; but, as we know, small good did it do Webb.

Should Watson have been pulled in, at the same time as Attilio and spoken to rather sharply? I rather think he should.

Attilio was arrested for living on the immoral earnings of Robina Dickson Torrance. She had been born on 25 October 1913 in Ayr, Scotland, had come to London in the 1940s and become an enthusiastic part of the Messina network, living with Attilio, fitting up Sally Wright for an alleged knife attack and collecting thirty-two convictions for soliciting.

Appearing at Bow Street Magistrates' Court on 31 October 1951, 41-year-old Attilio – he was described as 'a merchant' – faced charges of procuring a woman to become a common prostitute in 1945 and further, during 1945, 1946 and 1947 that he lived wholly or partly on the earnings of prostitution. He gave as his address Lancaster Lodge, that well known bolt-hole of the Messina tribe, used by Carmelo, Eugenio, Alfredo and Giuseppe – and of course, Attilio. Legal representation was not immediately forthcoming; neither Webb nor Watson appeared keen to offer their services. Eventually, an even more unwholesome member of the legal profession appeared. This was Judah Binstock, whose name later became synonymous with dodgy international currency deals and bribery of officials; when he passed away at his millionaire's home in Marbella aged eighty-eight in December 2016, he had been subject of investigations by the Metropolitan Police, the Spanish Police and the Department of Trade.

Mahon asked for a remand in custody and told the Chief Metropolitan Magistrate, Sir Lawrence Dunne, that owing to the time which had elapsed, the case was triable by jury. The reasons for the delay in bringing proceedings, he said, were new enquiries and the difficulty in finding Attilio.

Sir Lawrence was plainly troubled. 'Months, I could understand', he remarked, 'but this is a matter of six years; it is a long time.'

'The delay has not been on my part', replied Mahon. 'I started the enquiries early this year and I have been looking for Messina since March.'

'The question ought to be answered as to why the police had not begun their investigations for so long', said Sir Lawrence.

Mahon riposted by saying, 'Investigations had been made but so far as I can say, sufficient evidence had not been obtained before.'

However, Mahon had informed the court that Attilio had refused to provide his fingerprints, and a court order was made for them to be taken, as well as an order to inspect his banking account.

Attilio was told that now that the order had been made, police were entitled to use *such force as was necessary* to obtain his fingerprints. Those five pertinent words were delivered quietly, but in a pretty no-nonsense matter. Seeing the writing on the wall, Attilio peacefully submitted to having his dabs taken without further delay or hindrance. Ponces do not care to have their fingers broken, any more than more respectable members of the underworld do.

An unsuccessful application for bail was later made by Mr R. D. B. Davies, and Attilio was remanded in custody.

Eight days later, following a further appearance at court, Attilio was granted bail with sureties totalling £1,000 and a date was set – 20 November 1951 – for the case to be heard. On that date he pleaded guilty to living on the immoral earnings of Torrance, and the other charges were withdrawn.

It was said in court – by the prosecution – that the woman named in the other two charges was physically and mentally unfit to give evidence, and that because of the newspaper coverage of the Messina brothers, Attilio could not hope to receive a fair trial. This, it was thought – especially by Duncan Webb – was nonsense.

The Magistrate, Leo Gradwell DSC, RNVR, remarked that Attilio was not impoverished yet he had encouraged Torrance to go out soliciting, and when she returned, he had taken a fair share of her earnings from her. He then sentenced him to six months' imprisonment and ordered him to pay 30 guineas costs.

Did that make a difference? Not really.

Mahon penned a report dated 15 January 1952 to the Detective Chief Superintendent of the CID, informing him that even at the height of the Messinas' influence, in his opinion the total number of prostitutes under their control was no more than twenty.

In fact, by suggesting that he had broken the power of the Messina brothers, Mahon was doing no more than give himself a pat on the back. It had the ring of authenticity about it, with two of the brothers simultaneously in prison and the other three still out of the country. However, the report was either wishful thinking or bullshit (or perhaps a mixture of both), because other police officers were in no doubt that right at the time of the submission of that report, the number of prostitutes operating under the mantle of the Messinas was in the region of 200.

However cheering Mahon's report was intended to be, the stark reality of the situation was that in 1952 the Metropolitan Police was in a parlous state. When the Second World War ended – since recruiting had been suspended during the war years – it was perilously short of officers. The strength of London's police was no more than 14,500. Never mind, said the commissioner at the time, men will be returning from war service and we'll start a new recruitment drive. It should have worked, but it didn't. Some men did rejoin after their war service, others who had been conscripted into the armed services during the war joined the police and others were accepted from civilian occupations; but it was just a trickle of manpower and clearly not enough, especially since many officers who had been retained during the war were now resigning. Additionally, the ridiculous recommendations of the 1948 Oaksey Report with regard to pay increases put paid to any significant upsurge in manpower. Even a 20 per cent improvement in pay in 1951 failed to bring about the necessary improvement. And therefore, in 1952, given the number of post-war resignations, the police were still 4,000 men short.

The Commissioner, Sir Harold Scott (who in his heart was the civil servant he always had been and therefore well versed in the art of manipulating figures and statistics), was unnerved enough to write with candour in his 1952 report to the Home Secretary:

> The position is really far more serious than the overall percentage shortage would suggest, for when other duties have been provided for (and they have increased greatly in recent years), it is in the men available for beat and patrol duty that the shortage is really felt. Whereas in 1932, 87.6 per cent of the men required for beat and patrol duty were available, the percentage last year was only 44.6.

By late February 1952 Attilio had been released from prison and, using his alias of Raymond Maynard, leased 'Hideaway', a detached two-bedroom cottage in Bourne End, Buckinghamshire. Robina

Torrance moved in with him and leased two flats in her own name to be used as brothels in London, whilst Attilio acquired a flat in Shepherd Market for a similar purpose; a further flat in the same location was acquired by a long-time associate of the brothers, a prostitute named Jean Connolly.

But if the police were undermanned, the *People* was not, and Duncan Webb led his war-party down to the pleasant village of Bourne End to disrupt its tranquillity; Attilio and Torrance were glad that the railway station was just a couple of hundred yards from their idyllic cottage because it took the train just one hour and eight minutes to arrive at Paddington.

In 1953 a deportation order was made, but despite Attilio's birth being registered with the Italian authorities, they refused to accept him; neither would any other country. He and Torrance settled into an apartment at Rosehill Court, at the junction of St Helier Avenue and Bishopsford Road, Morden, almost as salubrious as their former residences. As an alien, he was obliged to report to the police once a week, and the nearest police station was Mitcham, which was where former Police Constable Thomas Proudfoot was serving at the time.

'I remember he was always smartly dressed, very polite and honoured the Widows and Orphans collection box which stood on the counter', he told me, sixty-five years after the event, adding, 'I felt in real life, he could have been a bit smarmy.'

It may have been a bore to have to trudge along to Mitcham police station once a week, but Attilio was more fortunate than he knew. Also stationed at Mitcham at that time was the highly unpredictable former SAS soldier, Harry Challenor MM. Noted at an early stage of his career for his casual disregard for suspects' human rights, he had just become an Aid to CID, and since he knew precisely where the unsavoury Attilio was going to be at a certain time each week, Attilio was highly fortunate not to become a statistic in the back of Challenor's CID diary; after all, he carried out an extremely controversial 105 arrests during the first seven months of his aiding service.[1]

We can leave lucky Attilio for the moment – but he'll surface again in grand style, never fear.

---

1. For further details of this officer's extraordinary lifestyle, see *The Scourge of Soho: The Controversial Career of SAS Hero, Detective Sergeant Harry Challenor, MM*, Pen & Sword True Crime, 2013.

CHAPTER 16

Ponces, Dodgy Cops and Bent Briefs

Time to take a break now from the Messinas and to concentrate on their legal representatives, their kinsman Tony Micallef, who whilst looking after some of the brothers' interests was also looking after his own, and others associated with the world of vice in London. All of them were of particular interest to Duncan Webb.

The first of these was 27-year-old Robert William Helas, who since he had three convictions in that name preferred to be known as Mark Langtry. He appeared at Marlborough Street Magistrates' Court on 12 January 1955 charged with living on the immoral earnings of prostitutes. Langtry had an office in Oxford Street where he conducted a semi-legitimate business providing social partners, escorts and introductions. However, when police officers went to Langtry's office they were charged one guinea for an introduction to a prostitute, and the prostitutes on his books paid Langtry a commission on their earnings.

Norman Beach, solicitor for the defence, roared, 'There is not one jot of evidence that prostitutes had paid money to Langtry! The prosecution could not prove their case if they called ten officers, each of whom said they had paid money, but there was no sexual immorality.'

Inspector Charles Reuben Jacobs gave fairly lacklustre evidence for the prosecution and, after Langtry pleaded not guilty and reserved his defence, he was committed to the Old Bailey for trial.

Six weeks later, Langtry had an epiphany and realized that he was indeed guilty of the offence; but despite his barrister, 'Billy' Rees-Davies, telling the Recorder of London, Sir Gerald Dodson, that at the time his client was not aware that he was guilty in law of any offence, it did him no good.

Telling Langtry, 'This sort of offence is very much against the public welfare and it is no excuse for anyone to say they did not know it is against the law. It is impossible to think or believe that you did not know that part of this business was against the law', the Recorder weighed him off with eighteen months' imprisonment.

The next case involved Micallef, a crooked solicitor and, once more, Inspector Jacobs, as well as another bent cop. In 1947 a 23-year-old Maltese national, Joseph Grech, had come to England but got into bad company in the form of Tony Micallef, with whom he opened a flat-letting partnership. In May 1954 Grech was fined £25 for permitting a premises to be used as a brothel, and then two months later, he was charged with housebreaking and stealing £500, two rings and other property. His solicitor, Ben Canter, had been admitted as a solicitor of the Supreme Court in May 1932; since 1937 he had also acted as solicitor for the Messina family.

At Canter's suggestion, Grech had paid £150, via an intermediary, Morris 'Spider' Page, to Detective Sergeant Robert James Robertson, a former member of the Ghost Squad, to say that a key found in Grech's possession which fitted the lock of the burgled premises also fitted the lock at Grech's home address. To this end, Robertson arranged for a duplicate lock to be made to replace the one on Grech's front door; when Grech was acquitted, he would pay Robertson another £150. In addition, despite knowing that Micallef had a fairly serious criminal record, both in this country and in Malta, Robertson accepted him as a surety so that Grech could be released on bail.

A reasonably ingenious plan, except that it didn't work, and Grech was sentenced to three years' imprisonment. Whilst serving his sentence, Grech was brought up to plead guilty to an additional charge of living on immoral earnings and was sentenced to twelve months' imprisonment, to run concurrently.

Grech was furious at what he saw as duplicity on the part of Robertson and others; in fact it wasn't, because that dodgy trio had done their best for Grech. It was the jury who had convicted him. But from his prison cell Grech made a series of very serious allegations to the Commissioner of the Police, now Sir John Reginald Hornby Nott-Bower KCVO, KPM, who appointed Detective Superintendent Herbert 'Suits' Hannam to investigate the matter. When he had done so, Canter, Page and Robertson were arrested and stood trial at the Old Bailey.

Grech was, of course, the prime prosecution witness (having been granted immunity from prosecution for his self-confessed complicity in the conspiracy) and apart from the foregoing matters he also alleged that Inspector Jacobs had demanded £500 from him in order to drop the case; but when he failed to pay, Jacobs had arranged for two of his officers to say that they had seen Grech in the vicinity of the burgled flat.

Unfortunately for all concerned, the trial judge was Lord Goddard, who on occasion was prone to interrupt counsel and conduct his own cross-examination. With Canter in the witness box, this was one of those occasions, and Goddard tore into him, saying, 'Do you think Mr Justice Davies would have granted bail to Grech if he had known that the surety put forward was a convicted brothel keeper or the partner of a convicted brothel keeper?'

Canter replied, 'I did not know that.'

Goddard snapped, 'Do you think any honest policeman would agree to accept Micallef as a surety for this man Grech?'

'That is a very difficult question to answer', replied Canter, but he was wriggling and Goddard knew it.

'I think it is a very simple question', he said and added, 'Try to answer it.'

'It depends on the circumstances', replied Canter, which gave Goddard the opening he was looking for.

'*These* circumstances!' he roared. 'These two men were partners in vice, amongst other things. The Judge in Chambers said, "I cannot bail a man unless the police are satisfied with the surety." Look at the surety the policeman was satisfied with! Unless you knew Robertson was going to accept him, would you not have tried to get someone who at any rate seemed more respectable?'

The unhappy Canter replied, 'Grech put forward Micallef', but the evidence was overpowering, the three men were found guilty of conspiring to pervert the course of justice and on 29 November 1955 Canter was sentenced to two years' imprisonment, as was Robertson (who was also dismissed from the Force), and Page received fifteen months' imprisonment.

It was thought that there was insufficient evidence to charge Jacobs; however, he was dealt with for disciplinary offences and, three months later, for assisting a prostitute to find a premises, failing to disclose a defendant's convictions in court and failing to account for property found in the possession of a man whom he had arrested, he was dismissed from the Force. For several years afterwards Jacobs continued to protest his innocence – as did Robertson – but it did them no good; nor was Grech helped when he brought civil proceedings for libel against Odhams Press. The case rumbled on until 22 May 1958, when Grech's appeal was finally dismissed; in addition, Grech received no remission of his 3-year sentence.

Those cases revealed the calibre of the legal representation employed by the Messinas and others engaged in the vice trade. Webb, Watson, Binstock and Canter, we already know about. The solicitor Norman Harry Beach who had been admitted in 1935 to the Supreme Court – and who routinely represented the Messinas' prostitutes – was adept at manufacturing defences for his clients and on one occasion arranged for a defendant to wear a wig in court in order that he could not be identified; Beach and his client later stood trial on a charge of conspiracy to pervert the course of public justice. The defence barrister in the original trial, Patrick Marrinan, was called by the defence, not that he did them any good. Marrinan was as bent as a nine-bob note; six weeks later, in respect of another piece of skulduggery, he was found guilty of three charges of conduct unbecoming a gentleman and a barrister and was disbarred and expelled from the Honourable Society of Lincolns Inn.[1]

Beach was found guilty and sentenced to twelve months' imprisonment but appealed and was later freed on a technicality. The Law Society later struck him off the Roll of Solicitors after Beach introduced a person to sit with solicitors in court during a porn trial to intimidate witnesses, and two years later, in 1979, the Divisional Court upheld that decision. In November 1981 his appeal in a matter involving income tax payments, in the words of the judge who ordered him to pay costs, 'failed utterly'.

Known as 'The One-Armed Bandit', William Rupert 'Billy' Rees-Davies (who had represented Langtry during his trial) was convicted on three occasions of offences including driving under the influence and was twice disqualified from driving; he routinely failed to appear for clients in court and was suspended twice for unprofessional conduct. He represented Stephen Ward in the Profumo enquiry and also acted as a go-between in respect of monetary payments to Christine Keeler. In the enquiry which followed, Lord Denning, describing Rees-Davies' actions, stated rather bitingly that he was 'presumably acting on behalf of Stephen Ward'.

These were some of the dross of the legal profession who constantly appeared for some the garbage from the world of London's vice to blare out their accusations in court of dishonesty and impropriety against honest police officers. All that separated the lawyers from their clients was a law degree – nothing more.

★

This brings us back to Anthony Micallef. On 13 June 1956 he was arrested for brothel-keeping, appeared at Marylebone Magistrates' Court and was remanded until 17 June, when he was committed to the London Sessions, which opened on 3 July, for trial. However . . .

---

1 For full details of Marrinan's disgraceful behaviour, see *London's Gangs at War*, Pen & Sword True Crime, 2017.

Duncan Webb still had the bit between his teeth when it came to exposing dodgy characters in the West End; these included Antonio 'Tony' Rossi (whom Webb dubbed 'The Jackal of Soho') and of course, Tony Micallef. On 15 July the *People* published a fairly explicit piece, with a damning headline which read 'ARREST THIS BEAST', together with a photograph of Micallef. Not only was the headline particularly critical, the rest of the article was hardly complimentary; it dealt with a premises situated at 57 Queen's Gardens, Paddington, in the basement of which was the Tango Garden Club; Micallef was denounced as being 'up to his eyes' in the foul business of purveying vice and managing prostitutes, as well as for his involvement with the Messina brothers.

In vain Webb protested that he was unaware that criminal proceedings had been launched against Micallef (and this was undoubtedly true; after all, why head an article 'Arrest this Beast' if the 'beast' had already been arrested one month earlier?). However, it was held in the High Court of Justice, in the Queen's Bench Division, by the Lord Chief Justice that there had been a contempt of court, that it would have been impossible for Micallef to have received a fair trial.

In fact, the matter was deemed to be so serious that proceedings were brought by the Attorney General, Sir Reginald Edward Manningham-Buller MP, QC, (later 1st Viscount Dilhorne PC), who outlined the article to the court (it provided details of Micallef's alleged 76 convictions, 'which, incidentally', as the Attorney General wittily put it, 'appeared to have been magnified tenfold'). The case resulted in Odhams Press Ltd. being fined £1,000. The editor of the *People*, Harry Ainsworth, and Webb were considered fortunate not to have prison sentences imposed on them and instead were fined £500 each. The respondents were ordered to pay the entire costs of the proceedings, and Micallef's costs as well.

Was justice done? In the eyes of the law it was seen to be done, and Odhams Press could certainly afford the fine and costs, especially since these latest revelations were, as the Lord Chief Justice so accurately stated, 'published with a view to increasing circulation and with no other object'.

On 21 October 1954 Webb had been attacked by gangland boss Jack Spot, who had broken his wrist; at Clerkenwell Magistrates' Court on 18 November Spot had a charge of possessing a knuckleduster dismissed, but for causing grievous bodily harm to Webb he was fined £50 with 20 guineas costs. At the Queen's Bench Division on 5 March 1956 Webb sued him for loss of earnings and was awarded £732 in damages. Spot failed to pay and on 21 February 1957 he attended bankruptcy proceedings, at which he filed a statement of affairs which revealed liabilities of £1,321 and assets of £125; he was gratuitously disbelieved.

Not that this did Webb any good; he died, aged forty-two, the following year, of leukaemia.

He was therefore unable to witness the downfall of another of his targets, Paul Cambridge Grubb. Superintendent C. S. Strath told Tower Bridge Magistrates' Court on 3 December 1958 that thirty-six men had been crowded into a room measuring 13ft by 12ft at the Seven Dials Club, Foubert's Place, W1 to watch a 14-year-old girl perform a strip-tease. The girl, who told the superintendent that she was paid £9 per week, was taken into police protection and was later admitted to hospital 'suffering from a serious disease'. For permitting unlicensed music and dancing, selling drinks to non-members and for selling drinks after the permitted hours, the club proprietor was fined a total of £220 and ordered to pay £31 costs.

The club was struck off the register and Grubb, the club secretary, was fined a total of £115; the magistrate gave him one week 'and no more!' to pay.

★

The last word on the subject of the Messinas' legal representatives should be in respect of John Scott-Henderson KC, who so valiantly – but unsuccessfully – sought the exculpation of Alfredo from the taint of bribery and poncing.

He went on to chair one or two committees, the most noted of which was the enquiry into the guilt of Timothy Evans, who had confessed to the police that he had murdered his wife and baby at their lodgings at 10 Rillington Place, Notting Hill. As was common in those days, only one charge of murder was preferred, and in Evans' case he was charged with (and found guilty of) the murder of his baby daughter. In his defence he tried to put the blame on his landlord, one John Reginald Halliday Christie, but Christie denied it, and Evans was hanged on 9 March 1950.

Later, a number of women's bodies were found in and around 10 Rillington Place, and Christie, a 54-year-old serial killer and sexual pervert, was arrested. He admitted the killings, including that of Evans' wife – but denied killing the baby – and although he tried a defence of diminished responsibility, it failed and he was sentenced to death.

The Home Secretary demanded an immediate enquiry into the guilt – or not – of Timothy Evans, and John Scott-Henderson was directed to head the committee. The enquiry was held in private and, it was later said, 'had been rushed through'. Scott-Henderson's findings were that Evans had indeed murdered both his daughter *and* his wife, and the report was published on 13 July 1953, two days before Christie was hanged.

But doubts still lingered and the burning question was: had there been a miscarriage of justice? Sydney Silverman MP, capital punishment's ardent abolitionist, certainly thought so, saying in the House, 'No honest man, on the evidence before Scott-Henderson, could have made the report he made . . . Scott-Henderson must have known it was not true.'

It was not Scott-Henderson's finest hour, because some of the Great and the Good agreed with Silverman's sentiments and Evans was granted a posthumous pardon.

CHAPTER 17

Attilio Revisited

Now it's time to return to the Messinas and to introduce two detectives who featured in Attilio's next arrest.

John Valentine Ralph Du Rose was known, certainly by the press if not by his colleagues, as 'Four-Day Johnnie', because of the speed with which he solved murder cases. There is little doubt that from the days that he first trod the beat on Soho's streets in 1931 as Police Constable 254 'C' he was a good police officer. The majority of the crimes he solved were due to pure, careful detective work, but unlike many of his contemporaries he seldom, if ever, used informants. It was the soubriquet of 'Four-Day Johnnie', bestowed on him by reporter Owen Summers of the *Daily Mail*, which made him an iconic figure to the general public, and it's true, he did have many successes. But when he came to write his memoirs at the conclusion of a 38-year career, having collected an OBE and retired as a deputy assistant commissioner, he filled them with exaggerations and downright lies.

It was suggested, for example, that Du Rose had been responsible for the arrest of serial murder John George Haigh, who thought he was immune from prosecution because he believed he had completely disposed of his victims' bodies by dissolving them in acid; in fact, Du Rose had interviewed Haigh, disbelieved his story and informed his senior officers – that was his sole input into the case. Guy Mahon had been the officer in charge.

Du Rose pretended that he knew the identity of the man dubbed 'Jack the Stripper' responsible for the series of 1960s nude murders, since by conveniently blaming a man who had committed suicide shortly after the last victim's body was found – and who, he said, he was just about to arrest – he could maintain the boast that he had solved all the murders which he had investigated. But this was wrong in two ways. One, Du Rose did not solve all of the murders he investigated. Two, he had never even heard of the man whom he stated was a suspect until three months after his death.

So it was with the Messinas. He suggested that, when Mahon first went after the brothers, 'as a chief inspector, I was a member of the team'. In fact, when Mahon commenced his investigations,

Du Rose was not a member of his team, nor was he a chief inspector: he was a detective sergeant (first-class) at Chelsea.

Heavily built, at one quarter of an inch over five feet ten and cheroot-smoking, it was as a chief inspector that he was posted to C1 Department at the Yard on 12 May 1958, nine months after Mahon had retired, and had dealings with Attilio Messina – and that was with a great deal of help.

★

Margaret Shaw Heald had been born in 1908 in Lytham, Lancashire and impressively educated at a number of private schools, so much so that when she joined the Metropolitan Police in 1940 she was exempt from sitting either the first- or second-class Civil Service examinations and passed the sergeants and inspectors exams at the first attempt. At three-quarters of an inch above the (then) minimum height requirement for women of five feet four inches, she was described as being 'a very quiet and gentle person who knew much about music, the theatre and the arts'.

She also knew much about police work, serving in the Inner London divisions and earning three commissioner's commendations in quick succession for undercover work detecting offences against the betting, gaming and licensing acts.

In 1948 she was promoted to detective inspector (this was very fast promotion indeed) and she arrived at C1 Department at the Yard six weeks after Du Rose's entrance, having just collected a further commendation from the commissioner for diligence in a complicated case of forging clothing coupons.

Their task was to gather sufficient evidence against the Messinas to convict them; but first the brothers had to be found. There was no help to be had from Duncan Webb since, as has been mentioned, he had died suddenly in September. There was no assistance from Du Rose either; after being promoted to detective sergeant and posted to Bow Street in 1943 he declared that it was very difficult to obtain information regarding crime and criminals since the Covent Garden porters were tight-lipped and 'clannish'. This was nonsense. The legendary Jack Capstick – known to the underworld as 'Charlie Artful' – at that time had just been posted back to the Flying Squad from Bow Street, where he had been the detective inspector prior to Du Rose's arrival. He had had no difficulty in recruiting informants from among the porters, who practically queued up to provide information. This was probably due to the fact that when the porters had cheeked Capstick, years before as a police constable, he had sorted them out by fighting with them rather than resorting to arrests, a course of action which earned their respect. So that, which resulted in his crewing the first 'Q'-Car which emerged from Vine Street police station in 1934, plus years of service with the Flying Squad – both of which had failed to attract Du Rose – were proof positive of the value of informants, a resource in which Du Rose was sadly deficient.

So Margaret Heald was tasked to find an informant who might assist with helping to hunt down one of the outstanding Messinas; described as having the appearance of 'an efficient school teacher, rather than an ace detective', her contribution was impressive and would later be recognized by the award of another commissioner's commendation.

Observations on Attilio were of little use, but Margaret Heald made contact with a prostitute's maid whom she met in a small café just off Oxford Street and who told Miss Heald that Attilio was living off the immoral earnings of a former dressmaker. It was a shocking story, even by Messina standards.

The dressmaker – her name was Edna Kallman, aged twenty-nine – had been walking home along the Edgware Road one night in 1947 when Attilio Messina pulled up in his car and offered her a lift. Separated from her husband, and living in a two-room flat in Kilburn, she accepted both the lift and an invitation to dinner, and later she spent the night with the man she initially knew as 'Pierre' in a flat at Winchester Court, Kensington Church Street.

Two years after they had first met, Attilio set her up in a flat at Egerton Gardens, Knightsbridge, where she was kept as a virtual prisoner for three months and where he told her she would be trained by someone to make easy money as a prostitute. The 'someone' was none other than Robina Dixon Torrance.

Initially, Edna worked as a prostitute from one of the Messina flats in Shepherd Market, followed by other addresses at King's Yard and New Bond Street. Each night, she returned to the Egerton Gardens flat, to where other girls had been brought. Describing Attilio's behaviour, she would later say:

> The first girl was there for about six days. I heard him hit her and I heard her crying. He said he was putting her out. She immediately packed and left.
>
> I had had a really good hiding in Egerton Gardens. I was absolutely terrified of him; that he would put me out in the street in my slippers and reduce me to nothing. He threatened that if I had any idea of getting away from him, he would cut my face. I had some nasty blows on the jaw which a doctor had to attend to.

She had initially earned £120 per week, but by 1959 her health had deteriorated to such an extent she was only making £50 per week, of which she was permitted to keep just £7 for her food and clothing. In addition, she was allowed free telephone calls and given a gold watch and a bracelet, a radio and a cheap fur coat. When a doctor advised her to take a month's rest, Attilio declared that this was 'rubbish' and not only ordered her back to work, but demanded that she worked harder. He derided her for her continuing ill-health and shouted, 'I could get a 17-year-old girl to work harder than you, and I could sleep with her as well.'

Attilio completely dominated her, making her work a beat so close to his premises that he was able to watch her from his window. Letters from Mrs Kallman's mother and stepfather were sent to Attilio's address so that he could intercept and read them first; her visits to them at their home in Derby were only permitted under his supervision.

On one occasion she had to call a police officer to eject a difficult client, and when Attilio heard about it he threatened to 'deal with her'. She was so panic-stricken that on 8 February she fled to Derby, where she stayed with a friend; but after Attilio saw her parents and explained that they'd had 'a silly row' he discovered where she was hiding. He sent Torrance to bring her back, but Mrs Kallman's friend kept her hidden. In the middle of the night, twelve years after she and Attilio had first met, she ran from the house on 20 February 1959, went to her parents and told them the whole story; providentially, she also wanted to talk to the police. She was able to tell them how much she had earned for Attilio during their liaison, and four days later, he was arrested.

CHAPTER 18

A Case of Procuration

A ttilio was seen in King Street, Hammersmith by Miss Heald and Du Rose, who said to him, 'Attilio Messina, you know who we are. I have something to say to you. Shall we go to your flat?'

Inside the flat, Du Rose continued, 'I have to arrest you for procuring Edna Kallman to become a common prostitute since 1947. It is also said that you have been handed £40,000 of her earnings by prostitution since that time and you will be charged with that offence.'

After being cautioned, Attilio replied, 'Edna Kallman? Who is she? I don't know anyone of that name. What is it all about?'

A search of the flat revealed a copy of Albert Londres' 1928 book about white slavery, *The Road to Buenos Ayres*. It appeared to be a Bible as far as Attilio was concerned; certain passages had been underlined in pencil and one chapter had been marked, 'The whole chapter worth reading twice'.

Taken to West End Central, he was charged with three offences: that on dates between 1947 and February 11 1959 in London he procured Edna Kallman to become a common prostitute; that on dates between August 1949 and December 31 1956, he knowingly lived, in London, wholly or in part on the earnings of prostitution; and that he knowingly lived wholly or in part on the earnings of prostitution on dates between January 1 1957 and February 11 1959. His response to these accusations was, 'It is fantastic. I have been framed. I cannot understand it. Tell me, what does procuring mean?'

When he appeared in the dock at Marlborough Street Magistrates' Court on 27 February 1959 he had been charged in the name of Raymond Maynard. The *Star* informed its readers, 'So crowded was the court that some of the public who wanted to get in had to be excluded', and there was indeed a great deal of publicity given to the case.

Du Rose asked for a remand in custody, which was opposed by Messina's barrister, David Tudor-Price (later His Honour Judge Tudor-Price QC), who asked Du Rose, 'Does Maynard have a furnished flat and an antiques business in Fulham, where he has been practising for seven years?'

'No, sir', replied Du Rose. 'He has a second-hand shop in Fulham which contains furniture which has been there for a considerable time. As far as I know, it has not been conducted as a business.'

In fact, Du Rose could have gone quite a bit further with his answer, stating that the bric-a-brac contained in that dump of a shop was covered in dust, the price tags were yellow and curled with age and there was no evidence to show that a sale had ever been made there; but he didn't, which allowed Tudor-Price to slip in, 'It is a matter of classification.' He then asked, 'Is it right that his nationality has been in dispute for seven years?'

'He has disputed it for seven years', replied Du Rose.

'On the other hand, so has the Home Office', stated the barrister. 'And the result has been that for seven long years he has reported once a week to the police station.'

'Yes, but there has been no dispute about his nationality as far as the Home Office is concerned', riposted Du Rose. 'They have said quite categorically that he is an alien.'

The Magistrate, Clyde Wilson, remanded the case until 4 March but nevertheless granted bail to Messina on his own recognizance of £2,000 plus two sureties of £1,000 each. Happily, those sureties were not forthcoming, and Attilio was carted off to Brixton prison that afternoon.

On the next appearance, Edna Kallman gave evidence that Attilio had told her that she should become a prostitute for between eighteen months to two years as a means to an end, after which 'they would have a life together'. She told the court, 'I was in Bond Street for eight years until February 8 this year. All that time I was earning money by prostitution – about £40,000. It was all handed over to the accused . . . I was absolutely terrified. There were always threats. He said if I ever had any ideas about getting away for him, he would cut my face.'

Other prostitutes – who were allowed to write down their names and addresses – gave evidence; one, dressed in black, wept as she told the court that she had met Attilio in 1943 or 1944 whilst she was waiting at a bus stop with a girlfriend. It was raining, and he stopped his car and offered them both a lift. Thereafter, she met him quite often and spent nights with him. She believed him to be a diamond merchant. She had returned home to the North of England but when she came back to London in 1953 she met Attilio again – coincidentally, once more at a bus stop – and they resumed their relationship. Taken in by his subtle flattery, she went to live with him at his flat at Rosehill Court, Morden – a very chancy business indeed, since Police Constables 251'W'

Peter Green and 266'V' Ray Brinsden were living at the same block of flats. Undaunted, Attilio suggested that he and his new *inamorata* might marry; ultimately, he persuaded her to become a prostitute. He introduced her to Edna Kallman, and the girl told the court, 'I met her at Bond Street. I was to stay at her flat for two or three days and she would introduce me to men until I knew how to go about things. I stayed only a few days.' She added, 'Edna was very kind and treated me well.'

A second woman, dressed in grey, said that when, in 1952, she was preparing to make a call from a public telephone box, Attilio drew up and she permitted him to make his call first. Afterwards, he offered her a lift and took her out to dinner. After several more meetings, she left her parents' home and she, too, went to live with him at his flat at Morden. Initially, he told her that he would get her a job in a sweetshop.

She knew him as 'Mr Maynard', until the day when he asked her to go to the wardrobe and get out a briefcase. He took out a long buff envelope which had written on it, 'The will of Attilio Messina'; she told the court that Attilio had said to her, 'Doesn't this mean anything to you?'

She replied, 'No – why, should it?'

His answer was, 'You must be greener than I thought you were.'

Three or four months later, Attilio took her to Edna's flat and told her, '[She] will teach you things', adding, 'Eventually, you will have your own flat and entertain a few very rich, well-known and influential people.' After a week, having earned £4 which she gave to Attilio, she left the flat, saying that she was frightened and that, 'I didn't want to do those things.'

Another girl told the court, 'For the first time in my life, I felt that someone wanted me. His voice was so soft, so ingratiating, I said to myself after our first meeting, "This man is a gentleman".'

A further witness – a friend of Mrs Kallman – was also permitted to write down her name and address and told the court that she had seen Mrs Kallman during March 1958 and that she was 'very sick and frightened . . . She was very distressed and had bruises on her knee and wrist. After that I continued to visit the flat more often than ever. I heard Messina yelling at Edna, using very abusive language and threatening to cut her up.'

She later saw Attilio at his flat at King's Court, and 'I told him she was a very sick and frightened girl.'

His reply was, 'Trouble. There is always trouble. One takes it in one's stride.'

The maid – who like the other witnesses was permitted to write down her name and address – gave particularly devastating evidence. She told the Bench that she started to work for Edna in 1949 at a flat in King's Yard, Mayfair; later, she met Attilio, whom she referred to as 'The Boss'.

'I was the maid for Edna and she was earning a living by prostitution', she said.

Oliver Nugent for the prosecution asked her, 'While you were at King's Yard, did you have anything to do with the money?'

'I collected the money until the end of the evening', replied the maid, 'and then it was handed back to Edna. The amount varied and it was anything from £10 to £30.'

After a short while both Edna and the maid moved to a new address in New Bond Street where, the maid said, matters continued exactly as before.

She was asked if she knew how Attilio treated Edna; to this, she replied, 'While I was in her presence there was nothing extraordinary, but several times I knew Edna had experienced beatings. The following day when I used to go in, she had bruises on her cheek and seemed to be very upset . . . I was reprimanded by the Boss once because I was told I was not helping her enough. One night in the car he asked me why Edna was not pulling her weight. He did not think she was making enough money. I said she was ill and needed a holiday.'

Nugent asked her, 'And did you ever hear him speaking to her when she was ill?'

'He called at her flat once and ordered a doctor to her', she replied. 'She remained in a bed about a week at that time.'

'Were there any other girls in that flat?' asked Nugent and was told, 'There were three in one year.'

'How long did they stay?'

'A very short time.'

'Did "the Boss" ever speak to you about any of those three girls?'

'No, he didn't speak to me about the girls, but I did everything I could to encourage them not to stay.'

With evidence like that, it was unsurprising that Attilio was committed in custody to stand his trial at the Old Bailey, after Du Rose had told the magistrate, 'The real objection to bail is that there is not the slightest doubt that witnesses will be interfered with.'

Four days later, Attilio made a spirited attempt for bail once more, this time at the Old Bailey before the Recorder of London, Sir Gerald Dodson. His barrister, David Tudor-Price, applied for the case to go over to the next session (commencing on 14 April) as there were many enquiries to be made, and the Recorder said that he would list it as soon as possible after Easter.

Alistair Morton, who appeared for the prosecution, said that bail was strongly opposed and called Detective Sergeant Dennis Welsh, who said, 'There is no doubt that if given the opportunity, the defendant will intimidate witnesses for the prosecution. The main witness, in fact, has disclosed that should the defendant be at large, she would herself "go missing", and we will have great difficulty in putting her before the court.'

From the dock, Attilio rather plaintively told the Recorder, 'I don't see why they should object to giving me bail. I have no passport and I have been reporting to the police for the last seven years. I have reported every week, regularly' – all to no avail.

'This application is opposed on grounds which cannot be ignored', said the Recorder, 'and this application must be refused.'

But when Attilio appeared before the Recorder again on 9 April 1959 he pleaded guilty to procuring Edna Kallman to become a prostitute and also to living on her immoral earnings; three other charges were not put to him.

Mr Mervyn Griffith-Jones (later, the Common Serjeant, Mr Justice Griffith-Jones, who had been junior counsel at the trial of Alfredo and would subsequently preside over the Mr Smith's Club murder trial featuring such luminaries as Eddie Richardson and 'Mad Frankie' Fraser), appeared for the prosecution and outlined the facts of the case. 'Exactly how these things develop in a woman's mind it is impossible to say', he said. 'No doubt to some extent she was infatuated with him but she was certainly cowed and subdued.'

Griffith-Jones described to the court how Edna had been 'incarcerated – that food was brought to her by Messina and she was ordered never to go out. That was the process of submission . . . Mrs Kallman was given rules to follow. She was to have no coloured clients and was not to talk to anyone but clients. She was also given a route by which to lead clients to her flat.'

The prosecution told the court that the maid was told that if Edna was with a client for longer than ten minutes, she was to knock on the bedroom door and 'get her out on the streets again'.

Robin Simpson said in mitigation that although his client had pleaded guilty, it did not mean that much of the evidence of Mrs Kallman was unchallenged. 'No sort of pressure was put on her to become a prostitute,' he said, adding, 'She could have walked out at any time she wished.' In addition, he said, 'There is no shred of proof other than Mrs Kallman's word to support the story of her £40,000 earnings and their disposal.'

They were words not likely to have endeared him to the 75-year-old Recorder, who could on occasion be persuaded to administer justice in quite a moderate way. Not, however, on this occasion, since he had read the witnesses' depositions.

> While many men make an honourable living in the merchandise of goods, you apparently for ten years have made a sumptuous but a revolting type of living from the suffering bodies of women you trapped or seduced and reduced to a form of slavery. It may be this woman Kallman was won over by your initial kindness. It was a false form of benevolence and was merely a cloak for your evil intentions. You have caused great suffering; it is only right and just that you should also suffer.

He then sentenced Attilio to four years' imprisonment and added a recommendation for deportation after Du Rose had informed him that there was no doubt he was an Italian subject. The Recorder added that it was up to the Home Office to decide whether or not to release him earlier so that the deportation could be carried out sooner.

Attilio's fortune was estimated at between £30,000 and £50,000, and it was said that he had the leases of forty properties in Mayfair with a prostitute in each of them. But now, this man who polished his nails three times a day and left the Old Bailey in an immaculately cut grey lounge suit was about to change his apparel for something more drab and, as a convicted prisoner, to earn just 1s 10d per day.

One week after Attilio's sentence the matter was raised in the House of Commons when Dr Donald Johnson, Conservative MP for Carlisle, asked the Home Secretary, Richard Austen 'Rab' Butler (later Baron Butler of Saffron Walden KG, CH, MP) how it was that Attilio had lived in England for twenty-five years as an Italian citizen and why he had not been deported following his conviction at Bow Street in 1951 when it was revealed that he was not entitled to British nationality.

'A deportation order was made against him at that time but proved unenforceable because the Italian Government did not then recognize him as an Italian national', replied Butler. 'I understand they are now prepared to do so, and I am giving urgent consideration to the question of his deportation.'

The rather fiery Labour MP for Easington, Emanuel Shinwell (later Lord Shinwell CH, PC) told Butler, 'The Home Secretary will exercise great wisdom if, instead of maintaining this criminal at public expense, he gets rid of him at once.'

Butler – as befitted someone who had enthusiastically advocated appeasement with Nazi Germany during 1938–1939 – rather wetly replied, 'I am not surprised to hear that reaction and it will be one of the things I will consider.'

Attilio obtained the maximum remission and on 17 November 1961, now aged fifty-one, was collected by police as he left Wandsworth prison and driven to London airport. There was a deputation waiting to see him off: eight officials from the Foreign Office, the Home Office, the Aliens Department and Special Branch. As he strolled across the tarmac, smartly dressed in a trilby and overcoat to protect him from a chilly British winter's morning, and boarded the waiting plane, Flight 206 to Rome, the assembled officials breathed a collective sigh of relief.

Upon his arrival, Italian police officials stated, 'We are not detaining him. There is no reason to do so.'

To this, Attilio, like the British deputation who had seen him leave, also expelled a sigh of relief, together with the comment, 'Thank God I am free.'

He settled down at 12 Via Privata Tivoli, San Remo, but before we bid adieu to him, there are two outstanding matters.

*

On the same day that Attilio was sent down, so was an equally well known character, by the same judge.

Reginald Kray, then aged twenty-five, was one of a three-man gang who had been found guilty of demanding money with menaces. He was fortunate to receive a lenient eighteen-month sentence from the Recorder. As his trial finished, so Attilio stood in the dock, since his was a plea of guilty.

As Reg and Attilio waited to be transported to Wandsworth prison to commence their sentences they apparently fell into conversation. In his unintentionally hilarious and wildly inaccurate memoirs Reg recounted that he was in that situation 'despite the fact I was innocent'; but he had found a soul mate in his companion, who informed him that he, too, was innocent and that 'prostitutes had given perjured evidence against him to gain a conviction'. Attilio obviously neglected to mention that he'd pleaded guilty, but his words must have carried a great deal of persuasion because, as Reg stated, 'I genuinely believed that he was innocent on this particular charge, even if he was a professional ponce.' That was quite all right, since he told Reg (as did others) that living off a woman was not immoral in Malta. It was, of course, an offence to live off immoral earnings in Malta; it always has been.

Reg's words would have carried more weight if he had not mentioned in one book that he believed it was Carmelo he was talking to and, further, that in 1967 Carmelo invited the Kray twins to Malta, where he had a proposition for them. This would have presented certain difficulties because Carmelo had died eight years previously. In another book he said he believed that he had shared the prison van with Eugenio, and in yet another Reg managed to reduce his own sentence from eighteen months to six.

None of which really matters. Hysterical Kray fans ('I loved the Krays', said one who had never met them) will be pleased to hear that Reg told some of the inmates at Wandsworth to 'look out' for Carmelo/Eugenio/Attilio because, well, that's the way Reg was. Not because he'd received a nice few bob from Attilio to do so.

*

The second matter arose when the body of a recluse named Raymond Maynard was found in the garage of his home in Oxford in April 2009; he had died two months previously on 5 February.

The former psychiatric nurse and self-trained concert pianist was aged seventy when he died, having been born on 21 April 1938 in Chelsea; a highly bizarre character, he was also known as Raymond Torrance, Count Ravenscastle and Lord Ravenscastle. He cut a strange figure, with his tattooed eyebrows and dressed in a shellsuit, and he spent much of his time writing anti-government pamphlets. He had left his house, 'Wuthering Heights' in Foxcombe Road, which was valued at £450,000, to some former patients, before moving into his garage. Unsurprisingly, he had no known close family.

But he did have some more distant relatives, and they approached probate researchers to discover who his legacy of £250,000 should go to. They discovered two birth certificates for Raymond: the first had no father's name on it, and the second – dated fifteen years later – revealed that his father's name was George Maynard aka Attilio Messina and that his mother was one Robina Dickson Torrance.

Torrance had a sister, Isabella, whose granddaughter, Mrs Elsie Powers, had no knowledge of her infamous relations. Mrs Powers, who lives in Motherwell, received a share in the estate – as did twenty-three Scottish cousins.

And now we really can bid farewell to two of the Messina family's most repellent members: Torrance, who died at Henley on 30 August 1992, and her paramour, Attilio, who departed this earth on 17 May 1991 at Costaraniera, Italy.

CHAPTER 19

Arrests in Belgium

W e now have to go back in time to see how the rest of the Messina clan were faring.

Eugenio and Carmelo had been stripped of their British citizenship – and not before time – since it was finally established (thanks to a great deal of help from Duncan Webb) that their births had been registered with the Italian authorities. Since that had occurred respectively forty-four and thirty-seven years previously, the British Government had to bear a great deal of responsibility for the wave of organized prostitution which swept the capital during the intervening years. And when the authorities refused to renew Eugenio's passport, his wife Andrée lost her British citizenship and was deported.

But in November 1953 something happened which prompted the brothers to think that Paris was not the safe haven that they had previously thought. Having spent an entertaining evening in a Parisian night club with his latest attraction, a girl named Eliane, Eugenio left in the early hours of the morning, whereupon he was unceremoniously grabbed by a group of men, shoved into a waiting car and driven off.

It was Eugenio's habit to telephone Marthe Watts practically every day; when, after two days, she had heard nothing from him, she telephoned Carmelo and Salvatore, but they, too, had had no contact with him.

The thought in all their minds was, had the French authorities arrested him? The *Sûreté* might not have, but what had been known as the *Deuxième Bureau* (and since the Second World War had been renamed *Service de documentation extérieure et de contre-espionnage* or *SDECE* – Foreign Documentation and Counter-Espionage Service) certainly could have done. This would have been a *coup de maître* for everyone: the French would have been rid of one exceedingly slimy character and, having dumped Eugenio like a tied-up parcel on a lonely British airfield, they would have received innumerable brownie points from their British counterparts who, if they failed to proffer any fresh charges against him, could certainly have him deported once and for all.

Marthe Watts and another girl, Augustine, flew to Paris; but Eugenio had still not arrived back at his apartment. It may have crossed Marthe's mind to knock on the door of 36 Quai des Orfèvres and ask any member of the *Police Judiciare*, 'Excuse me, but have you by any chance nicked a revoltingly sleazy *souteneur* who might answer to the name of Eugenio Messina?' But before that could happen, Eugenio turned up the following day.

And what a state he was in; shocked and covered in bruises, he told Marthe that he had been kidnapped by gangsters who had demanded a ransom of £15,000 for his release. He had eventually bartered his freedom for £2,000. Marthe sent for his brother and stayed with the two of them long enough for them to realize that Eugenio's attackers might return, possibly to confront them both, so they all departed with considerable haste for the sanctuary of Switzerland.

There is a school of thought which suggests that Duncan Webb, who had mixed with an unsavoury bunch of thugs during his quest for the brothers in Europe, might have been behind the attack. The Sicilian gang whom Webb had met in Genoa stated that they were very interested in obtaining protection money from the Messinas, and Webb had piously informed them, in the spirit of his habitual 'I made my excuses and left', that this was not a course of action to be recommended. But was there any truth in that? Who knows? Who, in fact, cares?

But in Eugenio's and Carmelo's rush to get away, even their belongings were left behind, and two of the Messina women came to pack the brothers' bags and put everything else into storage, before joining them at their new, temporary headquarters in Lausanne.

There was a falling-out between Marthe and Eugenio in June 1954 and she returned to London. It is possible that Eugenio felt that his split with Marthe was permanent, since he ensured that the house at 36 Shepherd Market which had been purchased in her name was now transferred to his.

He did not have the same reservations regarding Augustine, the girl who had accompanied Marthe to France on the rescue mission. She had been born Augustine Verlet and she had been working as a waitress in a Parisian restaurant when Eugenio met her, having beaten a hasty retreat to France following the *People*'s revelations. She arrived in London in 1951 and was promptly married to one Frederick Johans, who worked as a barman in a hotel in Charing Cross Road, a ceremony for which he was paid the princely sum of £35. As well as becoming Mrs Johans, she was additionally known as *La Souris* – 'The Mouse'. Her nickname would be of considerable interest later on.

Eugenio decided to move from Switzerland to Belgium, where certain aspects of the law governing prostitution were slightly more relaxed than elsewhere. During the German occupation of Belgium during the First World War, to try to prevent the spread of sexually transmitted diseases amongst their troops, the German authorities strictly regulated prostitutes' activities and insisted that they underwent regular health checks. Following on from the cessation of hostilities, prostitution was controlled by the municipalities and it became mandatory once more for prostitutes to be registered and to receive regular health checks. However, Isabelle Blume, a left-wing politician, teacher and a feminist who was active in women's rights, felt that this regulatory regime was discriminatory towards women. In 1946 a federal law was passed which decreed that prostitution was not prohibited and neither was paying for sexual services. Nonetheless, there was an aspect of the legislation which was less lenient regarding men, as Eugenio would later discover.

Initially, Eugenio stayed in a Brussels hotel, but before long he purchased an apartment at 177 Avenue Louise (or Louizalaan). This thoroughfare runs for 1½ miles between Place Louise and the Bois de la Cambre and is one of the most prestigious and expensive streets in Belgium's capital. He also ensured that the sale was in the name of Augustine Johan, who applied for, and got, a residence permit in Belgium. The reason for this was that any enquiries made with the British police regarding her suitability to become a Belgian resident would have revealed no convictions for soliciting; her customers had always been invited to one of the Messinas' apartments. So the beautifully spacious ten-bedroom flat in the Avenue Louise was filled with the furniture from Stafford Street which had been kept in storage, a maid was brought in for domestic purposes, a string of the Messina girls from London started visiting and Eugenio made a whole new bunch of attractive acquaintances for possible shipment to England.

However, Augustine's circumstances were about to change. On 10 February 1954 she purchased a house at 39 Curzon Street, Mayfair – she later 'sold' it to Eugenio on 10 October 1954 for £10,000 and ran it as a brothel. On 27 August 1955 the police raided the premises and Augustine was fined £25 for keeping a brothel; however, a search of a safe in the house, in the presence of five of the prostitutes, revealed the sum of £14,000. Augustine moved on to another Messina property at 7 Stafford Street, and 39 Curzon Street was taken over by Alfredo's mistress, Hermione Hindin; Marthe Watts (who had obviously resolved her and

Eugenio's differences) moved into the basement, whereupon it was business as usual.

The authorities were certainly aware that those two addresses, as well as those situated at 12 Chesterfield Street and 36 Shepherd Market, had been purchased by the Messinas since they had fled England four years earlier, as they were of the addresses in Paris, Hamburg and Vienna where the earnings of those establishments had been sent; but of course, whilst the likes of Augustine Johans could be fined a paltry £25 for brothel-keeping, the Messinas appeared to be bomb-proof.

In 1955 Eugenio had taken Marthe Watts to a sanatorium at Schönberg, near Fribourg in Germany, which would have provided a panoramic outlook over the Black Forest mountains, had not a heavy snowfall obliterated the view. Eugenio brought Marthe back to Belgium, where at Sisselles near Bruges a doctor's examination revealed that she had a collapsed lung. An operation was successfully carried out, and she convalesced in a sanatorium before returning to London.

In the meantime, it was said that Carmelo, using the alias of Gino Miller, was going to be the subject of a sting operation by Interpol for dealing in heroin; but for whatever reason – probably ineptitude on behalf of the authorities – an arrest failed to materialize.

Back in Belgium, Eugenio had obtained another British passport, No. 518230, this one in the name of Alexander Miller, which described him as being a merchant, born in Edinburgh; this had been issued in London. In addition, there was another which had been issued in Brazil and referred to him as Eugene de Bono. Carmelo, too, acquired other passports, one which described him as a Cuban national named Carlos Marino and another Turkish passport in the name of Carlos Moreno; and both men made trips to England completely undetected by the British authorities.

But not, however, by the Belgians. Their downfall came about because the brothers were initially believed to be East German spies. This was because they were attempting to import girls from Eastern Germany; telephone operators in Brussels realized that frequent telephone calls were being made from the Avenue Louise apartment to addresses in Communist-controlled East Germany and, believing (for the wrong reasons) that something was amiss, patriotically informed the authorities.

Robert de Foy, *Administrateur Général* of the Belgian State Security Service, *Sûreté de l'État* (SE), authorized telephone intercepts on the apartment's telephone, and counter-intelligence operatives got to work.

They soon discovered that the steamy telephone calls were nothing to with breaching state security and everything to do with procuration, and they passed their findings on to the Belgian CID.

The tall, bespectacled Belgian Police Commissioner, Anton Cuppens, discovered two matters of interest – first, that the brothers were indeed making journeys to England and second – and more importantly – that Belgian girls were disappearing from their homes.

Cuppens got to work; when Carmelo drove from France into Belgium in a Mercedes on 28 July 1955, that fact was noted. Individually and collectively, the brothers became part of an intense surveillance operation; they were followed from tea dances to night clubs and luxury apartments, until they arrived at the coastal town of Knokke-le-Zoute, where Eugenio took a suite at the very expensive hotel, Residence Albert, under one of his aliases. It was a town full of entertainment, including nightclubs, plus the Casino Mascotte and the Grand Casino Knokke.

It was there in Zoute on 30 July 1955 that Marthe Watts saw Eugenio at his hotel to tell him that she really had finished with him; perhaps she could see the writing on the wall. It is highly likely that, a few weeks later, Eugenio was in London using one of his false passports at the time of the police raid (or shortly afterwards) at 39 Curzon Street. The reason may have been the contents of the safe there. But if that were so, the police presence may have frightened him off and he made himself scarce, because two days later, he stepped off the boat from Dover at Ostend. From there he was followed, and at three minutes after midnight on 30 August the Belgian police swooped on Eugenio and Carmelo at Knokke-le-Zoute's luxury nightclub, the Horse's Neck. The brothers were found drinking champagne in the company of two glamorous women, a Belgian girl named Marie-Jeanne David and a French girl, Dominique Versini; the Messinas were also in possession of false passports which prompted the Belgian police to decide that this warranted further investigation.

Matters were not helped by the fact that both brothers were also in possession of loaded firearms. When they had previously crossed borders they had been astute enough to ensure that whatever weapons they possessed were safely ensconced in the handbags of their attractive escorts. The girls' ability to flirtatiously flutter their eyelashes at border guards ensured that their reticules were not searched, but the brothers had obviously thought that such legerdemain was not necessary in The Horse's Neck.

They were incarcerated in the fortress-style prison at Bruges before being driven, as two of a group of nine prisoners, to the grey stone Magistrates' Court, one mile away, just off the medieval City Square. It was necessary to convey them in a green post office van – no other transport was available – and they were led up a winding staircase and into a tiny book-lined office. Manacled to gendarmes who carried both revolvers and truncheons, the bothers were smartly dressed: Eugenio in a sober grey suit and wearing sunglasses, Carmelo in a smart brown suit; and as ushers shouted, *'L'affaire Messina!'* the examining magistrate, Judge Robert Claeys, entered and the preliminary hearing got underway.

The court was told that, apart from the false passports and the two firearms found in their possession when the brothers were arrested, two more loaded firearms were found at their suite at the Residence Albert, one in Eugenio's suitcase, the other in Carmelo's.

Maître Jose Van Der Veeren, who had been appointed by English solicitors to represent both brothers, asked for bail 'at any price' – this was knocked into touch by Judge Claeys, who told the court, 'It is essential they be kept in custody so that investigations can continue unhindered.'

Lawyer Van Der Veeren made a further, desperate plea for bail for Carmelo on the grounds that he was ill, suffering with heart trouble. His words fell on the unsympathetic ears of the Court President, Etienne Eeman, who curtly replied, 'He can be treated in the prison infirmary.'

The brothers were remanded in custody for a month, and having returned them to the fortress, the post van resumed its more usual activity of collecting and delivering the mail. The prison fare that evening was stewed pork and mashed potatoes, but not for these two celebrated residents.

The impudent message from the brothers was, 'We find Belgian prisons more comfortable than the British; and definitely better than other continental jails. We are extremely well treated and friends have sent us clothing, underwear and other luxuries.'

The messenger who brought that communication was their lawyer, Maître Van Der Veeren, who, when asked what these 'other luxuries' were, stated, 'The Messina brothers have money, you know. Friends bring them champagne, lobster and other delicacies.'

Those cocksure comments would have endeared them to 'The Queens of Maddox Street' but not, unfortunately, to the Belgium authorities.

Months went by; then on 16 March 1956 came their seventh and final remand at the courthouse at Bruges. On 26 March they would be formally indicted and they would be brought to trial on 16 April.

At their arraignment, the Court's President, Judge Leo Soenen, questioned the brothers. Addressing Eugenio, he asked, 'You were born in Alexandria?'

'No', replied Eugenio, mendaciously. 'In Sao Paulo, in Brazil', adding that he was domiciled in Frankfurt, Germany. The reason for his untruthfulness regarding his birth place was that if the Belgian authorities decided at any time to deport him, he could plead that he was Brazilian, the country to which he wished to be banished and which, coincidentally, did not have an extradition treaty with England.

Turning to Carmelo, Judge Soenen asked, 'You were born in Sao Paulo?' and received the answer, 'No, I was born in Alexandria.'

Judge Claeys stated he had built his case on evidence gathered from the Belgian, French and Italian police. He had hoped, he added, to have had an input from the British police, but although Belgian police officers had visited London (and were still there), nothing was forthcoming from the British authorities. In the event, Claeys told the court, it didn't really matter. He had sufficient evidence and did not now require Scotland Yard's assistance.

What on earth was going on? The Yard were aware that for seven months the brothers had been in custody. They had been unable to arrest them; surely this would be an ideal opportunity to give whatever assistance they could to the Belgian authorities, who had succeeded where they had failed? Not only that, but it would be completely cost-effective; England would be spared the cost of a trial, and the fares and expenses of British officers attending the court would be met by the Belgian authorities.

For whatever reason, several matters now changed. The Belgian prosecutors had demanded the attendance of seven women at the trial; five of them answered, but now two of them, Elizabeth de Meester and Marie Therese Vervaecke, who had made written statements to the authorities, refused to attend. Not only that, they had vanished; the police believed they had left the country. It weakened their very strong case; how many more women would refuse to come to the trial? Next, two Scotland Yard officers *would* attend the trial. Whether this was at the insistence of the Belgian Foreign office or because of a softening of policy at the Home Office is not known. Lastly, the venue of the trial was altered. The court in Bruges used Flemish as its working language, which the brothers claimed not to understand. Their lawyers successfully argued that their trial should be moved to an equivalent court at Tournai, which used either Flemish or French, and after a 28-minute adjournment, Judge Soenen agreed.

The brothers left the courtroom for the last time at 9.45 that morning. For reasons best known to himself, the head of the gendarme guard told the press, 'They are such perfect gentlemen.' Drip.

There we can leave the brothers for the next three months. Apart from stuffing themselves silly with chicken à la mode and other delicacies brought in by their adoring entourage, there wasn't anything – apart from cooking up a defence to the charges – to concern us.

Something far more interesting was happening 199 miles away, across the Channel. It was occurring in London and it was that one thing which prompts politicians to change their underwear more often than would be thought strictly necessary; it is called 'Public Disquiet'.

CHAPTER 20

Questions in the House

This affair had really started as an offshoot, a year previously, of the trial of the crooked cop Robertson, the dodgy solicitor Canter and their involvement with Tony Micallef; this has been dealt with in Chapter 14.

There had been a report in the 17 November 1955 edition of the *Daily Mail* which stated that as a result of Superintendent Hannam's enquiries into the investigation of Robertson & Co he had submitted a confidential report to the Commissioner, Sir John Nott-Bower. This report allegedly contained details of forty men serving prison sentences who were associated with night-life in London's West End whom Hannam had interviewed; and as a result, it was suggested that there was widespread corruption amongst the men of West End Central, where some constables were receiving bribes of up to £60 per week for tipping off club owners of impending raids, watering down evidence and arranging a rota system for arresting prostitutes for soliciting. If that allegation was true, and since a constable's weekly wage at that time was £10 16s 7d, any of the West End Central personnel who were that way inclined must have felt that copping six times their weekly pay was well worth having.

That was quite enough to divert the commissioner from his planned whist drive; the same afternoon, he went straight to West End Central, jumped up on to a table in the canteen and addressed the massed personnel. The following day, 18 November, in the House of Commons, James Callaghan, Labour MP for Cardiff South-east (and later Lord Callaghan of Cardiff KG, PC) asked Sir Hugh Lucas-Tooth, Under Secretary of State for the Home Office (who was standing in for the Home Secretary), for a statement regarding the matter. Fortunately, the commissioner had already forwarded such a statement to him. As he informed the house:

> The general accusations made in certain quarters about the police are unwarranted and unsubstantiated. The Metropolitan Police are a fine and conscientious body of men and women whose good relations with the public

whom they serve might be impaired by irresponsible charges made against them. There is no truth whatever in a suggestion that 450 men, which practically constitutes the whole establishment of 'C' Division, may be transferred from that Division. No transfers from 'C' Division are in contemplation. Certain matters which may lead to disciplinary or criminal proceedings are under rigorous investigation; and it would not be proper . . . to comment on them in any way.

That appeared to appease Callaghan, but more was to come. The same day, the Chief Metropolitan Magistrate, Sir Laurence Dunne, in the company of his brother magistrates, Mr Bertram Reece, Mr R. H. Blundell and Mr Cecil Campion, made a statement from the bench at Bow Street Magistrates' Court in which he too drew attention to the piece in the *Daily Mail*:

I feel it would be wrong to allow this article to pass without comment . . . its effect cannot be other than to sap the confidence of the public in law enforcement, both outside, and perhaps of even greater importance, inside this court . . . The writer pretends to have inside knowledge of – and to reproduce – the matter in a report submitted by Superintendent Hannam to the commissioner. I am satisfied that in so far as this article pretends to reproduce the gravamen of that report, it is utterly misleading and most mischievous . . . I believe that the only matters of fact in that article are that Superintendent Hannam has indeed submitted a report and that that report does deal with certain aspects of what is compendiously known as vice in the West End . . . I hope it may help to allay any sense of public unease if I say that my brother magistrates and I retain complete confidence in the probity of the Metropolitan Police as a Force and in view of the unwarranted attack upon them, of 'C' Division, in particular.

So that was that, until about three weeks later, when the Home Secretary, Major Lloyd-George (later Major the Right Honourable Viscount Tenby TD, PC), was pressed by Emmanuel Shinwell, Labour MP for Easington, and Arthur Lewis, Labour MP for West Ham North, to hold a public enquiry into the goings-on at West End Central; it was Shinwell who used the words 'public disquiet'.

Refusing a public enquiry, the Home Secretary told Lewis that 'he talked as though he believed the recent statement made in a newspaper about 'C' Division', which was undoubtedly the case. A deeply unpleasant character, in 1983 Lewis would be de-selected by his constituency.

But the arrest of the Messina brothers in Belgium the previous year was sufficient for the *Daily Mirror* to take up the cudgels in respect of public tranquillity. For six weeks the newspaper had been promoting a 'clean up London' campaign, and the headlines for the 20 June 1956 edition roared, 'AT LAST! A MOVE TO CLEAN UP THE SHOCKING CITY', and it stated that the following day, questions would be raised in the House by three Members of Parliament.

They were. The case involving the slashing of Jack Spot took prominence – quite rightly – with allegations of 'blatant perjury' and tales of how gangs of up to a dozen thugs swaggered about outside the Old Bailey in an attempt to intimidate witnesses; this was trumpeted in the paper's blazing comment: 'WHEN WILL THESE COWARDLY HOODLUMS BE CURBED?'

But next came the Messinas. Major Richard Rapier Stokes MC & Bar, *Croix de Guerre*, MP for Ipswich, had been doing his homework, no error there. He bombarded the Home Secretary with facts regarding the addresses owned by the Messinas and used by prostitutes, the dates when they had been acquired, the payments the Messinas were still receiving and details of twenty-two of the prostitutes under their control.

Referring to the brothers, the Home Secretary said rather vaguely, 'I think two of them left this country four years ago', which sounded rather wet and, of course, was. When he said in, one supposes, an attempt at humour, 'I should not like to tell the House the amount of information we have at Scotland Yard about these people', it brought forth cries from the floor, 'What are you doing about it?'

Allegations of ineffectiveness in respect of law and order are sufficient to put any Home Secretary on his mettle; the answer, then as now, is to hit back at the accusers with statistics, and Major Lloyd-George was able to inform the House that arrests for soliciting in the West End had risen from 4,969 in 1951 to 7,230 in 1955. Indeed, in the same period, arrests for the whole of the Metropolitan Police in respect of soliciting had risen from 7,566 to 11,173, and arrests for men living on the immoral earnings of prostitutes had risen from 57 to 91.

He bolstered these statistics by mentioning that, in addition to the normal police coverage in the West End, there were fourteen two-man patrols to deal with rowdyism and prostitution, plus two patrols of women police between 3.30 pm and 7.30 am.

Responding to accusations that no action was taken against the Messinas after Augustine Johans was convicted for brothel-keeping, the Home Secretary said:

> If nothing is done about premises which are known to be occupied by prostitutes, it is quite wrong to assume that the police are blind or negligent. The police cannot do anything unless there is something to be done about. No police action could have been taken in this case. Mrs Johans was fined for keeping a brothel but there is no action the police can take against these two men . . . there is no evidence; suspicion is one thing and certainty, another. In this case, there was no evidence before the police of a breach of the law.

But Major Stokes was not going to let the matter drop. 'The evidence I have is practically conclusive', he stated. 'I put these questions down not only to draw attention to the Messina brothers but also to the fact that the whole of the West End is permeated by gangs of this kind who are exploiting prostitution to their own ends and not for the purpose for which it is intended' – which brought loud laughter from the floor.

To cheers (which may have been ironic, if not downright derisive), the Home Secretary replied that he would avail himself of Major Stokes' help and get what information he could.

It wasn't very much. On 2 July, in answer to further questions in the House, the Home Secretary referred to the Wolfenden Committee and doubted that their report would be ready before the end of the year. Whilst the committee was aware that he was anxious to have the report as soon as possible, 'it would be a mistake to hurry them into snap decisions'. He referred to two of the premises which were being used as brothels, saying that neighbours had got an injunction to prevent the use of them by prostitutes but that the police were satisfied that there was no case at present for proceedings in relation to them.

Newspapers other than the *Daily Mirror* were now taking up the cudgels. The Canadian-born Sir Arthur Beverley Baxter FRSL, Conservative MP – during service with the Royal Engineers in the First World War he stated that he had received no decorations due to 'neither being sufficiently forward, nor far enough back' – who had worked for the *Daily Express* and had been a theatre critic for the *Evening Standard*, now made his contribution, mentioning how

Chicago had brought down the reign of Al Capone by charging him with income-tax evasion and suggesting that in the absence of new legislation the present situation might be addressed in a similar fashion:

> Suppose we have a gentleman in Soho with a house in which there are five, six or seven girls, all in different rooms – cannot we have a statement where his earnings come from?
>
> I have some friends living in Bayswater, just off Hyde Park, and they tell me that practically every night – and I have seen it for myself – up comes a car with a couple of men who take money from the prostitutes in that area.
>
> There are screams, quarrels, blows. That is the regular technique. But apparently, that is not regarded as 'causing a disturbance'.
>
> The other night, I walked up Park Lane to Marble Arch . . . These women were drawn up like a guard of honour – or dishonour – three yards apart. Was there any doubt of their purpose? But these women, according to our quaint laws, are not causing a disturbance.
>
> We love London, but its streets are the most disgraceful in the world. I do not pretend that New York is a model of morality but you simply never see a prostitute plying her trade there. Even Paris, so long hailed as the gay city – you don't see it there, either.

The Home Office's Parliamentary Secretary, William Francis Deedes, the Conservative MP for Ashford (and later Baron Deedes KBE, MC, PC), shied away from Sir Beverley's Al Capone-style suggestions when he told the House, 'No one would attempt to defend the law as it stands. Nor do I think the House would accept any serious change in the law before the Wolfenden Committee reports.'

But John Hall, Conservative MP for Wycombe (later Sir Frederick John Frank Hall OBE, TD), backed up Sir Beverley's condemnation, saying, 'I live not very far from Hyde Park and the situation there is such that I cannot allow my young daughter to walk there unattended.'

Back now, to the Home Secretary who went on to say:

> It is all very well to say the streets of London must be cleaned up and vice must be put down. The House, rightly, would be quick to criticise me if the police began

arresting people against whom they could bring no charge, or if I interfered with activities which, although possibly morally obnoxious, were not criminal. Solicitation is only an offence if it annoys a pedestrian, passer-by or resident. The police cannot arrest a prostitute merely for being on the street and to get proof of annoyance is not the easiest task. It is often assumed that if you drive prostitutes off the streets you solve the problem of prostitution. But unless you remove the demand (and I should be interested in suggestions about how that is to be done) prostitution will go on in some form. It would be premature and unwise to legislate on any aspect of the subject until the committee's report has been studied.

The Home Secretary concluded by saying that the establishment of West End Central at the time he was speaking would reach 670 (a 50 per cent increase on the previous year), and on the subject of gangs – he was referring to the likes of Billy Hill, Albert Dimes and Jack Spot – there was no evidence to suggest that they were engaged in 'closely organized activities'; they were mainly engaged with clubs and betting. The fact that it was common knowledge, not only to the police but to the man in the street as well, that Albert Dimes had been part of a three-man gang involved in an affray at the Palm Beach Bottle Club when Eddie Fleischer had been stabbed to death, that Jack Spot had masterminded the attempt to rob London Airport employees of goods worth £237,900 and Billy Hill had been responsible for two major robberies which had netted him £332,500, appeared to be neither here nor there.

At any rate, the Home Secretary told the House, he was quite satisfied that the police were doing all that they could to put down violence, before in strident tones returning to his original theme: 'Nothing can do a greater disservice to that highly skilled and disciplined body of men, the Metropolitan Police, than to make sweeping allegations of bribery' – and, on that high note, he sat down.

Seconds later, the proceedings turned into farce. Bessie Braddock, the 56-year-old heavyweight Labour MP for Liverpool County Borough Council, stood up as the Home Secretary sat down, produced two unloaded air pistols and, pointing them at the ceiling, pulled the triggers which 'created two dull plops'. This brought censure from the Deputy Chairman, Sir Rhys Hopkin Morris QC, which increased considerably after she crossed the floor of the house to deposit the pistols besides the Government dispatch box. Told that she was out of order, Mrs Braddock replied, 'I know I am; I did it deliberately' and informed the bewildered members, 'You see, I have to startle the House before anyone does anything about anything.'

As a publicity stunt it was quite imaginative; but the fact remained that nobody was going to do anything about anything.

Now it's time to return to Belgium.

CHAPTER 21

Enter Scotland Yard

Tournai, situated on the River Scheldt in the province of Hainaut, 53 miles south-west of Brussels, is one of Belgium's oldest cities and an important cultural site. The picturesque Cathedral Notre Dame de Tournai possesses the oldest belfry in the country, and the city, like much of Belgium, is littered with attractive bars, cafés and restaurants which serve the population – amounting in 1956 to 68,000 – as well as tourists.

Two such visitors – albeit unwilling ones – arrived on 26 June 1956 by train, travelling rather ignominiously under armed guard in a third-class carriage. When the trial of the Messina brothers got underway in the courthouse, the court dossier containing the amassed evidence was twelve inches thick.

The brothers were charged with bearing false names, using false British and Cuban passports, falsification of official, trade and banking documents, possession of prohibited arms and incitement to prostitution.

Article 380 of the 1946 legislation regarding prostitution covered the offence of procuring through the provision of premises – such as running a brothel or providing a premises for prostitution for unjust gain; also aggravated pimping – using violence, threats, deception or exploitation of a vulnerable situation. It appeared that both brothers (Eugenio especially) fitted the bill perfectly.

Eugenio had been in possession of a safe deposit box; when Commissioner Cuppens of the Belgium police opened it, it contained the title deeds to four Mayfair properties which also revealed that the true owners of those properties were Eugenio de Bono and Edward Marshall, both aliases of Eugenio Messina.

This was damning evidence; the details of the buying and selling of the property at 39 Curzon Street have already been mentioned. At the time that Eugenio had acquired that property on 20 October 1955 he was already under arrest. But there was also 7 Stafford Street, bought by a Raymond Carter for £10,150 on 16 May 1951. A declaration of trust was made out to Edward Marshall (Eugenio) on 20 May 1951.

Then there was 36 Shepherd Market, purchased by Marthe Watts for £8,500 on 1 December 1951 and sold to Eugene de Bono (Eugenio) on 23 April 1954 for £8,500.

Lastly, there was 12 Chesterfield Street, which had been sold to Eugene de Bono for £11,250 on 16 June 1955 – six weeks before his arrest.

Unfortunately for Eugenio, the safe also contained jewellery, money and progress reports on the various girls written by both Augustine Johans, who had also rented the safety deposit box, and Marthe Watts. One report was addressed, in French, to 'My dear Gino', the diminutive of 'Eugenio', which was habitually used by Watts. It appeared that when Watts stated that 'she was through, for good' with Eugenio when she visited him at Zoute on 30 July 1955, she was not being entirely truthful.

With justification, Watts wrote that 'business was good at "Staff",' the codename for the Stafford Street premises; the girls were referred to by their initials.

One of the reports featured Marie Therese Vervaecke, a 24-year-old former nurse from Harelbecke; Eugenio – in his guise as Alexander Miller – had posed as her fiancé and asked her parents' permission to marry her. He told them he was an ardent Catholic and produced a picture of St Anthony (known for his love and devotion to the poor and the sick) which he said he always kept in his wallet. On 7 July 1954 she left for England telling her parents she was going to attend the London School of English to learn the language. Her parents became concerned because no wedding photographs appeared, and friends (not to mention her family) were astonished when instead of becoming Mrs Miller, Marie became Mrs George William Smith on 11 August 1954 – her husband vanished following the sham wedding and was seen no more. She collected her first conviction for soliciting prostitution on 1 November and became known as 'Thérèse'; in one of her progress reports to Eugenio, Marthe Watts revealed that she was 'One of the best girls we have', since over a six-week period she had earned Eugenio £2,368. She certainly was a brisk worker. Another was 'Betty', identified as Elizabeth McCann, who had earned £2,490. Three of the other girls, however, managed to make no more than £4,000 between them during the same period.

In the safe deposit box in Brussels there was a will signed by Eugenio in which he left 'Thérèse' £160,000 plus all of his property if she should still be living with him as his wife at the time of his death.

The sister of Thérèse later told the court that Thérèse was now a London prostitute and had recently telephoned her in order to ask her to say as little as possible in court.

Eugenio posed as a lovelorn fiancé once more in the case of a 21-year-old typist, Elisabeth de Meester; instead, she married James McCann in Paddington on 16 May 1955, and on 27 June, she acquired her first conviction as a prostitute.

It was hardly surprising that those two witnesses decided not to attend.

Three further girls – Marie-Jeanne David of Liège, Jacqueline Delport and Anne-Marie Bruyneel, both of Brussels – were, fortunately for them, unsuccessful candidates for Eugenio's and Carmelo's line of work.

Eugenio was represented by a divorced Parisian advocate, 39-year-old Mme Germaine Seneschal, who had been decorated by the French Resistance for wartime bravery in Paris. Assisting her were two attractive members of the Brussels Bar: blonde Simone Letroye and brunette Colette Remacle.

The Public Prosecutor, Monsieur Jean de Bettencourt, told the court (with a decided flair for hyperbole) that the brothers were known to 'the police of the whole world'. At the time of their arrest, Eugenio was carrying a loaded Mauser pistol which, the accused stated, was for his protection; and whilst Carmelo was also in possession of a firearm, he stated that he had declared it to the Belgian customs officials. Both denied being engaged in white slave traffic. Eugenio said that he earned his living as a dealer in, amongst other things, American surplus stocks but that he did not keep books recording this trade.

The court was told that the Messinas' technique was to strike up an acquaintance with a good-looking and probably susceptible girl, introduce her to their own opulent lifestyle and then seduce her, if necessary by the promise of marriage. Once the girl had become accustomed to a life of luxury, it would be suggested that she should go to England to take up prostitution.

'The methods used today are the same as applied twenty years ago', said the prosecutor, adding, 'Their father was known by the Egyptian police in 1908 as a wholesale dealer in human flesh and he formed an international company with his five sons acting as branch managers. As long as twenty years ago he (Eugenio) seduced a young girl in Charleroi. He was introduced to her family and friends and told them he was taking her to England to marry her. In fact, he married her off to somebody else.'

Two Scotland Yard officers attended to give evidence. One would have thought that Guy Mahon was the most suitable candidate for such a task, having such a wealth of information about the brothers, but no. Since leaving C1 Department in 1954 he had been promoted to detective chief superintendent and been posted to the Research and Planning Department, where he had lasted seven months. Then he became the head of the Flying Squad – this time his tenure was just four months.

This reason for this short-lived posting may have been that three weeks after his appointment, Billy Hill's gang carried out an audacious raid, stealing gold bullion valued at £45,500 from a lorry outside the KLM Dutch Airlines office in broad daylight. All of the gang members were impressively alibied, the best of all being Billy Hill, who at the time of the raid was in the company of Duncan Webb in the offices of the *People* dictating his memoirs for serialization in that newspaper. That was painful enough; matters worsened when, three weeks later, the newspaper concluded Hill's memoirs by explaining, in great detail, exactly how the KLM raid was carried out. The Squad officers undoubtedly breathed a sigh of relief when Mahon departed and the charismatic Reggie Spooner stepped into the breach.

Mahon's next appointment, to No. 2 District Headquarters, continued for a year; then at the time of the Tournai trial it was back to the Research and Planning Department; and it was evidently felt that he was too precious to be released from such a thrilling and demanding employment.

So one of the officers to arrive at the court house was Woman Detective Inspector Margaret Heald, who of course was an excellent choice; the other was Detective Sergeant Syd Gentle. He had joined the Metropolitan Police on 16 May 1938 and within a few weeks had been walking the streets of Soho as Police Constable 195'C'. Joining the CID, on 12 July 1948 he had been posted as a detective sergeant to the Flying Squad, where he collected four commissioner's commendations in quick succession for ability in cases of larceny, receiving and attempted warehousebreaking. He was also much in demand to act on information provided by the informants used by the ultra-secret post-war Ghost Squad, which resulted in arrests for a number of cases involving receiving stolen property. He had arrived at C1 Department on 4 July 1955.

Ken Davies, then a detective constable at Marylebone Lane police station, recalled Syd Gentle, saying, 'He was a quiet and thoughtful chap as I remember, and far more inclined to help you rather than give you a bollocking' – but sadly for them, that benevolence did not extend to the brothers Messina.

After Gentle produced documentation from the Yard's Criminal Record Office, Eugenio's counsel, Monsieur Van de Vereen, objected on the grounds that this was hearsay. Leaping to his feet, he cried, 'It is scandalous! The London police not only failed to convict the Messina brothers, but send people over here who know practically nothing about them. Do we have to take what they say as evidence?'

Not so, replied Gentle; he had personal experience of the Messinas and had once been offered a bribe of £200 by one of them. He knew their records, had never known any of them to have worked for a living, and yet they were all rich men. It could be proved, he said, that Eugenio and Carmelo owned property in London which had been used for the purposes of prostitution, and he had personally inspected records held by the Westminster County Council which proved that they paid the rates on those properties.

He went on to say, 'I know that they never did work of national importance during the war, as they should have done. They all have a lot of money. One of the brothers, Alfredo, has served two years' imprisonment for living on immoral earnings. The director of a Piccadilly jeweller's shop has told me he remembers Eugenio Messina taking various girls to his shop and to a branch in Bond Street at Christmas time and other times, and purchasing for them on their selection, pieces of jewellery. He had no records of these sales, as they were always paid for in cash.'

He told the court that there were hundreds of prostitutes in London, that he had interviewed ten girls, all of whom had convictions for prostitution, 'some of them as many as 250 times', and that amongst them were Augustine Johans, Marie Vervaecke and Elisabeth de Meester – but they, like the other seven, had 'no intention of coming to Belgium'.

Asked about Eugenio's nationality, Gentle replied, 'He was born in Egypt, obtained a British passport but is not now a British subject. If he comes back, he will be turned away as undesirable by the immigration authorities', adding, 'The same applies to his brother.'

Gentle was shown blank cheques which had been found in the safe deposit box. All of them had been signed by the girls, and this had been done to discourage them from leaving the Messinas' gang. In that event, the cheques would be filled in for an extravagant amount and presented for payment. The girls were told that should payment on the cheque default, they would then be prosecuted for passing a dud cheque and, following criminal charges, payment would be pursued through the civil courts to reimburse the brothers. Now Gentle was asked if he knew the names on the cheques.

'They are all prostitutes', he said.

The court's president, Robert Derbaix, asked Gentle if they were connected with the Messinas. 'Yes, some of them have lived with the Messina brothers', he replied. 'Others live in property owned by the Messinas. One girl lived at No. 5 Stafford Street; these premises belong to Carmelo Messina.'

'Is he the owner?' asked the president.

'He is the rateable occupier recorded by Westminster City Council', replied Gentle.

Mme Seneschal told the court, 'Sergeant Gentle has admitted there are hundreds of prostitutes in London. If prostitution is so rife, why haven't police taken drastic measures to stamp it out? And why didn't they get a conviction against the Messinas when they prosecuted them for living on immoral earnings?'

This was an unfortunate remark to make, because the brothers had never been prosecuted for living on immoral earnings in England. She had obviously been told that the brothers had been prosecuted in 1947, Eugenio for grievous bodily harm and Carmelo for attempted bribery, and had undoubtedly, and boastfully, been told by Eugenio, 'They couldn't make charges of immoral earnings stick'; but that wasn't the same thing as being unsuccessfully prosecuted.

Woman Detective Inspector Heald gave evidence that she had participated in the raid at the Curzon Street brothel and personally knew some of the prostitutes who worked in London whose names had been mentioned during the trial, also some of the men who had married them so that they would acquire British passports; she added that once the marriage formalities were over, the husbands were seen no more; these were nothing more, said Miss Heald, 'than marriages of convenience'.

Someone who provided devastating evidence was Anne-Marie Bruyneel, who told the court that she had met Eugenio at the *Grand Siècle* cabaret in Brussels, where he introduced himself as a British diamond merchant. A week later, in February 1955, she went to his flat in the Avenue Louise and became his mistress; he then suggested that she go to London to become a prostitute. She told the court, 'He told me I would be rich. I would not have to walk the streets but I would have a flat, a car, a fur coat and so on.'

By a stroke of good fortune, Anne-Marie's mother was one of the few women not to be taken in by Eugenio's charm and flattery; she asked him point-blank if he was 'a white slaver', something he had little difficulty in hotly denying. Nevertheless, her mother managed to prevent Anne-Marie from going to England.

The same applied to 20-year-old Marie-Jeanne David, who was one of the girls present at the brothers' arrest. Dressed smartly in a pale blue pork pie hat, a silver grey coat and high heeled shoes, she described in a quiet voice how she had met Eugenio in a Blankenberghe dance hall. He had told her that he earned £700 per week, and she had visited both brothers at their Brussels apartment. Asked if she had been offered a Mercedes sports car as a gift, she replied that she had been in a sports car which she thought was German. 'Carmelo told me that if I wanted a car like that one, I should have to earn it,' she replied, but added demurely, 'He did not say how I should earn it.'

She said that on the evening of their visit to The Horse's Neck, Eugenio had told her that she would have a life of luxury if she went to London for him. Unfortunately, before he could elaborate on what she would have to do to achieve this luxurious lifestyle, and how often and with whom, the police arrived.

CHAPTER 22

The Messinas Fight Back

Much of this testimony was strenuously denied by Eugenio in court. He described himself as both an estate agent and a dealer in stocks and shares. He was obliged to admit that Augustine Johans was an acquaintance – the safe deposit box was registered in her name and the code to open it were the letters S-O-U-R, the first four letters of Eugenio's nickname for her (*Souris*) – but of course, he denied knowing that she was a prostitute. He said he had known her since 1946, that she had no profession but at one time had been a secretary at the Portuguese Embassy in Paris.

'If she has no profession', said the prosecutor, 'how can she pay 15,000 francs (about £107) a month for her flat in Brussels?'

Amidst howls of laughter, Eugenio replied, 'She works for the secret service.'

Similarly, he denied knowing the professions of Elizabeth McCann or Marie-Thérèse Vervaecke, let alone that they were convicted prostitutes.

Turning his attention to Carmelo, the public prosecutor asked him, 'When you were arrested, why did you deny Eugene was your brother?'

'I was arrested in a nightclub in the early morning' – as though he felt that that was sufficient explanation.

'Why were you described as a bachelor on your forged passport?' asked Monsieur de Bettenbourg.

'I was married for such a short time that I did not think it was worth mentioning', replied Carmelo.

He then stated that the girls who were present at the time of their arrest were simply 'friends' and that he was not attempting to procure them.

The defence attempted by Eugenio's lawyer, Mme Seneschal, was almost as amusing as her client's explanation had been regarding Augustine Johan's profession. She tried to convince the court that the Mayfair premises were not brothels at all, but gambling saloons. In addition, she said, many countries tolerated prostitution, and prostitutes in London added to the state revenue since they were fined an average of £2 every fortnight.

Odd though this might have seemed, it did have a basis, if not in fact, certainly in practice. John Falconer, who was a station sergeant when he was posted to West End Central in 1957, told me:

> At that time, prostitution was flourishing with soliciting on the street commonplace. Among the well-known 'ladies' of the era were Marie Theresa Smith and Christine Tolan, who were run by the notorious Messina brothers. There was an unwritten law that prostitutes would plead guilty if they were allowed fourteen days between arrests. It used to annoy me to see PCs go up to prostitutes who were obviously soliciting and then take no action when the woman produced her last bail notice showing it was less than fourteen days since she was last arrested. On the occasions I was patrolling officer, I would arrest those two in Curzon Street or Shepherd Market. I did not worry about the fourteen-day syndrome and as a consequence, they always pleaded not guilty. They were always represented by solicitor Norman Beach. One day when I was station officer, Norman Beach came to the counter and said he wished to make a complaint about a PC who was preventing his clients from working! This was too much for Inspector Harry Morgan who had been listening. With a straight face, he said, 'Mr Beach, if you can prove that one of my officers has prevented your clients from going about their lawful business, I'll have the uniform off his back!'

In an impassioned speech, Mme Seneschal told the court:

> If the English authorities could bring no conviction against the Messinas, neither can this court. The English apparently regard the evidence as insufficient, but want Belgian justice to act where they cannot.
>
> The evidence against him is nothing but fake reports from across the Channel. He is a victim of British law.
>
> Prostitution is, always has been and always will be with us. In England as well as every other country, they are incapable of stamping it out. Known prostitutes are summoned every week or two in England, are fined and immediately return to their soliciting.

In fact, she did have a point.

Maître Maurice Garçon, representing Carmelo, stated that there was no evidence upon which to convict him for white slavery offences and that 'All this amounts to is that a few Belgian prostitutes have changed their addresses. What do the charges amount to? Nothing but brief and shady statements by Scotland Yard who seem to have a particular grudge against the Messina family.' There was no denying that Dominique Versini, who had been the second girl present at the time of the brothers' arrest, had become Carmelo's mistress in June 1955. However, he continued:

> We all know that summer is the most tiring season of the year. This girl told Carmelo that life was not very amusing with a man with whom she was at that time living, and she said she would like a holiday. Carmelo took her away for a holiday, but he did not try to persuade her to become a prostitute.
>
> I rather fancy that his brother Eugene is more fickle and often changes his girlfriends. But fickleness is not normally a reason for suspecting a man of being engaged in white slavery. In any event, it has nothing to do with my client.

Mme Seneschal's final words were less convincing and led to a great deal of amusement in court when she said, 'The morality of Eugene Messina is, admittedly, not of the highest quality.'

The case closed on 24 June with the public prosecutor asking for 'the maximum sentences'. He told the court, 'They are a public evil who should be removed from circulation', adding, 'I have no doubt they are millionaires.'

The brothers appeared upbeat about the proceedings, although rather disappointed that the court's judgement had not been delivered immediately. Eugenio boasted to reporters, 'I *do* own property in London. Let there be questions in Parliament – I don't care.'

After a week's deliberations, on 6 July the presiding judge delivered the court's decision and the sentences. Carmelo had admitted possessing a gun and a forged passport but denied ever trying to procure a girl for the purposes of prostitution and he was acquitted of that charge. The President told the court, 'We must be indulgent with him because he is in bad health', and then sentenced him to a total of ten months' imprisonment; this consisted of three months' imprisonment and a fine of 2,000 francs for bearing a false name and using a forged passport, six months' imprisonment and a fine of 4,000 francs for possessing arms and one month and a fine of 2,000 francs for illegal residence in Belgium. On top of the total fines of 8,000 francs, Carmelo was required to pay one quarter of the total trial costs of 29,516 francs, or £109.

Since he had already spent the ten months of his sentence in custody, he was released and told to leave Belgium within 24 hours. He replied that since he was a British subject, it was to Britain that he would return. The Home Office, apparently forgetting that he and Eugenio had been stripped of their British citizenship some five years previously, nervously muttered that his passport had lapsed and that 'there would be strict scrutiny of any documents he produced to support his application for a new passport'.

But Carmelo did not return to London; not immediately, anyway.

As Eugenio nervously bit his fingers, the President of the court, Monsieur Robert Derbaix, told him, 'Evidence from London convicted you', and went on to commend Syd Gentle and Margaret Heald (who almost three years later on 3 June 1959 was finally commended by the commissioner for her work in the case), saying that their evidence had clearly shown that Eugenio had recruited women from Belgium and sent them to walk London's streets as prostitutes.

'It is evident he is in touch with numerous prostitutes who carry on their sordid business on property he owns in London and who account for their earnings to him', said the President, adding, 'The law must be strictly applied to foreigners of very bad reputation who carry arms and seek to act in an anti-social way.'

For procuring Marie Vervacke Smith and Elisabeth de Meester McCann, plus attempting to procure Anne-Marie Bruyneel, he was sentenced to five years' imprisonment and fined 100,000 francs. For bearing a false name he received another year's imprisonment and a fine of 6,000 francs, plus an extra year's imprisonment for using a false passport, falsifying documents and possessing prohibited arms. He was also required to pay three quarters of the court costs, so the total of fines and costs amounted to £814.

'Could have been worse', muttered Eugenio to his counsel, although since he had received the maximum sentence for procuration and then had two years added on top, it's difficult to see how much worse it could have been – this was nothing more than braggadocio, rather like the English criminals who in similar circumstances inform the court, 'I'll do that standing in my prick!' and then go down to the cells and burst into tears.

Now it was time to bid adieu to the lobster and champagne and to say hello to a rather queasy lunch of boiled cod and watery cabbage. Off came the brown Savile Row suit, the silk shirt, tie and pocket handkerchief – they and the handmade shoes from Peal & Co. Ltd went into storage – and out came an itchy, grey prison uniform, bearing his convict number, A/140823.

On 15 July 1956 retired Detective Superintendent Bob Fabian, now working for the *Empire News*, penned an article directed at the Messinas which referred to 'The dung heap mountain of vice that is our capital city', and the following day, Eugenio lodged notice of appeal against his conviction; so did the public prosecutor, in respect of the sentences. The appeal was heard on 19 November 1956 at the Court of Appeal in Brussels. Eugenio arrived in a horse-drawn Black Maria, and when a reporter asked him how he was enjoying the prison food, he replied, 'Not bad at all', although given his colossal arrogance, no one really expected him to say, 'Actually, it tastes like shit!'

Judge Auguste Schuermans read from the dossier for two hours; he commented on the earnings of the prostitutes, details of which had been found in the safe deposit box. Eugenio replied that he made £14,000 per year from his property in London, including the earnings of the girls employed as hostesses in these properties, which were not so much brothels as gaming rooms. In addition, he obtained further income from smuggling gold, currency and jewels. He insisted that the court records were wrong about his place of birth, stating that it was Sao Paulo, not Alexandria.

Judge Schuermans commented on the arrest of the brothers, saying, 'You were both carrying loaded automatic pistols. What were they – playthings?'

Eugenio replied, 'My life has been threatened', and now tempers became a little frayed. Leaping to his feet, the Belgian Attorney General, Maître Henri Dykmans, produced a light brown leather briefcase.

'And this?' he shouted. 'It was found in your seaside flat after your arrest.'

'It belongs to Madame Johans', replied Eugenio, dismissively. 'She left it there.'

Opening the briefcase, the Attorney General produced a dismountable sub-machine gun. 'And this plaything?' asked the Judge. Then two Luger pistols were produced from the case. 'And this and that?' commented the Judge. 'Do they belong to Madame Johans?'

The appeal went into a second day, and Maître Dykmans described how a 'battalion' of prostitutes working for Eugenio was run on army lines, complete with discipline.

He named the 'Sergeant Major' responsible for the girls' discipline as Marthe Watts; the 'paymaster' was Augustine Johans; and the 'quartermaster' was Blanche Costaki – but not according to Eugenio's lawyer, Mme Seneschal, who told the court:

He has nothing to do with these women in England. He has not been to England for many years, so how can he control them? He liked the company of young girls. So do many men. The only crime he has committed has been to tell young girls that he was a bachelor, when he was married. But many other married men do exactly the same thing.

It was not the most persuasive of arguments, but on 5 December, whilst his conviction stood, the court reduced his term of imprisonment to six years and five months and his fines to 108,000 francs – or £771.

However, Carmelo's sentence was increased to two years' imprisonment and his fines increased to 20,000 francs – £114, the exchange rate by then, having presumably altered. This, of course, was in Carmelo's absence.

Eugenio refused to give up. On 21 January 1957 he appealed against the decision in his appeal, saying that the appointment of an interpreter at the appeal court had been irregular, but it did him no good. And then, one year after his sentence, he was interviewed again, twice within the same week, by Anton Cuppens, the head of the CID. As a result, Cuppens issued an order for the immediate arrest of both Salvatore (who incidentally had been expelled from Belgium in 1953), and Carmelo. Had a little horse-trading gone on? Quite possibly. Eugenio achieved maximum remission and on 31 July 1959, having spent almost four years behind bars, he was released, taken to the French frontier and deported to Italy.

But where on earth was Carmelo?

CHAPTER 23

The Hunt for Carmelo

Following his release, Carmelo had been driven away from the courthouse in a hired black Chrysler. He held an impromptu press conference as he sipped iced lager at a roadside café in Tournai:

> I'm glad to be out. They could not hold me. Now, I want to go to England. I'm British and Britain is my home. I intend to apply for a new British passport tomorrow morning at the British Consulate in Brussels. I am not wanted for anything in England. Britain cannot refuse me a passport. While in gaol, I was investigated all over the world. Not a single country has anything against me. I don't know anything about Eugenio's business. I want to get back to my export business and open a London office.

But after Carmelo got back into the Chrysler and headed to Brussels, according to the chauffeur, 'We drove off very fast. He kept looking out of the rear window. He told me to stop in the main square. There, he paid his bill – and I last saw him standing in the square with his suitcase in his hand.'

The concierge at 177 Avenue Louise stated, 'Carmelo has not been near here lately', and his belongings at the luxury hotel at Knocke were untouched.

The 24-hour deadline to get out of Belgium given to Carmelo by the court had come and gone. He had not gone to the British Consulate. It would have done him little good if he had, because although the Belgian police had telephoned the British Acting Consul saying, 'We consider Carmelo Messina is British. He was born of a Maltese father and both before and after the last war, he entered Belgium on a genuine British passport', the Consulate begged to differ. They stated that if Carmelo attempted to re-enter England, they would treat him as being Italian.

His lawyer stated that he was unable to assist. 'I haven't any idea where he is', he said. 'I think he is probably staying with friends in Brussels. It's quite easy to disappear in a big city like Brussels.'

The Belgian police appeared to be affronted at Carmelo's disappearance; it was bad enough that he had – initially, at any rate – got away with procuration charges; now, after being given a generous 24-hour *laissez-passer*, it appeared that he'd thumbed his nose at the authorities once again. Consequently, his name was circulated as being wanted for 'illegal residence in Belgium', which carried a prison sentence of up to one year. The Belgian *Police Gazette* almost filled a page with his photograph, description and fingerprints, and his details were forwarded to border posts at the French frontier. One report said that in order to apprehend him, all police leave had been cancelled, although that does sound as though the pudding was being seriously over-egged. An official from the *Sûreté National* stated that Carmelo had telephoned from Belgium for permission to enter France; he was told to renew his application the following day, although the official was under the impression that that request might well be refused. So what to do? Poor Carmelo was thought to be undesirable in three countries.

Over a period of several months he was supposed to have been seen in Belfast and Dublin, but it was Margaret Heald who got to work with her contacts and was finally able to report that Carmelo was going to meet a prostitute in the Kensington area. It was a set-up. At the appointed time and place, on 3 October 1958, Miss Heald and John du Rose kept observation from a taxi and saw Carmelo, sporting a handsome suntan, in a car in the Brompton Road, Knightsbridge. 'You are Carmelo Messina', said Du Rose to him and received the reply, 'No, I am not'. He went on to say his name was Charles and produced a bill in that name from the New Court Hotel, but after a new more questions Carmelo admitted, 'Yes, all right. I am Carmelo Messina but I am not wanted anywhere.'

He was taken to Chelsea police station, where a search of his person revealed some interesting documentation. Carmelo was charged that, being an alien, he had been found in the United Kingdom, having landed without leave of an immigration officer; and that not having furnished particulars required under Article 14 of the Aliens Order 1953, he did not produce on demand a passport containing a photograph of himself or some other document satisfactorily establishing his identity or nationality or give a satisfactory reason for not producing such a document. The forged Cuban passport which he possessed in the name of Carlos Marino was a good try, but not good enough.

But swiftly getting over the shock of his arrest, within hours Carmelo had secured the services of one of Britain's top legal representatives, so that when he appeared at Marlborough Street

Magistrates' Court the following day, Saturday, 4 October, it was not a solicitor who appeared on his behalf but Bernard Gillies QC (later, His Honour Judge Gillies).

The Magistrate was Eugene Paul Bennett VC, MC, whose courteous demeanour once prompted a journalist to say, 'It was an absolute pleasure to be fined by him for illegal parking.'

After Du Rose applied for a remand in custody, Bennett's courtesy was demonstrated when, in disbelieving tones, he asked Gillies, 'You are not asking for bail, surely, on this charge?'

But he was; Gillies had his instructions. 'This man claims to be a British subject and fully entitled to be in this country. It will be incumbent on those who make these charges to satisfy you that they are well founded in law.'

Affecting a rather dazed manner, Bennett said, 'Anyone landing in this country . . . you think that the onus of proof that he is not a British subject is upon the Home Secretary? . . . When do you say he arrived?'

'He has been here some weeks', replied Gillies. 'He came from Scotland. Subject to proper sureties and other conditions, I ask you to consider bail.'

'If a person goes out of this country, they go with a passport, do they not – and so return with one?' said Bennett. 'It is not disputed, is it, that he failed to produce a passport?'

For one so eloquent, Gillies could only mutter, 'I haven't gone into that', and Carmelo was remanded in custody.

One week later, Gillies was back in court, still asserting that his client was a British subject; but after hearing evidence of the arrest from Du Rose, Paul Bennett said, 'There is evidence so far that he admits he is Carmelo Messina. I know nothing about Mr Carmelo Messina except that at first, he said he was Mr Charles.' Granting a further remand, and refusing a further bail application, Bennett added, 'In these circumstances, it is very difficult for me even to consider the question of bail.'

By now, Gillies must have been reasonably demoralized, because when Carmelo appeared at the Magistrates' Court again on 28 October he was represented by Basil Thomas Wigoder QC (later Baron Wigoder); and despite Carmelo shouting, 'I am not guilty – I am British!' he was committed in custody to stand his trial at the Old Bailey.

In view of the baptismal certificate which had been produced by Carmelo when he had acquired a British passport in Alexandria in 1933 and which showed him to be a Maltese citizen – and if that were true, a British subject – the prosecutor for the Crown, Reggie Seaton (later Chairman of the London Quarter Sessions), stated that enquiries had been made in Malta which revealed that there was no record at all of Carmelo being a Maltese citizen.

The defence argued that Carmelo was a British protected person because he was born in Alexandria when Egypt was a British protectorate – which was half true.

However, Dr Pietro del Giudice, a member of the Italian Bar and legal advisor to the Italian Consul General in London, next gave damning evidence. He produced an authenticated copy of a birth certificate from Catania, Sicily, of Carmelo's father, Giuseppe Messina, which showed that he was born in Sicily on 6 October 1878. Other documents, he said, recorded the births of Eugenio and Attilio Messina at Alexandria. Under Italian law, said Dr Del Giudice, the child always bore the nationality of the father – wherever the birth took place.

Summing up to the jury, the Recorder of London, Sir Gerald Dodson (who with considerable understatement later described Carmelo as 'a member of a somewhat notorious family') said, 'So far as the question of law is concerned, I am bound to tell you, this man is an alien and also as a matter of law, in my view, he is not a British protected person.'

It took the jury no time at all to find Carmelo guilty, and after Du Rose helpfully informed the court that the defendant was one of five brothers who since 1936 had between them held the leases of 38 West End properties, mostly for the purposes of prostitution, on 25 November 1958, and one year away from retirement, the Recorder sentenced Carmelo to six months' imprisonment and recommended him for deportation.

The Yard contacted their Belgian counterparts – did they still want Carmelo for illegally staying in their country to serve the rest of his increased sentence, for whatever reasons Commissioner Cuppens had demanded his and Salvatore's arrest? Well – no, they didn't.

There was sufficient evidence to prosecute him in England for living on the immoral earnings of prostitutes; however, there were three reasons why he was not dealt with in a more robust fashion. One was his poor state of health. Then there was the availability of witnesses and the cost involved in a trial. Lastly, it was known that the Italian authorities would accept him, so it was expeditious (as well as cost-effective) just to kick him out of the country and let some other nation look after him.

Released from Wandsworth Prison, he was escorted to London Airport by two Scotland Yard officers, boarding a BEA Viscount airliner and turning to wave cheerily to the police officers and press, and was deported on 20 March 1959. Following his arrival in Rome, and after a two-hour interview during which the police told him they would not stand any nonsense from him, he was transferred to Catania, Sicily. He finished up in Linguaglossa but within two days was caught trying to fly back to Rome.

The Sicilian police were not going to stand for any of Carmelo's shenanigans any more than their mainland counterparts were, and he was told that he had to report daily to the local police station. Oddly – because he had plenty of money to pay boys to run errands for him, purchasing cigarettes and bottles of wine, for which he would tip them lavishly – he was living in a dump, a seedy, flyblown boarding house with a threadbare carpet. All that commended it was that it was situated almost opposite the police station, so at least he didn't have to walk very far to report.

Carmelo collapsed from a stroke and the following day, 27 September 1959, in that dingy boarding house with his landlady and a priest as his companions, the youngest of the five brothers was the first to die, aged forty-three.

So in the same place where his father had begun his life some eighty years previously, Carmelo ended his. Incidentally, the literal meaning of the town's name – Linguaglossa – is 'Smooth-Tongued'.

Did the irony of that cause a great deal of amusement to Carmelo and those who knew him? I rather think it did.

By his will, which was proved five years later, he was found to have left just £7,000 to his heirs and beneficiaries; but nobody was in any doubt that that was just a fraction of his wealth.

His money had been surreptitiously invested in any number of places, which included the South Western Building Society and the State Building Society, both in London. Using the alias of Charles Maitland, he had opened those accounts in 1955, and the £1,400 invested in the State Building Society had, by 1963, increased with interest to £1,885.

This came to light when 54-year-old Mrs Mary Carmen Davies forged a withdrawal form at the South Western Building Society and obtained a cheque for £400. She pleaded guilty at the Old Bailey on 8 May 1964, when she was conditionally discharged and ordered to pay £50 costs.

Her husband, Trevor Davies – at twenty-six, just under half her age – pleaded guilty to five charges of uttering forged State Building Society forms, having forged the signature of 'Charles Maitland' and obtained £1,119. He was fined £250 and also ordered to pay £50 costs, with nine months' imprisonment in default of payment.

Mrs Davies of Kensington Park Gardens, Notting Hill believed that she had a right to 'her money', which was not too far from the truth. A few years earlier, she had been known as Marie Sanderson and, with her sister harpies, Marthe Watts and Blanche Costaki, had carried out a sustained attack on Duncan Webb.

As it turned out, Mrs Davies née Sanderson was not the only one of the Messina ladies who thought she was owed some recompense.

CHAPTER 24

A Very Dodgy Marriage

Life went on in London; during 1958 there were 16,990 arrests for prostitution in the Metropolitan Police Area. It was estimated that 5,000 prostitutes were working the streets, but the Street Offences Act 1959, designed to drive them off the streets due to increased penalties, was drawing nearer.

One by one, the detectives in the various investigations drifted away. After nine months service in the Technical Support Unit, Mahon retired in 1957. Syd Gentle (who had been promoted to detective inspector) similarly retired, as did Margaret Heald. She left with the rank of Woman Detective Superintendent, having spent seventeen years in C1 Department; she was highly respected and much admired. John Du Rose who had successfully overseen the enquiries into the Richardson and Kray gangs, retired in 1970 with the rank of deputy assistant commissioner.

Marie Smith was sometimes enticing punters back to 49 Curzon Street, the property owned by Eugenio Messina, who after his release started importing drugs from Afghanistan to England. Salvatore was living in Switzerland and in 1967 he and Eugenio were still paying the rates on Mayfair properties.

But not for long. Eugenio had gone to live in San Remo, Italy where on 12 March 1970 he married 39-year-old Marie Smith, who was also known as Maria Thérèse Rachelle Versaeke – and also Smith and, of course, Messina. If that sounds rather complicated, matters were about to become even more so when, six hours after the wedding ceremony and on his wedding night, Eugenio suddenly breathed his last. When his remaining brothers – Salvatore and Attilio – arrived to offer their condolences, they discovered that Eugenio's safe had been emptied.

Marie Smith was the lady mentioned in Eugenio's will, produced at Tournai court, who would receive £160,000 if she was still living with him as his wife, at the time of his death, plus all of his properties. Well, that seemed to be fairly open and shut. She was not only living with Eugenio 'as his wife' at the time of his demise; she was in fact his legally married spouse. And if that was so, what was the problem? Quite a lot, according to the rest of the

Messina family. Having spent most of their lives evading the law, they now used the courts to suit their own ends.

Eugenio's fortune was originally estimated to be in the region of £17 million (later, quickly reduced to a more modest £800,000), and under Italian law the widow was entitled to half of his estate. However, Salvatore, Attilio and their sister, Margherita – believed to be also graced with the surname Nasser and/or Micallef – commenced proceedings at San Remo Civil Court on 17 June 1970 to request an annulment of the marriage. They produced documentation to show that at the time of the wedding their sister-in-law was already married. The San Remo court decided to defer the proceedings until 8 July.

In the meantime, Marie had not been idle. Her antecedents have already been mentioned in this book, but the same month that proceedings had been launched in Italy, she had gone to the Divorce Court in London, where she offered Judge Forrest a slightly different story.

Apparently, she was just seventeen when she met Eugenio in a Belgian teashop, and for the following five years, the two could only modestly converse through a grille in the gate of a convent, where she was studying to become a nurse. When she was twenty-three, Eugenio had proposed marriage to her, and she came to England 'with some women' and was put into a house in Stafford Street; Eugenio was nowhere to be seen.

Let Judge Forrest take up the tale of her forced and unlawful marriage to William Smith ('a tragedy for Mrs Messina'), from the evidence supplied by Marie:

> She says that she was locked in her room and from time to time the Messinas threatened her with a revolver. Threats were also made against her family.
>
> Mrs Messina had never intended marrying Smith and did not know that she had, until after the death of Eugenio this year when Salvatore told her what had happened.
>
> She says that on the evening of August 10, 1954 they came to her room, one with a revolver, and told her that next day she was to be ready at 10 am to go to an office and say 'Yes' when questioned. This, she was told, was to get her papers in order so that she would have no trouble with the police and be able to stay in England.
>
> The next day she was taken by taxi to an office where there was the man Smith. She had never met him before.
>
> She did what she was told, said, 'Yes' and signed her name, when she was required to sign her name.

She says she never saw Smith again but was taken back
to Stafford Street and was there until 1960 under constant
surveillance of the Messinas or their staff.

Marie's solicitors had hired a handwriting expert to say that the
signature, 'Marie Thérèse Smith', that appeared on the application
for British nationality following the marriage ceremony had not
been written by her. This was backed up by Marie, who stated that
she had never gone to the office in Lincoln's Inn Fields where the
oath of allegiance had been taken and confirmed that she had not
signed the document.

Smith had been traced through a newspaper advertisement and
had made a statement in which he said he had been paid a sum of
money to go through with the ceremony.

As the result of a telephone call, Marie had gone to the
Continent, where she met Eugenio once more and lived with
him for ten years, prior to his shuffling off this moral coil on his
wedding night.

'I can well understand she was frightened and unhappy,' said
Judge Forrest, referring to her time in London. 'She spoke only
Flemish, she was in strange surroundings and was surrounded by
hostility.'

It appeared that even after years of prostitution in London,
Marie still only spoke Flemish, because she was provided with
an interpreter for the court proceedings. However, although the
Judge was not satisfied that a case of duress had been made out in
respect of the marriage ceremony, he was satisfied that she had not
known what was happening at the time. Marie had impressed him
as 'a truthful witness and I believe her story'. Since he believed
that Marie was ignorant of the nature of the ceremony, he would
declare the marriage null and void. In fact, the Judge hurried up
proceedings so that the decree could be made final in 28 days,
instead of the usual three months. However, the Judge did add a
codicil to his findings: 'But I am bound to say I was a little surprised
by her story of the subsequent sixteen years. She must have had a
lot of experience of the more unfortunate parts of life in this world.'

Do you think the learned Judge had his tongue in his cheek
when he made that statement? No, I don't think so either. He had
taken Marie's story and swallowed it, hook, line and sinker.

Marie's barrister, Mrs Betty Knightly, told the court that no
costs would be claimed against Mr Smith; her client, still speaking
through the interpreter, claimed that she was 'So 'appy'.

Her solicitor, speaking after the hearing, said that the decision
was an important one because of the litigation in Italy, where a wife

was legally entitled to half of her late husband's estate. However, he added, 'But things are still complicated and we really don't know what the amount of the estate will be.'

Marie had no such reservations, because through the interpreter she stated that Eugenio's estate was estimated to be £17 million.

But at the High Court in London, on 7 August 1970, an application was lodged to overturn Judge Forrest's ruling. A member of the public had shown cause why the nullity decree should be set aside. It was practically unheard of for a private individual to intervene in a case such as this; in fact, the last time this had happened had been twenty years previously. Normally, such proceedings were undertaken by the Queen's Proctor, a solicitor representing the Crown in matters of divorce or probate.

The matter was heard at the Probate, Divorce and Admiralty Division on 7 May 1971 before Mr Justice Ormrod. Mr John le Quesne QC (later His Honour Judge Sir Godfray le Quesne) and Mrs Knightly appeared for Marie, Mr F. J. White appeared for the person who had caused the intervention and Mr Peter Hopkin Morgan for the Queen's Proctor. In a second petition Marie had alleged that the marriage to Smith was null and void since at the time he was married to another woman. In late 1937 Smith had married a Russian woman, Helen Gavrilkina, at the British consulate in Shanghai. However, further enquiries revealed that in 1946 a court in the US state of Nevada had granted a decree to her on the grounds of separation. It was a bilateral decree, Smith had submitted to the jurisdiction and nothing was known of his wife thereafter. The presumption was that she was still alive when Smith had married Marie in 1954, and therefore the question which arose was this: was the Nevada decree one which effectively dissolved the first marriage? It was decided that the interests of justice could not be served by continuing to regard Smith – who had not been in England for nearly twenty years – or Gavrilkina, who had never had any connexion with England, as still being married by the law of England.

Mr Justice Ormrod was far less impressed with Marie than Judge Forrest had been. Furthermore, it was just as well that Marie was not present in court because he had some fairly harsh things to say about her:

> The principal figures in the story have lived for many years in close association with one another in an illicit underworld in which normal standards of behaviour had little or no place. The application of normal standards to the relationship between prostitute and ponce could lead to wholly erroneous conclusions . . .

I am satisfied her case was false and misleading.

She has tried to create the impression that Salvatore was scheming to get his hands on as much of Eugenio's property as possible.

Yet she admits she has his Rolls-Royce in Belgium and that the various safes were empty, particularly of jewellery, when Salvatore was able to open them . . .

If it is true, no woman was ever more diabolically treated by the man she loved. Yet she hurried to Paris to meet him on his release from prison in 1960 and lived with him for at least six years as his wife before they married.

Far from being a more or less secluded convent girl, Marie trained as a midwife in Brussels and practised there from 1950 to 1954.

Common sense revolts at the suggestion that in 1954 a qualified midwife could be forced into prostitution against her will and kept at it for nine or ten years.

Consequently, the judge held that she knew perfectly well what she was doing when she married William George Smith at the Paddington Registry Office and that it had been 'a mere marriage of convenience' so that she couldn't be deported as a prostitute or as an undesirable alien; and with that, he cancelled her decree nisi.

On 23 June 1971 Marie appealed the ruling, but the following year, on 8 March, she abandoned the appeal.

The concerned 'member of the public' who had brought his anxieties to the attention of the High Court was, of course, Salvatore Messina. It is quite possible that Eugenio's fortune was indeed £17 million and that Salvatore had artificially lowered the amount to £800,000, so that in the event that Marie had won her case she would only have had to have been paid £400,000 and the other beneficiaries would have been £16,600,000 better off.

The unkindest cut of all was that Marie had to pay Salvatore £7,000 in legal costs. Still, as Mr Justice Ormrod mentioned, she still had Eugenio's Rolls-Royce.

CHAPTER 25

Miscellaneous Ponces

It's now time to pull down the curtains on the Messinas and their womenfolk. Marie Messina – sorry, Smith as she was legally now known – went back to live with mum and dad in Brussels and probably looked through the Belgian equivalent of 'Yellow Pages' to find a car dealer desirous of purchasing a rather aging Rolls-Royce.

Marthe Watts, her mental and physical health now in tatters, hobbled out of the limelight of Mayfair on her trademark 'beer bottle' legs. She had allegedly earned £150,000 for Eugenio during their 15-year liaison and as the sorrowful possessor of over 400 convictions for prostitution wrote a self-serving memoir in which she made no mention of several incidents in her life, including the Vassalo blackmail trial when she lied her head off, or many other instances when she was ever so parsimonious with the *actualité*. The 3 September 1960 edition of the *Sydney Morning Herald* described it, thus:

> One strongly suspects editorial fiddling with the manuscript or a ghost writer who has tried, with lamentable results, to equate the harsh facts with what he hazily believes to be public taste . . . otherwise, its main interest must be to Britain's Internal Revenue Department who will be chagrined to discover what they missed from the 14-hour day operations of Mme Watts.

So much publicity had been generated about vice in general and the Messinas in particular (especially with regard to the Belgian trial of Eugenio and Carmelo) that the Government decided that it was high time for something to be done about it. The Home Secretary, Sir David Maxwell Fyfe, set out a confidential cabinet memorandum in which heavier penalties for repeat offenders were proposed in an effort to cleanse the streets of prostitutes.

This led to the formation of a committee comprised of three women and twelve men under Lord John Frederick Wolfenden CBE which produced *The Report of the Committee on Homosexual Offences and Prostitution*, published on 4 September

1957. It became known as the Wolfenden Report, and its findings were wide-ranging and – for the time – considered by some to be controversial. The thin end of the wedge was the legalization of homosexual acts between consenting adults, a proposal which provoked varying points of view. Noël Coward noted in his diary on Sunday, 29 September 1957 that whilst he was attending a dinner at Government House, Bermuda, 'We discussed wickedly the Wolfenden Report on Homosexuality' and then went on to say:

> The Governor takes a casual and fairly irreverent view of the whole boring subject. He said that at one period of his army career he had to lecture several hundred young cadets. He told them that, as far as he was concerned, they could get pigs in trouble, goats in trouble and themselves in trouble, but if they got any NCOs or officers in trouble, they would be OUT! This, I need hardly say, I enjoyed enormously.

A rather different view was taken by the former Commander-in-Chief of Allied Forces Northern Europe, General Sir Walter Colyear Walker KCB, CBE, DSO & two bars, who had rather forceful opinions on a variety of subjects, including equal treatment for homosexuals in the armed forces. There could be no place for such people, he said, 'who use the main sewer of the human body as a playground'.

That was the homosexual side of Wolfenden's report dealt with; with regard to the matter of prostitution, which Wolfenden proclaimed was 'a weakening of the family' and led to 'community instability', it produced the Street Offences Act, 1959.

Section 54(11) of the Metropolitan Police Act, 1839 and its ludicrous forty-shilling fine was repealed. Now, a woman who had been seen soliciting men and had twice been warned as to her behaviour, could be charged with being a common prostitute and fined £10 for a first offence; for a second (or subsequent) offence it was a fine of £25 or three months' imprisonment, or both. In addition – and this, no doubt was due to the Messinas' influence – the two-year sentence for living off immoral earnings was increased to one of seven years.

Overnight, the prostitutes seemed to vanish. I was a 16-year-old working in London and I well remember Monday, 17 August 1959, which was the day following the date when the act was implemented. The prostitutes who inhabited the flats above a baker's shop in Drury Lane and who made me blush as they cheerily waved to me from the windows and had called out highly suggestive remarks on the previous Friday, had all disappeared.

Not all of the prostitutes had actually vanished (although it appeared that they had), because between then and 30 September 1963, 2,856 of them were sent to prison. Many had moved out of Soho and Mayfair to less salubrious areas, such as Notting Hill and Hammersmith, where they charged risible amounts for sex, usually in the back of cars in dark, dismal and often very dangerous places.[1]

Nevertheless, some remained, and the Messinas still controlled properties in Mayfair. But vice had changed. Printed cards were now put up in public telephone boxes (so many of them that it was often difficult to see if anyone was using the box) bearing invitations to telephone a number and discover exactly what was meant by 'Large chest needs polishing' or to secure the attention of 'A French maid offering services'. The risk of arrest for soliciting on the streets was slowly disappearing.

The area had never been regarded as one particularly displaying moral rectitude, but now it was downright sleazy.

However, the ponces were of the same high calibre.

With the decline of the Messinas, a new clique was emerging, mainly from the East End. Many of them were Maltese; one such was Philip Louis Ellul, who had convictions for possessing a gun and living on immoral earnings and was described as running a chain of 'second- or third-rate prostitutes'. He came to prominence when he murdered Tommy Smithson, a former fairground boxer, who had become rather troublesome after 'putting the black'[2] on Maltese ponces and club owners. In fact, it was one of those club owners, George Caruana, who had lured Smithson to a property he owned at 88 Carlton Vale, NW6. Smithson really should have realized something was amiss, because less than two weeks previously he had head-butted Caruana and had an associate slash Caruana with a knife, in order to extort £100 from him. Unfortunately, Smithson himself was not the sharpest knife in the drawer; although he possessed limitless courage, he was also the owner of at least 105 stitches (and possibly more) as the result of two razor attacks. Nevertheless, he duly arrived at Carlton Vale and was just as duly shot to death.

The ponce behind Smithson's murder was Bernie Silver, who was not Maltese but an East End Jew. On 9 February 1956 Silver was one of eight male defendants (and one woman) who walked free from the dock following a three-week trial, after a reasonably

---

1 And for details of what happened to some of them, see *Laid Bare: The Nude Murders and The Hunt for 'Jack the Stripper'*, The History Press, 2016.
2 Blackmailing.

dopey judge decided that they had no case to answer on a charge of living on immoral earnings.

When Silver moved into the West End he did so seamlessly, in much the same way as the Messinas had moved into the area two decades previously. Why not? It was common knowledge that Eugenio and Carmelo were banged up in Belgium, awaiting trial. Alfredo was a spent force, Attilio was keeping a reasonably low profile and Salvatore was keeping out of England altogether.

Silver was the only non-Maltese member of what became known as 'The Syndicate'; he took up an alliance with Tony Micallef, 'Big Frank' Saviour Mifsud (weighing in at 18 stone and a former Maltese policeman), Romeo Saliba (who had formed part of the Vassalo gang) and many others. Thanks to the protection from a cadre of very crooked cops, they flourished for almost twenty years, and it was not until the resourceful gangbuster Bert Wickstead got to work that Silver and a number of his unsavoury associates stood in the dock at the Old Bailey; on 19 December 1974, for conspiracy to live off the immoral earnings of prostitution, Silver, Anthony Mangion, Emmanuel Bartolo, Victor Micallef and Joseph Mifsud received lengthy prison sentences and fines. It was a real 'dog-eat-dog' trial, with Romeo Saliba giving evidence for the Crown, but there were other trials, before and after.[3]

Ten years before the Silver trial, Joseph Micallef and seven other defendants with occupations such as club proprietor, doorman, waiter and tout, appeared at Bow Street Magistrates' Court charged with conspiracy to cheat and defraud and to contravene the Pharmacy and Poisons act by offering phials marked 'Morphine' to frequenters of the 41 Club in Dean Street. In fact, they contained potentially harmful watered-down penicillin.

And ten years after the Silver affair, six men stood trial at the Old Bailey, charged with fraud offences and conspiracy to live on immoral earnings. A Maltese, Jean Aguis, was said by the prosecution to be 'the principal figure in this organization'. But after a two-month trial which resulted in everyone being acquitted, quite obviously he couldn't have been, and he left the court complaining of 'a police vendetta' against him.

★

---

3 For fuller details of these offences and trials, see *London's Gangs at War*, Pen & Sword True Crime, 2017, *Operation Countryman: The Flawed Enquiry into London Police Corruption*, Pen & Sword True Crime, 2018 and *Scotland Yard's Gangbuster: Bert Wickstead's Most Celebrated Cases*, Pen & Sword True Crime, 2018.

So it goes on. There is a current spate of revelations, mainly from the Midlands, of girls from troubled backgrounds who have been dragooned into thoroughly organized prostitution by men who gave them presents, clothes, mobile phones and computer tablets, plied them with drink and cigarettes and offered them the sort of affection which they craved for and had previously been denied. It's absolutely no good attempting to provide details of individual cases; it appears to me that there are fresh exposés, if not weekly, then certainly on a monthly basis.

It involves hundreds of defendants and thousands of victims, many of them underage. Charges of child prostitution rings, child pornography and rape have been levelled at men who used their victims as sexual playthings, passing them from one to another. The comments of the judges at their trials make shocking reading: 'Your victim became a sexual plaything to the four of you'; 'You took it in turns to abuse her and each of you behaved like an animal'; 'You made them feel worthless, dirty, unloved.'

One gang made their victims kiss their feet and drink from a lavatory bowl, and in a case where five men were jailed for a total of eighty-nine years, one of the victims was made compliant with heroin; when she reported her abuse to the police she was turned away, being told that 'she needed more evidence'.

And why was this? The answer is simple. The vast majority of the perpetrators came from minority ethnic backgrounds – often Pakistani or Bangladeshi – and their accusers were white, underage girls, many of them in care of the local authorities. The intention of the culprits was clear: to submit the girls to as much degradation as possible. Almost as an attempt at justification, one of the defendants said, 'They're white, so they're slags.' It was an explanation which many of the other perpetrators had no difficulty in accepting. Many have found assistance from the silicon chip; there are now 'pop-up' brothels to be found on the internet, which can be taken down just as quickly as they're posted, controlled and visited by drooling perverts.

The police and council officials were terrified of upsetting the delicate balance of political correctness, of being accused of racism and certainly of losing the chance of advancement in their occupations as well as being denied inclusion in the Honours Lists. The complainants were fobbed off and ignored, the gangs grew stronger and more arrogant, and when the lid did eventually come off, those pusillanimous officials looked like children who, fearing a scolding, hoping to ward it off with tears, put their index fingers in the corner of their mouths and whimpered, 'Golly!' followed with that good old stand-by, 'Well . . . lessons have been learned.'

Not one of the so-called police officers and none of those alleged care workers have yet to stand in the dock. It's an absolute disgrace.

Just before I close, to go on to the epilogue, my thoughts on the matter of prostitution.

I believe – as I've always believed – that soliciting prostitution could be outlawed by having Government-run brothels. In that way, the girls could work in a decent environment, they would receive regular, medical check-ups and they would be relatively safe from physical molestation. They'd keep much of the money they'd earn – I assume they'd have to make a contribution to the upkeep of the brothel – and in addition, they would be liable to pay income tax and National Insurance contributions, so that when they were too old (or too whacked-out) to practise their profession, at least there'd be a state pension for them.

Is that too simplistic a solution? Well, I suppose it is. Because there are always going to be vulnerable girls, seduced by unscrupulous men offering gifts and the promises of a glittering lifestyle, who'll be enticed into a world of degradation.

Epilogue

People never seem to visit cemeteries on sunny days, do they? Probably because the person who's the subject of their attention has died during the winter months, when resistance is at its lowest.

It wasn't winter when I visited Gunnersbury Cemetery, London, W4, but the weather played up for me, in keeping with the solemnity of the occasion: a light spattering of rain, a slightly chilly wind and leaves which swirled around my ankles.

I looked at the inscription on the gravestone:

A LA MEMOIRE BIEN-AIMEE

DE

GIUSEPPE MESSINA

1879 – 1946

'Friend of yours, was he?'

I turned, and standing behind me was someone – I don't know who – a council worker, I suppose, someone employed to prepare or tend the graves. I was deep in thought, otherwise I'd love to tell you that with a bit of quick-wittedness I'd replied with that line from *Hamlet*, 'How long hast thou been gravemaker?' But I didn't, so I just scowled at him, he wandered off and I turned again to the grave and its inscription.

Why was it in French? Giuseppe had been Sicilian, his wife, Maltese and three of his sons, Italian. All of them purported to be English. I shrugged. So what?

The father of all these troubles, Giuseppe, had died on 25 February 1946, aged sixty-nine, at St Charles' Hospital, Exmoor Street, W10. He'd died from heart failure, said Dr A. J. Luchecki, and the body of the man described as a retired carpenter and who prior to his hospital admission had been living at 3 Lancaster Lodge, Lancaster Road, reached his final resting place, here, three days later. The funeral arrangements had been made by Carmelo Messina, who gave his address as 11 Market Mews, W1, which may or may not have been true.

But the monumental stonemason had done a good job. He had skilfully used his mallet and chisel to produce the words which, when translated would read: 'To the memory of well-beloved Giuseppe Messina'. The type of sentiment that any family would wish for a father.

And then I thought of the suffering, the terror that must have been experienced by those unfortunate young women when dear old Giuseppe sold them to the scum of the Moroccan markets, all those years before. Of course, he wouldn't have said, 'Well, ladies, it won't be too long before you're in the clutches of the dregs of North Africa; what a fun time you'll have, being beaten, raped and passed around like a piece of meat!'

No, he'd have jollied them along with rich, expansive promises of goodness-knows-what until it was too late, when they finally realized that they would be subjected to the ultimate shame, pain and degradation for what remained of their lives.

And this was the creature who spawned five sons to carry on the family traditions, tricking silly, gullible young women into a life of squalor and humiliation.

The rain intensified and I walked away.

Well-beloved?

Well-beloved, my arse.

Bibliography

Bingham, Adrian	*Family Newspapers? Sex, Private Life and the Popular British Press, 1918–1978*	Oxford University Press, 2009
Browne, Douglas G.	*The Rise of Scotland Yard*	George G. Harrap & Co. Ltd., 1956
Davies, David Twiston (ed.)	*The Daily Telegraph Book of Military Obituaries*	Grub Street, 2003
Denning, Lord	*Lord Denning's Report*	Cmnd. 2152, HMSO, 1963
Dodson, Sir Gerald	*Consider Your Verdict*	Hutchinson & Co Ltd., 1967
Du Rose, John	*Murder was my Business*	W.H. Allen Ltd., 1971
Fido, Martin and Skinner, Keith	*The Official Encyclopedia of Scotland Yard*	Virgin Books, 1999
Fido, Martin	*The Krays: Unfinished Business*	Carlton Books, 2000
Finmore, Rhoda Lee	*Immoral Earnings or Mr Martin's Profession*	M.H. Publications 1951
Flynn, Errol	*My Wicked, Wicked Ways*	Pan Books, 1961
Higgins, Robert	*In the Name of the Law*	John Long, 1958
Howe, Sir Ronald	*The Story of Scotland Yard*	Arthur Barker Ltd., 1965
Jackson, Sir Richard	*Occupied with Crime*	George G. Harrap & Co. Ltd., 1967
Kelland, Gilbert	*Crime in London*	Harper Collins 1993
Kirby, Dick	*The Guv'nors: Ten of Scotland Yard's Greatest Detectives*	Wharncliffe True Crime, 2010

Kirby, Dick	*The Sweeney: The First Sixty Years of Scotland Yard's Crimebusting Flying Squad 1919–1978*	Wharncliffe True Crime 2011
Kirby, Dick	*Scotland Yard's Ghost Squad: The Secret Weapon against Post-War Crime*	Wharncliffe True Crime, 2011
Kirby, Dick	*Death on the Beat: Police Officers Killed In the Line of Duty*	Wharncliffe True Crime, 2012
Kirby, Dick	*The Scourge of Soho: The Controversial Career of SAS Hero, Detective Sergeant Harry Challenor MM*	Pen & Sword, 2013
Kirby, Dick	*Laid Bare: The Nude Murders and The Hunt for 'Jack the Stripper'*	History Press 2016
Kirby, Dick	*London's Gangs at War*	Pen & Sword, 2017
Kirby, Dick	*Operation Countryman: The Flawed Enquiry into London Police Corruption*	Pen & Sword, 2018
Kirby, Dick	*Scotland Yard's Gangbuster: Bert Wickstead's Most Celebrated Cases*	Pen & Sword, 2018
Kray, Reg	*Villains We Have Known*	Arrow Books Ltd., 1996
Laite, Julia	*Common Prostitutes and Ordinary Citizens: Commercial Sex in London 1885–1960*	Palgrave, Macmillan, 2012
Levine, Joshua	*The Secret History of the Blitz*	Simon & Schuster, 2015
Linane, Fergus	*London: The Wicked City. A Thousand Years of Prostitution and Vice*	Robson Books Ltd., 2003
Lock, Joan	*Marlborough Street: The Story of a London Court*	Robert Hale Ltd., 1980
Lucas, Norman	*Britain's Gangland*	W.H. Allen Ltd., 1969

Morton, James	*Gangland: The Lawyers*	Virgin Books, 2003
Morton, James	*Gangland, Volumes 1 & 2*	Time Warner, 2003
Morton, James and Parker, Gerry	*Gangland Bosses: The Lives of Jack Spot and Billy Hill*	Time Warner, 2004
Morton, James	*Gangland Soho*	Piatkus, 2008
Murphy, Robert	*Smash and Grab*	Faber & Faber 1993
Payne, Graham & Morley, Sheridan (ed.)	*The Noël Coward Diaries*	Weidenfeld & Nicolson, 1982
Pearson, John	*The Profession of Violence*	Panther Books, 1977
Scott, Sir Harold	*Scotland Yard*	André Deutsch Ltd., 1954
Sharpe, F. D.	*Sharpe of the Flying Squad*	John Long, 1938
Slater, Stefan	*Pimps, Police and Filles de Joie: Foreign Prostitution in Interwar London*	The London Journal, 18.07.2013
Straw, Jack, MP	*Interception of Communications in the United Kingdom: A Consultation Paper*	Home Office 1999, Cm. 4368
Thomas, Donald	*Villains' Paradise*	John Murray, 2005
Tullett, Tom	*Inside Interpol*	Frederick Muller Ltd., 1963
Watts, Marthe	*The Men in My Life*	Christopher Johnson, 1960
Webb, Duncan	*Crime is My Business*	Frederick Muller, Ltd., 1953
Whitcomb, J. F.	*The Trial of Alfredo Messina*	W.L.A. Publications, 1956
Wilkinson, Laurence	*Behind the Face of Crime*	Frederick Muller Ltd., 1957
Willetts, Paul	*North Soho 999*	Dewi Lewis Publishing, 2007
Williams, John	*Hume: Portrait of a Double Murderer*	William Heinemann, 1960

| Wolfenden, Lord | *The Report of the Committee on Homosexual Offences and Prostitution* | Cmnd. 367, HMSO, 1957 |
| Wyatt, H. V. | Journal of Maltese History, Vol. 3, No. 2 | University of Malta, Department of History |

Index